THE MEANING OF MAN

THE
MEANING OF MAN

by

JEAN MOUROUX

TRANSLATED BY A. H. G. DOWNES

SHEED & WARD · *New York*

1948

NIHIL OBSTAT
REV. R. G. PHILLIPS, S.TH.L.
Censor deputatus

IMPRIMATUR
E. MORROGH BERNARD
Vic. Gen.

Westmonasterii, die 28 Aprilis, 1948

PRINTED IN THE UNITED STATES OF AMERICA

PREFACE

This book makes no pretence to be anything more than a witness. It is impossible to try to live by Christian truth, to think it and to teach it, without being profoundly struck, not only by the treasures of divine wisdom it contains, but also by its internal coherence, its explanatory potency, above all by its profound "humanity." Yet we live in the midst of a world persuaded that Christianity is a doctrine alien to man and his genuine problems, unavailing in the face of his tragic condition, and careless alike of his misery and his greatness. The pages that follow may serve to show on the contrary that the Christian mystery is filled with a murmur of divine friendship for man, that it is able to explain both his misery and his greatness, that it has power to bind up his wounds, and by divinising to save him.

Here then we shall try to elucidate the meaning of man for the Christian according to the simplest of plans. Two chapters, which may serve as a kind of introduction, define man's place among temporal values, and in the bosom of the "mysterious universe" in which he plays his part. Three chapters follow on the human body—this body of ours which Christianity is so freely accused of slighting, anathematising and persecuting. Five chapters next on the spiritual values— the person, liberty, love—which give man his unique dignity, and which, according to the respect or indifference in which they are held, condition the very existence of a civilization. These are so many problems among others, and we are well

aware of the incomplete character of this sketch. The questions
in particular which concern "the Holy" and the "Community,"
though lightly touched on here and there, have not been taken
up for themselves. The questions treated bear at any rate on the
crucial points, that is to say on those essential values which, in
organic interconnection, solicit man on each of the main levels
of his being. How are these values rooted in Christian thought?
How do they fare there? That is what we propose to discuss.

Thus the book is a long theological reflection. It was not
written primarily for specialists. For the most part these studies
were conferences before being thought out afresh to go to the
making of a book. Save only for the chapter on the person, the
notes (here collected at the end of the volume) attempt no
justification for the theses advanced; they are simply references,
pointers, invitations occasionally for those who might like to
control the work or follow it up. If nevertheless the theologians
consent to peruse these pages they will encounter, we hope, at
every turn, their own familiar thoughts. Our originality, if it
exists, consists entirely in this two-fold effort, which is quite conscious on our part: to explore on certain capital points the
concrete paradox of a being nobly fashioned in his creation,
miserable in his fall, and become more admirable than ever in
his redemption—a thing which is not to be done without some
regrouping of the themes; and to carry this out, not only by
availing ourselves of the resources of the classical theology,
but by returning deliberately to the Source, by brooding piously
over the living waters and—let us say it without metaphor—
by allowing ourselves to be penetrated and carried away by the
major themes of the Word of God.

As for others, Christians bent on a better understanding of
their Christian life, even unbelievers who might wish to know
something about it, we hope they will find here some few good

reasons the more for pride in their Catholic faith, or at least for holding it in sympathetic respect. Much has been written in recent years on the subject of Christian humanism. We shall make no attempt to re-open the theoretical debate, nor to go over the ground covered in such fine works as *l'Humanisme Chrétien* of Canon Masure, or *l'Humanisme Intégral* of Maritain ("True Humanism" in the English translation). We have simply wished to show that certain essential human values have already, in point of fact, been set in their true place and magnificently appreciated and saved by Christianity. Pray God that our witness may not be unworthy of so great a theme.

CONTENTS

ix

CARNAL VALUES

TEMPORAL VALUES

CHAPTER ONE

HOW THE CHRISTIAN SEES THE TEMPORAL

Man is a creature destined to live in two worlds. He is surrounded first by the realities of this world, he lives among things and plants and animals and in the society of other persons like himself, and is active among them in thought and work and love. On the other hand he is called to live with divine realities. Christ is present in the world and in the depths of his soul to introduce him to the society of the Divine Persons and to achieve his consummation in God. Thus he has simultaneously to breathe an eternal and a temporal air.[1] As a first approximation, and availing ourselves of the traditional formulas,[2] we may say that the temporal and the eternal are to be distinguished as the *earthly,* realized here below, and the *heavenly,* which comes to full realization hereafter; as the *human,* terminating in human tasks and human persons, and the *divine,* terminating in the deiform life, in the Church, and in the Trinity; as the *natural,* comprising everything that lies within our own powers, and the *supernatural,* attainable only by the power of God, become ours, and in the very mystery of God Himself. Our task is here to define this temporal order and to indicate its relations with the eternal.

We can say at once that this "temporal" designates a

I

totality of hierarchised values: all that is loved, desired and realized by men as inhabitants of this world. To be more precise we shall have to examine the various levels on which human activity develops; and here it seems we shall have to distinguish three.

There is an activity proceeding from the soul inasmuch as it animates a body, an activity therefore engaged in the world of sense. Its domain lies in the carnal and the material, the organic and the organizable, and we may define it as *organizing activity:* one that aims at understanding, ordering and mastering the world around us so as to assure, at the limit, the triumph of man over matter and over his own body.

But the soul also transcends the body, it is a spirit—no longer simply *anima* but *spiritus.* The soul, inasmuch as it lives in itself and for itself, looks to an interior and spiritual universe made up of magnificent things: of thought and love, of self-achievement through liberty, of communion with other persons. This is the realm of immanent activity, immaterial, inviolable, secret even when it gives itself, the realm of the sage, the poet and the hero.

Then there remain the final depths, the soul in its living relations with God and in so far as it lives for God—no longer simply *spiritus* but *mens.* For more than itself the soul desires God; and even to be itself it must needs seek something higher than itself. Thus the spirit is a capacity and a desire for the Infinite Being, a living aspiration to God, and its highest activity is religious activity.

Needless to say, these activities, though distinct, are hierarchised and interlinked. Thus, a pure organizing activity does not exist; it is always animated and spurred on by a love. Again, a pure immanent activity does not exist; either it will shut itself up in itself and become a kind of self-centred religion, or else it will open itself to God, and flourish in the shadow of a better love. But the intercrossing of these activities does not do away with their distinction, and that should help to enlighten us. And we can say, returning to our problem, that the organizing and immanent activities cover the field of the temporal—they terminate in man; while religious activity covers that of the eternal—it terminates in God. The first two activities go to realize the temporal, while the third introduces us to the eternal.

To set out now the hierarchy of the temporal in greater detail, we have, to start with, *material* values, that is to say "nature," the whole totality of God's creatures, whether useful or beautiful; the material elements of a civilization, bread and wine and the "well-built house," tools and clothing and the monstrous power of money. Such as these serve higher values, *human values* properly so called and two-fold like man himself, namely *vital* (or carnal) values—the body, its health, strength and beauty; and *spiritual* values, the noblest and most typically human. These latter include the person taken precisely as spiritual—the sole absolute value here below— and all his activities in the face of things and men.

And first, *activities of effort,* comprising all the immense labour of subduing the earth and setting the human race on its feet. A scientific, theoretical and technical effort issuing in the mastery of man over matter; a social effort, seeking a minimum of ease, security and culture for every member of the human community; a political effort, to give the group a common purpose, a common means of action, a typical structure and a definite part to play among the nations; an artistic effort, expressing the double mystery of the soul and the world; and finally a moral effort, tending to raise up men who shall be capable, courageous, fit for service. In this immense effort our temporal activities are largely absorbed, and yet it could not be made at all unless sustained by other and deeper activities, more secret, more irresistible—by *activities of communion*. Communion with truth, with grandeur, with beauty, with other spiritual persons—there is the innermost heart of man. This is the plenitude, at once tranquilizing and exalting, to which he always aspires, often enough without knowing it. If there is joy in successful effort, there is a greater in realized communion. And it is because it achieves the deepest of communions, the communion of living persons with each other, that love is the unparalleled force it is, and source of a joy that does not pass. When effort and communion merge at their point of highest intensity, throwing all their power into some great work to be done, then they culminate in *activities of heroism*. For when we speak of heroism we speak of a love that takes possession of the whole person, a tension that absorbs all his forces, a mortal combat with the obstacle or the task, demanding—and already involving—the sacrifice of self. But all this fails to issue in a true heroism unless it be expended for an object, a value, an ideal that surpasses man and can therefore raise him above himself. Every other heroism, whatever its origins, condemns him in the end to homicidal adventures. Finally, all these values, far from existing in separation, mutually call for each other. A certain number of material, vital and spiritual values, bound up with each other in definite structure and tension, go to make up a type of civilization. United by ties of blood and soil, of traditions and hopes, men form families, cities and nations. And these organic wholes confer an overplus of value on all that they embrace, and set in order and develop from within.

Now we can understand better why the temporal order must necessarily comprise both material and spiritual elements:

these are always and everywhere united as body and soul. The material universe itself is an expression of the divine thought, and a distant reflection of the beauty of God; it is all alive with light and with love. Civilization is the outcome of a spiritual work, it is born of man's need to fulfil himself by bringing the universe to fulfilment. And spiritual persons, conversely, exist only in engagement with matter: they communicate with each other—and with God—by way of the flesh, by way of these corporeal signs and ties through which their mutual presence is brought about. But if matter and spirit are everywhere in close embrace, nowhere are they wholly achieved; they are given us so that by humanizing we may achieve them. The whole world is one great call; and human effort, groping but glorious, is man's response to this call. Hence it is equally true to say that the temporal order is the universe along with all its material and spiritual riches, but taken in hand and developed by human effort; or, on the other hand, that the temporal is human activity, but wholly thrown into the work of transforming and humanizing a universe of things and persons. To create intelligent and generous men, in a brotherly and habitable city, in the bosom of an ordered and spiritualized universe —that is the work for which the man of the temporal order is and lives. And if that is not the whole of our human vocation it is assuredly one of its essential parts.

In the face of all this magnificent reality what will be the attitude of the Christian? It would seem so easy to reply: a frank and joyful acceptance and an enthusiastic collaboration! But this reply is not in fact accepted. Modern man—as the outcome of how many tragic misunderstandings!—regards the Christian as the sworn enemy of all things temporal. We have all fallen in with some part at least of the total indictment formulated against us. The Christian, they say, is a man of the next world, devoid accordingly of all interest in this one. He rejects and contemns everything that goes to make life worth while—ephemeral things no doubt and frail, but nevertheless our all. Christianity is the enemy of beauty: it imprisons the Carmelite behind blank walls, cuts her off from God's earth; it regards a fair face as a dangerous seduction. The Christian mistrusts art; he thinks it pagan, cramps it with all kinds of moral restrictions and does his best to exorcise furtively what he dares not openly suppress. The Christian is the enemy of civilization: he cares nothing for human ease and comfort, he regards material progress as subversive, and laments the new facilities that undermine the old traditions. At bottom, he is the enemy of all human joys. He has perforce to extend them a sort of toleration, but he hedges it round with rules and re-strictions: whether there is question of sport or friendship or love he accords but a grudging allowance accompanied by warnings, prohibitions and threats. Under pretext of loving God he merely hates the world, and wants everybody else to hate it likewise. Very well then—let not these Christians be astonished! They may go their own way if they like, but the man of this world will go his, build up his own temporal city and organize his own happiness for himself. Since they, for their part, prefer to remain in a vale of tears in order to gain a paradise hereafter, we, for ours, shall work for the advent of a paradise on earth—a task sufficiently hard and sufficiently glorious, one would think, for anyone. These Christians must be good enough to leave us to save ourselves. . . .

In the face of everything contained in this indictment—or despairing outburst—which may indeed touch certain Catholics but wholly misses the genuine Catholic spirit—we propose to show that the Christian attitude, and the Christian attitude alone, has power to embrace the temporal order in its entirety, and to save it. All that has to be done is to bring out the essential characteristics of the Christian love of the temporal.

* * *

The first characteristic of this love is that it is real and positive. The Christian loves the temporal first of all because it comes from God. Things, persons and all their innumerable activities spring from the Creative Power of God, and consequently all are good; that is to say full of the power and sap of being, consistent, nutritive, invigorating, desirable, and capable of enriching and exalting man. *And God saw that it was good*—that is the refrain which punctuates the account of creation in Genesis, and St. Paul echoes it back from the other end of the Book: *For every creature of God is good, and nothing to be rejected but rather received with thanksgiving* (I Tim. IV, 4). In this thanksgiving God's honour is involved: from the very moment that anything exists, that thing is good and worthy of our love. Moreover, every reality is an image of God. Before He brought it into being He conceived it in His Mind, it was born of His knowledge and of His love; and that is why it always carries with it—for those who have eyes to see—a reflection of His beauty. An indestructible reflection even in the sinner, who in spite of his sin is still called by God, and is still a son of God in expectation and hope; even in the damned, who are still spirits and tragically destined to know and love the God they have rejected. All activity reflects the divine activity. God gives existence and gives life, and the effort by which man discovers, makes and brings to realization is a distant image of the divine activity. God knows Himself and loves Himself; and human knowledge and love are an image of God's life. How then should not all this be admirable? How should there be anything or any activity incapable of attracting our love?

True, there is sin. But if sin has wounded everything it has corrupted nothing. In spite of the original transgression everything still bears the divine imprint, everything remains capable of a true orientation and a genuine use, what is wounded can be healed. All is redeemed in Christ in principle; and the divine benediction redescends on things and men and the efforts of men. The Church has never thought that things are bad; it is man's heart that is bad when he uses things ill,[3] and makes them groan beneath a perverted yoke. But the heavens never cease to declare the glory of God; man has received and retains a vocation as son of God; human endeavour remains always destined to perfect the universe and to save souls. Temporal realities and temporal values may be wounded and dangerous, but they remain innocent, and always worthy of love.

Moreover the law for us who are Christians is no mere abstract principle, but a Person at once divine and human, Christ. Need we recall how often Christ showed His love for temporal things and how His brotherly heart went out towards His Father's creatures? In each of them He read the message left by the touch of the Divine Love. Birds and flowers spoke to Him of the creative Goodness; the harvests ripened in His eyes to the image of another Harvest; the cockle mingled in the corn pictured that other terrible mingling with which His own would have to live. And when He recited the Psalms it was all the universe that glorified God on His lips; for He alone, the centre of all the cries, desires and supplications of this prayer, could sovereignly gather up the praise of the whole creation and offer it to His Father in one immeasurable act of homage. If it was thus with the humblest creatures, how much more were the properly human values accepted, lived and consecrated by Christ! He did not sing the glory of work, but He worked Himself at the carpenter's bench to the point of being identified with His profession. He gives us a glimpse of His taste for good work in some of His parables. In one (the wheat and the cockle) we have the misery of work spoilt; in another (good and bad servants) the need for religious earnestness in the daily task; in yet another (talents) the call to serve with all our strength. He chose His Apostles from the ranks of the workers; and for the last, the thirteenth, He would have a Hebrew of the Hebrews, a Greek in formation and withal a Roman citizen, thus combining all human resources—religious, cultural, political—in him who was to be the conqueror of the Graeco-Roman world. He made a point of sharing men's sufferings, of providing for their humblest needs, of healing all their most fleshly ills. He knew affection and friendship. He acknowledged His racial ties with His own people and, foreseeing the doom of Jerusalem, He did as the weakest among us would do, and wept her fall.

The Lord Jesus therefore loved and sanctified every temporal reality. His attitude is our law and our rule of life. The love of God's creatures, of human endeavour, of human joys, is not merely permitted us but commanded: we too have to love these things if we would be like Christ and accomplish our task. The Christian is Catholic precisely because he thankfully accepts this temporal order that God offers him and Christ has redeemed. The express command moreover may be found in St. Paul: *For the rest, brethren, whatsoever things are true, whatsoever modest, whatsoever just, whatsoever holy, whatsoever lovely, whatsoever of good fame, if there be any virtue, if any praise of discipline, think on these things* (Phil. IV, 8).

* * *

But man in his present condition no longer knows what equilibrium is. He is not content to give his love to the temporal, he gives it his preference, he makes it his be-all and his end-all, so that his love, now become idolatry, ends in a positive exclusion of the divine and eternal from his life. This attitude, conscious, deliberate, ruthlessly applied and defended is, without doubt, the most typical and terrible of the errors of our time. Let us try to understand it and do what we can to set it right.

The root of the mischief lies in the fact that temporal values have been severed from God. All come from God and are gifts of His love; all therefore should lead us to God and help us to achieve and fulfil our being by entering into union with God. Divorced from God alike as regards their source and as regards their term, torn out of their rightful context, these values have become catastrophic. "Whoever takes the race, or the people, or the State, or the form of the State, or the depositaries of power, or any other fundamental value of the human community—all with their necessary and honourable place in the terrestrial order—whoever takes these notions and proceeds to withdraw them from the scale of earthly values in order to divinise them in an idolatrous cult, this man reverses the order that God has decreed and created," and, in consequence, he works for chaos. For when these values are isolated and closed on themselves, they become, precisely because of their genuine potency, so many direct and permanent sources of temptation. Since our life is bounded by the cradle and the grave, it will have to be squeezed like a fruit for the last drop of juice. Since human effort suffers no law but its own, every means will have to be enlisted for the subjugation of the world,—the only solid achievement. Since human joy is the supreme value, since to miss it is to miss everything, it must be sought with a pertinacity amounting to frenzy. Then man becomes like a beast, governed henceforth not by his aspirations but by his lusts: carnal lusts for money or for pleasure, spiritual lusts for dominion over matter or men. All this gradually takes shape in a collective mentality and organization that become practically irresistible, and disaster very naturally ensues. The cult of money issues in general misery, the cult of the body in physical or moral collapse, the cult of power in war; and when all three scourges join forces and fall on us at once the end of the world may seem to be at hand. Now at the source of all these ills there lies in the first place a rupture: the temporal world divorced from God; and then a perversion: human love given exclusively to the temporal. Here again the Christian reaction will not be simply to condemn but to rectify, and to transform a strayed into an orientated love.

The true path is indicated in the Gospel texts: "Seek first the Kingdom of God and his justice, and all these things shall be added unto you"—"What shall it profit a man to gain the whole world and lose his own soul?"—"No one can serve two masters"—"It is better for thee with one eye to enter into the Kingdom of God than, having two eyes, to be cast into the hell of fire." The meaning is clear: for the Christian there is but one absolute love, the love of God and beatitude in God. Let God be the first desired, the first sought, the first served, since He is not only the Source and the End, but also the God of Benediction. Now as always, in Jesus Christ, He envelops us in His creative and redemptive love. In giving us Christ He gave us Himself, and through Christ He calls us to a share in His own Joy. God, His Glory and our Beatitude—that is the first aim and the first law of Christian love. In the order of values that is the absolute rule; and to seek first the Kingdom of God is the Kingdom itself. This does not imply the abandonment of the sick and hungry for a so-called service of God. It means that we must care for the wretched and comfort them in body and soul, so that, through this service, a human being may be touched, helped, opened to the presence of the Lord, and, if it may be, totally healed. When therefore we affirm the absolute primacy of the love of God we speak of this love as it is in the soul, and not of exterior actions; we envisage the motivating force behind the free act, and not the matter to which the act is applied; we indicate the principle which is to call forth and unify the whole of our spiritual activity.

Consequently "all these other things" will be loved with a love in accord with that first love, animated and safeguarded by that love, in short, with a love that has already received its orientation. The Christian will treasure all temporal values as a gift, welcoming all of them day by day with ever renewed thanksgiving. I love the sun, and life, and health, and beauty; but I love them as so many riches that God has heaped upon me. Standing behind them at their source is God, and through them it is still God that I love, and never shall I love any of them more than I love God—how much less then shall I love them in opposition to God! If the temporal comes from God, it goes to God and points to God, and the Christian will love it as a way to God. Things have a meaning, they carry a call from on high, they are there to remind us of God and bring us nearer to God. That is why this Christian love is penetrated through and through with desire—with desire to pass beyond creatures by entering into their natural movement. I love the light, but as a reflection of the beatifying light that is in God; and health, but as an image of that fullness of life in joy eternal that God would give me; and beauty, but as the call of that divine Countenance that I hope to see at last in heaven.

Moreover the Christian has to labour here below, and he will love temporal things finally as *servants*. If it be a question of material values, he will put them to good use: money, abundance, technical progress,—so many bad masters, certainly, but potentially good servants in the hands of a rightful love. Human values on the other hand are too high to be simply used, but the Christian will see them in their context and give them their rightful orientation; and thanks to them he will achieve his destiny. His effort is thrown into the service of his ideal; in joy he finds his repose, and preparation for a better activity; and he opens himself to love that he may reach his consummation in union with his brothers and with his God. But when the servant becomes a danger and an obstacle on the path, then he has to be sacrificed. Cut off thy hand, pluck out thine eye, if so it must be to enter into life! In other cases, when a temporal good is a proper means to something better than itself, when its purpose is fulfilled in its disappearance as the flower in the fruit, then once more the Christian makes the sacrifice; and he gives his temporal life for his country, or to save his suffering brethren, or to remain faithful to his God.

Thus the Christian loves the temporal as something that shall help him to rejoin his God. His love is detached and freed from bondage because it goes first to God and to the eternal; and in attachment to God he finds detachment from the world, in adherence to God a deliverance from the yoke of the human. The risk he runs is not the risk of too much love for the fair things here below—who ever loved them like the saints?— but rather the risk of too little love for God, for his own soul, and for his brothers, and so therefore of a disordered love for "these other things," and of loving himself in them. Let him but love the Lord with all his strength, and then, with a purified heart, he can extend a joyful welcome to the whole creation. This evangelical love of temporal things is one of the most effectual testimonies a Christian can bear amongst men, since it is a love of the visible based on a love of the invisible, a love of things created straining past them to the Creator, a temporal love proclaiming an eternal. This possession shot through with detachment, this love renouncing itself to fulfil another, is precisely the attitude St. Paul would have us adopt: *Brethren, the time is short: it remaineth that they also who have wives be as if they had none; and they that weep as if they wept not; and they that rejoice as if they rejoiced not; and they that buy as if they possessed not; and they that use this world as if they used it not* . . . (I Cor. VII, 29 et seq.).

We may now easily perceive that what the Christian so emphatically condemns is not the love but the *idolatry* of the temporal. For this idolatry is a complete reversal of values, it changes their signification, and ends by falsifying temporal things along with man himself. It is a degradation: *There where thy treasure is, there will thy heart be also.* The Law avenges itself inexorably whenever man disregards it. He was made for the love of something higher than himself, and when temporal things usurp the first place in his affections then, inevitably, he falls beneath himself; and according to the type of error to which he succumbs he becomes a means of production, or an accumulator of money, or an instrument of pleasure, or a beast of prey—in any event a creature discrowned. Nor do the consequences stop there: *Whosoever would save his soul in this world shall lose it.* The violation of order brings its own reckoning: disorder felt in the bones, wholly crippling and destructive. If we attempt to hold a desire for the infinite within the narrow limits of the finite, if we love a thing or a fair face as if it could give us God, then the poor thing we have chosen ends by crumbling beneath our eyes, and leaves nothing behind in the fingers but a little pinch of dust. Let us add finally that to put the temporal in the place of God, when done with full deliberation, is the sin of pride in all its gravity. This was

Adam's sin when he preferred his liberty and his full mastery of himself to the homage he owed to God. The wound is always open, always a danger. The grace of God alone can heal it and open our hearts to this evangelical love, detached from created things and orientated to God, which is the only true love of the earthly and the human.

* * *

We might be tempted to halt our analysis at this point, but that would be to do so too soon. For we have still to explain the possibility and the prevalence of this idolatry against which the Christian always has to react; and to say why, in certain cases, the temporal has to be sacrificed. In a word, we have to account not only for the presence but also the intensity of the tragic element so deeply interwoven in every human destiny and so visible in all our human problems. Here again the Christian, and the Christian alone, is armed with the answer. He knows that the temporal has been wounded, and that he has to love it with a redeeming love.

For the entire world was affected by the first transgression. Not that it was corrupted in itself and made the bearer of a hidden poison; that is a type of pessimism the Church has always condemned. But man is one with the creation and it was for him to give it its meaning and effect its fulfilment. As long as his heart remained within the divine order, things also worked harmoniously with him in the service of God. From the day when his heart was alienated from God, when his interior powers were dislocated because he no longer loved God above all things, when his eyes were blinded to the light that lit up things with all their meaning—then, for him, all things fell apart into disunity and disorientation, each reverted to its own brute value, and became pliable to any and every end. Man's interior powers disordered, his flesh turned rebel, the universe become ambiguous, and sin fermenting in the soul and in the world, and every kind of misery along with sin—such is the debt of a fallen world. The values of which we have been speaking no longer exist in a pure state; they are no longer in any spontaneous accord with each other; they are often hidden and indiscernible, sometimes even overwhelmed and destroyed by the load of evil. Love of the temporal must henceforth be a love at grips with evil, ever striving to sift out the good from the evil and to save it. In a world that has ceased to be simply the world that God created, the Christian loves the real possibilities of things and sets himself the task of arousing, releasing and developing the buried values. An admirable work of purification and liberation, none other in fact than one particular aspect of the work of redemption; but a work that is painful and tragic, and one in which the trembling human creature runs a considerable risk of coming to grief.

When it is a question of things the Christian will try to look at them with purified eyes, to put them to use with a rectified will and re-orientate them to God by adoration and thanksgiving. When it is a question of his own body, he will set out to master its rebel energies, to make it amenable to the spirit, and turn it into a good fellow-servant. When it is a question of his spiritual activities, he will purify them and consecrate them to the Lord. None of these things can be done without effort and suffering and renunciation of a large part of himself and of the world—the vitiated part, all that is warped and become a temptation. This explains both the ease with which we fall into idolatry and the necessity for sacrifice in our love of temporal things. There is here no incoherence, no fear of real values, and—to speak like Nietzsche—no "resentment." The Christian is not a faint-heart who fears to say "yes" to life, nor a weakling shrinking from joy, nor a failure contemning a beauty beyond his grasp. He is a clear-eyed and decided man who knows that everything stands in need of a purification—nature, work, love, the very person himself—and that, with the help of Christ, he is capable of purifying all.

So true is this that we must now say: a love of the temporal cannot be positive and orientated save on condition of being redemptive. It is not enough to love men simply for what they are, for they are not what they should be. A love that lacks power to make a new creature of things and men is a love that lacks reality. It halts on the road, begins to stray, brings nothing to success. To take but one example, the Christian alone can love *man* as he should be loved. First, because he loves him truly for himself and not for something that is not himself—for superficial qualities, for services rendered, or with this merely partial fraternity that unites men in groups (of class or nationality) and keep the groups apart in sullen hostility. He loves men for what they truly are: persons, free agents, made to the image of God, redeemed in Christ; brothers by birth and destiny. But then, how often is the image unrecognizable, the greatness smothered beneath a load of misery, the redemption to all appearance a dream! How shall a love that is merely "positive" not find itself here disarmed and defeated? But then, precisely, the true love is not merely positive but also redemptive. And that is why, without illusion and without fear, but with a great hope in his heart, the Christian stoops to his guilty and miserable brothers. He knows that he was once as they, and that Christ has redeemed him; he knows that even from the most stale and corrupted of men new and innocent forces can still be drawn; he knows that the task will be hard, that he will burn his own fingers at it, but that it must be undertaken and should succeed. And so he endeavours, humbly, to love his brothers as they are, so that, through their miseries and through his labours there may arise—when God wills—the new creature of which as yet he sees no sign. Such love is real because it is redemptive.

The Christian then is never an escapist. Quite the contrary, there is no one more deeply committed than he to assure the progress, the success, and the salvation of the world. He knows that the universe has but one principle of consistence, of movement, of fulfilment, and that this principle is Christ. For *in him were all things created in heaven, and on earth, visible and invisible . . . all things were created by him and in him, and he is before all, and by him all things consist* (Col. I, 16–18). Christ is thus the great Assembler who works in the depths of souls and in the depths of things to sanctify all, and unify all, and consecrate all to the glory of God. To this gigantic enterprise the Christian freely pledges himself—at his place, in his hour, and with all his resources. He does not work alone: he collaborates. He obeys an impulsion that rises up within him from depths beyond him, an impulsion which acts on the totality of things as it acts on himself, and makes everything work together to the same end. Divinely called, divinely drawn, he works for his own part with docility, because the impulsion is given; and with courage, because the task is hard; and with faith, because it is mysterious and disproportionate to human power. He works for the progress of the universe, for the success of a world redeemed, for the birth of a new creation: through a chaos of painful labour, full of hopes, full of distresses which are not those of a death-agony but of a childbirth. He may perish, but he knows that his temporal work will not perish. Consummated at last in Christ, a new heavens and a new earth will one day gather up its fruits—"and the fruits will surpass the promise of the flowers."

CHAPTER TWO

HOW THE CHRISTIAN SEES THE UNIVERSE

I

M ODERN MAN SEES himself more and more as a fragment—or a summit—of the universe. He has become aware that his own history is a chapter in the history of the world. He scrutinizes the world with more interest, more appetite, and more hope than ever before. He wants to master it, to rule it, to make it more habitable, to make it yield more and more sustenance for body and soul. So intent is he upon it that ultimately it becomes in his eyes a kind of god that hides and takes the place of the true God. It is a matter of urgent necessity to re-establish the Catholic sense of creation in our minds.

The first character of the Christian world is this: it has been created. It was created by God out of pure generosity, that He might manifest His goodness and bestow it in participation on beings other than Himself. The universe therefore is a distant but real expression of God, it reveals His presence, it is "sacramental." His creatures are very really things; they exist in themselves; they are definable by generic, specific and individual characters; they are possible objects of science. But more profoundly they are signs, and signs that speak to us of God. The most rigorously formal of all theologians did not hesitate to write: "God, like a good teacher, has taken care to compose most excellent writings that we may be instructed in all perfection. *All that is written,* says the Apostle, *is written for our instruction.* And these writings are in two books: the book of the creation and the book of the Holy Scriptures. In the former are so many creatures, so many excellent writings that deliver the truth without falsehood. Wherefore Aristotle, when asked whence it was that he had his admirable learning, replied: "From things, which do not know how to lie." [4]

Because it was created, the world is necessarily an image of God. All realities, living or lifeless, express a creative idea; this idea they obscurely reflect; and the spiritual reflection is what we call beauty. Each one speaks on its own account, and the organic whole more clearly still; creation teems with variety and inequality because an ordered and hierarchised multitude will better—or less inadequately—express the infinite riches of God. If all creatures reflect God they present us with a double analogy, or, as Baudelaire would say, a double "correspondence": they resemble God, and there is correspondence between heaven and earth; and they agree with each other in a common origin, a common likeness, and a common end, all equally divine, and there is correspondence between the things themselves. The entire universe thus becomes an immense book, pregnant with meaning, inexhaustible, in which things declare themselves to each other, and declare God to us. But this book is nevertheless mysterious. The divine ideas are embodied in a matter which at once expresses and veils them. They do not reach us distinctly, but, as St. Gregory says, like a murmur.[5] Consequently, creation is a book that we have to learn to decipher, and those who are privileged here are neither the scientists nor the philosophers, but the poets and the saints. The poets, because the divination of the spiritual in the sensible is precisely their proper gift; and the saints, because they look at their Father's world with the unspoilt eyes of children, and because they recognise in its beauty the love and the power of the Lord—in heaven *the throne of God,* and in the earth *his footstool* (Matt. V, 34–35). On two different levels that do not lie at the same depth but "correspond," they also, poet and saint, work together in brotherly harmony. That is why it is so easy for the saint to be a poet; and why the Bible is not only the word of God but glorious poetry. The Old Testament takes up the theme of the great divine likenesses: light, the garment of God and the glory of His Countenance; water springing up in the desert, like a fountain of grace in the parched soul; winds and tempests that fulfil His word; the tree rooted beside living waters, as the just in God Himself. And Christ in His turn takes up these themes to reveal His own mystery to our minds: I am the light that enlightens every man who cometh into the world; I am the living water springing up to life everlasting; I am the vine that sends the sap through all its branches. And lastly, to give us His name, this admirable image which almost closes the revelation: *I am the bright and morning star* (Apoc. XXII, 16). The Christian can look at the stars and find them beautiful: they prefigure and call to the star he shall one day see: *when the day dawns, and the Day-Star arises in your hearts.* (II Pet. I, 19.)

The creation however does not stand fixed in dead immobility; it is living and active, it presses tensely towards its end. It is a movement and an aspiration to God. Every creature, even the humblest, is made at once to give glory to God and to attain to its own perfection: two ends, but one reality. For God calls all things to existence, to life, to activity; not from without, but from within; not by uttering a word, but by forming beings,

endowing them with a structure and an orientation. He calls to
the torrent as it breaks from the foot of the glacier to bound
uproariously over the rocks and cry aloud its joy as it leaps
and flashes in the sun. He calls to the rose to bloom in its crim-
son robe, and to throw around its beauty this veil of perfume
that delights the gods. He calls to the birds to spread their
wings to the wind, to soar and to sing, each with a note of its
own, from the humble chirping of the sparrow to the pure and
liquid plaint of the nightingale. Every creature answers the call.
They yield to the vital impulse that sweeps them along, they
give free way to their own abounding energies, and, in this
happy obedience, the thing they seek is their own fulfilment
and their own perfection: which for water is to flow, for the
rose to bloom, for the bird to utter its song. More deeply still,
it is an image of God they seek in this fruition of their being,
it is God Himself whom they seek and find without knowing
it.[6] *And the stars give light in their watches and rejoice. They
are called and they say: Here we are! And joyously do they
shine forth to Him that made them."* (Baruch III, 34–35.)
By all this activity Nature praises God, since her activity is a
call and a desire for God: and thus in virtue of its tendency to
its own perfection the whole world is one immense aspiration
to God.

By that very fact it is a *call to man.* We can appreciate
better than our fathers could that all things were made for
man. Numerous new sciences, unveiling the history of life,
invite us to conceive the universe as an immense living creature
struggling up towards a more perfect organization, towards a
more highly developed nervous system, towards a larger brain,
towards consciousness—that is to say towards man. What is
suggested by science on its own plane is affirmed as a religious
truth by Genesis when it distributes the work of creation into

three stages: first the elements, then living things, and lastly
man; and when it represents man—this magnificent fruit of
the earth and proper work of the divine hands—as the head of
all creation. Man is linked with nature in the vital, moral and
religious orders; along with her he forms an organic whole
which finds its meaning and definitive fulfilment in the glory of
God. But man alone is conscious of it. He alone is able to
present the world to God in thought and love and to glorify
God through the world. Thus he is bound up with nature,
but only to rule, complete and achieve it: he is the *animal that
commands,*[7] but commands in order to serve and do homage;
and thus he is truly creation's priest. And fraternal nature, not
unhelpful, but seeking, desiring, looks up to him who alone can
fulfil her desire by giving her a soul and a voice wherewith to
honour her God.

II

These luminous aspects of creation are real. They belong to
its essence. But shadows are there too and sometimes darkness,
coming of its wounded state; and unknown splendours due to
the Redemption. The tragic aspect of the universe is emphasized in the famous and difficult text of St. Paul (Rom. VIII,
19–23): *For the expectation of the creature waiteth for the
revelation of the sons of God. For the creature was made subject to vanity; not willingly, but by reason of him that made it
subject, in hope. Because the creature also itself shall be delivered from the servitude of corruption, into the liberty of the
glory of the children of God. For we know that every creature
groaneth and travaileth in pain, even until now. And not only
it, but ourselves also. . . .* This, we repeat, is not to be taken
in any physical or scientific, but simply in a spiritual or religious sense. Nature and man make up this whole we call the

universe. Man sinned and fell, and nature was also affected and fell in her turn. Genesis marks the fact, and underlines the sullen hostility of nature to man in his fallen state: *Cursed is the earth in thy work; with labour and toil shalt thou eat thereof all the days of thy life. Thorns and thistles shall it bring forth to thee; and thou shalt eat the herbs of the earth. In the sweat of thy face shalt thou eat bread till thou return to the earth out of which thou wast taken: for dust thou art, and unto dust thou shalt return* (Gen. III, 17–19). St. Paul insists on the slavery to which man's sin has reduced the creature: it becomes subject to " vanity," that is to say to irrational misuse, to emptiness and futility; it is even delivered over to the "servitude of corruption," that is, to the sinful and criminal enterprises of mankind.

If we venture to strip this page of its dramatic character, it still remains the affirmation of the necessary bond between the state of man and the state of the "cosmos." The latter has no meaning apart from man; he is its epitome and normative type. When he fell into the first sin something of the tie between soul and body was, if not broken, at any rate strained; and by that very fact the ties between man and the universe became relaxed, undecided, pliable to any and every end. The soul had ceased to hold the body in the same direct grasp as hitherto; and the world, a kind of extension of the body, was so much the less firmly ruled.[8] Just as the body, up to a point, had ceased to be made for the soul, so the world, up to a point, had ceased to be made for the body. It became, like the flesh, opaque, unwilling, fraught with temptation; to a large extent it now hid God instead of revealing Him, hindered our effort instead of helping it; and its very beauty became an enticement. All that of course was against the grain, against its most radical tendency, and solely due to the fault of man by whom the accord was broken.[9] Till grace shall give back power to the soul to transform its body the world will not be delivered from bondage. This unity between man and nature, which may seem a bold assertion,[10] was expressly noted by the Ancients, as witness St. John Chrysostom: "The creature will be delivered from the servitude of corruption, that is to say it will cease to be corruptible and fall in with the transformation of thy body. *As once thy body became corruptible so also the creature became corruptible; and when thy body shall put on incorruption, then the creature too will follow thee and will be subject to thee anew.*" [11] The soul, the body, the world—how terrible a continuity, how wide a field for the ravages of sin!

But the same field also lies open to grace. Christ came, and the whole world was redeemed. By His Incarnation—in which God took a human soul and body and became man like to ourselves—He entered into union with all the most spiritual, but also with all the most carnal elements of the universe. As sin had thrown everything out of joint, so the coming of God in the flesh brought everything renewal and healing. God's benediction, made present and active in Christ, restored the divine face of men and things, and gave them back their spiritual meaning. And for example, in the waters of Jordan that bathed the limbs of the Saviour and received that day their "right of baptism," [12] it was the whole creation that Christ sanctified and re-orientated to God: "He came up out of the waters. He uplifted all the world along with Himself and saw the heaven opened that Adam had shut for himself and for all his race." [13] This was but a beginning and a hope. The Redemption is realized as yet only in principle, in germ, and in expectation; here below it is in the state of first-fruits, an adumbration and a foretaste. Nothing is definitive, nothing fulfilled, nothing material or carnal in particular is truly transfigured; and in the creation, as in baptised man, good and evil are still at grips. But we hear the new call that goes up from the world, the call for deliverance, the daily appeal for redemption, the longing in the heart of things for the final transformation when man at last shall be fully filial, liberated and glorious, and the world, now cleared of its shadows, shall be nothing more than an instrument of praise and benediction in the hands of the sons of God.

As long as everything is still in expectation and travail creation remains ambiguous. Fallen and redeemed, lending itself equally to sin and to sanctity, it is given over defenceless into the hands of man and it will be what his spiritual liberty shall make of it. According as his eyes are opened by grace or dimmed by evil; according as he yields obedience to the ineradicable dictates of the spirit, or to the carnal forces that too often come uppermost; according as he breathes in an atmosphere of sin, or in the peace of God, so the world changes its face. There he finds the thing that he is and the thing that he seeks; sometimes even the thing that his will refuses to seek, and unruly desire seeks for him. Guardini, in a page that goes deep, has noted this ambivalence of creation in connection with water: "This daemonic ambiguity of water, so forcibly expressed in the ritual of the Blessing of the Font, is something we have all felt at times: in the ceaseless flux of the great river, in the swirling eddy, in the sullen liquid murmur that rises from its hidden depths. For water is at once gentle and terrible; it refreshes and it kills; it is transparent and full of enigma. Evil is in it, and magic, something alluring, something pagan. He who does not know it does not know nature. But the Liturgy knows it, and knows that in nature the same powers sleep as in the soul. The Satanic lives in things, and they cannot avail for God's service until they are purified. The malign and pagan

spirit must be cast out. The Liturgy throws light on the mystery
of the profound ambiguity of nature and the power of the
elementary forces, of which the thing we would know above
all is in whose hands they are. There we may see how little we
are lords and masters of ourselves, and how in the depths of
the essence of all things created the hand of a master may be
felt. . . . As far as things are concerned the mission of the
Liturgy is to transfer them from evil hands to good, from the
hands of the Prince of this world to the hands of the Father.
Thus it is that from water, from the evil and perilous element
that can fill us at times with shuddering fear, is born that pure
and limpid thing 'very useful and precious and chaste.' It is
pure and it purifies; it is fruitful; it has become the living symbol of supernatural life." [14]

We may thus understand how it is that every literature voices
the contradictory calls of one and the same creation, now to a
sensual, carnal and pantheistic intoxication, and now to purity,
joy and the praise of God. Examples will leap to every mind.
Taking those that lie nearest, consider for instance what is read
into nature—by themselves or by their heroes, for we pass no
judgments on persons—by such writers as the Comtesse de
Noailles, Giono, and the earlier Mauriac on the one hand, and
by Ramuz, Péguy, and Claudel on the other. And if you would
see the two themes juxtaposed you have only to open the *Contemplations* of Victor Hugo and there you will find a nature
that is one great summons to pleasure and to carnal love, and
another, altogether maternal, breathing purity, and singing with
full voice to God. Nature will always set before us both the
Dionysian and the Christian lesson, because she is big with both
possibilities, and because it is for man to actualize the one or
the other, saving or submerging the creation in the act of fulfilling or maiming himself.

III

The Christian attitude is determined by these truths. Man remains creation's head and priest, and he has to present it to its Creator; but since it is wounded he has to redeem it in Christ in order to offer it to God. The task will demand all his activities in all their forms.

First he has to subdue the earth. God has confided it to his care that he may put his stamp upon it, give it a human face and figure, integrate it with his own life and so fulfil it. One whole side of his activity, that which we have ventured to call his organizing activity, is absorbed in the task. Man, in this respect, is very truly *Homo faber*; but far from imprisoning himself in his own techniques, he invents his means and instruments only to realize his spiritual aims. The Christian engaged in such labour seeks to release the energies and riches of nature, to rid the earth of thorns and briars, to penetrate it with intelligible intentions and results, and thus make all things sing together. Toil of the husbandman, whose age-long effort brings corn and vine to fruition; toil of the engineer, who opens up the world to human enterprise with his roads and bridges and dams; toil of the scientist, who harnesses its hidden forces with his dynamos, aeroplanes and radio—all are so many efforts to humanize the universe and to make it better than it was even in God's eyes.[15] Because it issues in use and beauty the work is admirably human, and it is not in the least surprising to see it give birth to a practical *mystique* in which intelligent energy, industrious courage, and a consuming passion for efficiency can all be employed to the full.

There are deeper things in man than the activities of organization. There are those of his interior life. Deeper therefore than work, which is only a means, there is contemplation which is already an end. Surrounded as he is by God's holy reality he has to discover its intelligible significance, to taste its spiritual savour and to discern the beauty that comes to it from above. In thus disengaging the traces of God that lie hid in things, in giving them a name and a voice, the Christian fulfils the world from within. And we must not suppose that by any kind of "angelism" he scans creation for nothing more than an abstract sign of the presence of God. Things exist, they are rich with the creative generosity, they abound with being and with goodness. That is why the Christian has to recognize the Beauty of things in all its forms, at all its various depths, and particularly, it would seem, at three distinct levels of increasing interiority.

Sometimes he will contemplate reality simply as existent, in all the beauty that comes of its very existence, in all the abundance and savour and grace that attaches to the least particle of being in the least of its details, as well as in all the dark grandeur that emanates from forest and mountain and sea. This predilection for being, for reality, for life, is a perfectly Christian thing. St. Francis of Assisi had it in a truly extraordinary degree.[16] His mind did not trail away to the abstractly religious message of things; he seized them in their individual values, he entered into their own joy in being and in life. He sang of the sun which is "beautiful and bright," of water, which is "very useful and humble and precious and chaste," of fire, which "is beautiful and jocund and strong." Each several creature, in virtue of its being and its difference, was to him an image and a word of God, and thus we may see him "so greatly rejoice interiorly and exteriorly in things created *that he had but to see or to touch them* and his spirit seemed to be no longer on earth but rapt away to heaven." [17] Thus, a wondering attention to all the real is perfectly Christian, and all that expresses it with spirit will be a joy. We shall find ourselves at home with the beasts of Ronsard [18] or of Colette, with the flowers and foliage of Katherine Mansfield, no less than with the immense intelligible and delectable universe of the "Satin Slipper."

We may also contemplate reality as *brotherly*, that is to say as a source and echo of our own emotions, as an image of ourselves since it is born of the same Father, as calling us to lament or rejoice, as an invitation to use it as means to express our inner life. So deep is the brotherhood between these two creatures of God, that every human soul finds itself spontaneously in tune with the whole creation. That is why nature has always spoken to men of their life and their death, of their loves and their griefs, and of their frailty in the face of the Infinite.

And lastly the Christian will contemplate reality as *divine*, as the direct reflection and the living call of God. Creation is here taken as a natural revelation of God according to the words of St. Paul: *For the invisible things of him, from the creation of the world are clearly seen, being understood by the things that are made.*[19] But this contemplation can move in two different directions according as we regard creatures more especially as *things*, or more especially as *signs*. In the first case we enter on the path of purely philosophical thought, abstract, technical, thoroughly purified. The essential thing here is the argument: if anything exists, then God exists. The starting-point matters little, or rather the more removed it is from sense the better. The classical metaphysics will simply set aside the fair and changeful face of things and concentrate on nothing but intelligible existence. It is not the *spectacle* but the *analysis* of creation that is in question here, and the analysis will lead us to a sufficient reason for the being of all things, and, in short, to that absolute Plenitude of Being we call God. This mode of knowledge is unshakeable, and on its own plane indispensable; but in its fully elaborated and strict form it will remain the preserve of the technician.[20] We shall not speak of it in these pages, but of another, more spontaneous and simpler, aiming rather at a vision than at an analysis of creation.

For man possesses what may well be called spiritual instincts[21] making him capable and desirous of the supreme values: truth, goodness, beauty. He has one instinct moreover that synthetizes and transcends all the others, and aspires to the possession of Him Who is at once Truth and Goodness and Beauty. This is the religious instinct. Thanks to it, God is on the horizon of human thought; He is divined and desired in advance; and so, on the least contact, He will be discovered. At the spectacle of these created things which call to him with familiar looks, man will recognize—confusedly no doubt, but surely—the hand of the Divine Workman; and as to the others, the sea, the forest and the mountain, they speak to him of God by their power, their immensity and their purity. Normally, this mode of knowing depends on the whole state of the soul. It can be developed or spoilt by education; it comes to true fruition only in souls with clear and candid eyes, and their vision will gain immeasurably by humility, and purity and detachment. By humility: for at bottom it is a question of a tryst with God, Who does not give Himself except to the humble; and even creatures do not give up their secret save to those who open their hearts to receive it. By purity: for that alone gives the clear eye and the heart fraternal even to God, and so makes all reality transparent to the divine rays. By detachment: since he who lays hold on creatures egoistically drags them down to his own level, and imprisons and darkens them by that very fact. He who has no will to make himself poor will have his eyes blinded by his own riches, be they never so miserable, and things, for him, will lack savour and light. The true contemplative approach to nature gains by a life of hardship. A whole ascesis will be needed to achieve it, and that is why the wretched tourist will always miss the joy the climber knows as he pulls himself up to the topmost rock, exhausted by toil and parched with thirst, and there, between the silent snows and the dazzling sky, listens to the hymn of praise that goes up from all the earth to God.

We shall need something more however than a purely personal effort, we shall need a gift of God, a grace that lights up the soul and material things, opens them to each other, and makes them enter into discourse together on their common Lord. I have just now cited Guardini on the daemonic quality of water. But water, for the purified soul, is another thing altogether—an instrument, an image, one of the most "speaking" of God's creatures. Tertullian, almost without intending it, wrote the "praises of water" in connection with the sacrament of baptism: "In the beginning God created the heavens and the earth. And the earth was without form and void, and darkness covered the face of the deep, and the Spirit of God moved over the waters. There, O man, art thou called upon to venerate in the first place the antiquity of the waters, that ancient substance; and next their dignity inasmuch as they were the seat of the divine Spirit, to Him, no doubt, more beautiful than all the rest. For as yet there was but formless darkness without the adornment of stars, a gloomy deep, an earth unordered, a heaven unwrought; and water alone, always a perfect, joyous, and simple material substance, pure in itself, lay spread beneath the feet of God, as worthy to bear Him. Why then be surprised that it was by the waters, mothers of harmony, that the ordering of the world was henceforth carried on by God?" [22]

At the other pole of the Christian universe we have St. Cyril of Jerusalem developing the evangelical theme of water and grace: "Why then does the Saviour refer to the grace of the Spirit as water? Because it was by water that all things were constituted; because it is water that forms the tender grass and everywhere diffuses life, because it is from heaven that the sweet rains fall, because this rain is everywhere the same, but its fruits are varied. For one spring watered Paradise, one sole and same rain fell on all the earth. And it became white in the lily, red in the rose, purple in the violet and iris, varied in every species and one thing in the palm, another in the vine, and yet another in other things; of essence unique, never differing. For the rain changes not itself to fall as one thing here, another there, but adapting itself to the forms of things that shall receive it, it becomes for each the thing that befits each. So also the Holy Spirit, Who is one, and of essence unique and indivisible, distributes grace to each as He wills." [23]

St. Teresa of Avila seized on water as a means of expressing herself: "Ignorant and slow-witted as I am, I can find nothing better than water to convey the idea of certain spiritual things. I am particularly attracted to this element and have observed it with special attention." [24] What wonder, then, that a Christian poet in his turn has sung of water and singled out some of the symbols with which it abounds: of the spirit, of grace, of penitent tears, and of man himself transfigured by God:

Vous ensemencez avec l'eau baptismale nôtre eau humaine,
Agile, glorieuse, impassible, impérissable. [25]

With the water of baptism Thou sowest this our human water, Agile, glorious, impassible, imperishable.

Moreover, far from being a perilous or barely tolerated pastime, the consideration of creatures is traditional in the Church as a method of union with God. To cite but one master, at once a mystic, a theologian and a poet, St. John of the Cross has left us a sketch of this way of return to God. The soul that loves God seeks Him out by way of creatures, questions them— that is to say considers in them the work of their Creator— rejoices in this "trace of God," and finally "in its vivid contemplation and knowledge of created things the soul beholds such a multiplicity of graces, powers and beauties wherewith God has endowed them, that they seem to be clothed with admirable beauty and supernatural virtue derived from the infinite supernatural beauty of the very Face of God, whose beholding of them clothes the heavens and the earth with beauty and joy, as it is written: *Thou openest Thy hand and fillest with blessing every living creature.*"[26] And all this beauty serves but to wound the soul and increase the anguish of its longing for the Beloved.

But the Christian does not merely contemplate creation, he does better: he consecrates it to God. That is what it is for. So fair it is that when he stands in its presence he has no choice: he must either adore it, or present it to the Lord. Man's final rôle is to bring about the return of all things to God by adoring, through them, Him who created them: *Benedicite opera omnia Domini Domino.* In point of fact this return is not to be effected save through Christ. He it is who stands at the source of creation as its Exemplar; He it is who redeemed it and made it penetrable by grace; He it is who makes use of it to bring His own life to mankind; He it is who consecrates it to God; and this consecration is the Eucharist. This is no merely poetical phrase, but a strict truth: it is by way of Christ that all things return to God, and so also inclusively the material creation. It is, moreover, a traditional truth. St. Irenaeus developed it very early with astonishing realism when he presented the Eucharist as the sacrifice of the first-fruits, bringing about the return of the creature to God. Let us cite some fragments of this splendid text: "Christ commanded His disciples to offer up to God the first-fruits of His own creatures, not as if He stood in need of them, but that they themselves might be neither unfruitful nor thankless. He took into His hands His own creature of bread, saying: This is my Body. And likewise the cup, another part of our created world, and this He confessed to be His Blood, teaching that this is the new oblation of the New Testament announced by the Prophet Malachi . . . For it behoves us to make an oblation to God, and in all things to be found thankful to God our Maker, offering up to Him with a pure mind, in faith unfeigned, in firmest hope and fervent love, the first-fruits of His own creation.

"The Church alone offers this pure oblation to the Creator in offering Him with thanksgiving some small part of His creation. But the Jews did not offer thus, for their hands were stained with blood, and the Word who is offered to God they had not received. Neither do any of the sects of the heretics. For some, who maintain that the Father is other than the Creator, do, when they offer Him something of this creation, set Him forth as covetous of another's property, and desirous of what is not His own. And those who say that this world originated from some primaeval apostasy, or ignorance, or passion, when they offer the Father the fruits thereof they rather sin against Him and insult Him than give Him thanks. How should it be true for them that this bread, over which a thanksgiving has been pronounced, should be made the Body of their Lord, how should the cup contain His Blood, if they do not acknowledge Him as the Son of the Creator of the world, that is to say His Word, by whom the trees bear fruit, the waters flow, and the earth sends forth *first the blade, then the ear, then the full corn in the ear?* . . . So therefore we

offer to God, not as though He stood in need, but giving thanks
for His gift, and sanctifying His creation." [27]

We may bring this to a point and say: the world, tainted by
sin but saved by Christ, returns to God at the Mass. The bread
and the wine are fruits at once of the earth and of human
effort: the Host and the Chalice represent the whole creation
and all the toil of man—

> *Car sur la fleur des pains et sur la fleur des vins,*
> *Fruit de la force humaine en tous lieux répartie,*
> *Dieu moissonne et vendange, et dispose à ses fins*
> *La Chair et le Sang pour le calice et l'hostie.*

> From the flower of bread and the flower of wine,
> Fruit of the earth and the toil of men,
> God has His harvest too, and His vintage,
> For ends of His own He gathers them up—
> For the Body and for the Blood,
> For Chalice and Host.

Many days were needed and much labour and weariness, to
bring corn and grape to fruition, and make of them bread and
wine; and thus all human labour is resumed and offered and
sanctified in the Eucharist. The Christian contemplation of the
universe is here pushed to its limit. God's holy creation is present before us in bread and in wine; but the substances of bread
and wine have disappeared, they have become the Body and
Blood of Christ. The material veils remain which enable Christ
to be present in our midst: veils that are real and consistent,
for what remains of the bread and wine does not fail to nourish
and refresh; veils that are tenuous and transparent, since that
which supports them and makes them to be there is Christ
Himself. And thus, when our eyes are fixed on the Host they
contemplate the earth in these real veils, in these true appearances, and faith, through them, seizes and recognizes its God.

And further: since bread and wine become the Body and Blood of Christ, they are not simply *sanctified* but *sanctifying*. They communicate to us the very Principle of all life and of all sanctity. An astonishing mystery, and withal so beautiful! This dull, opaque, and perilous matter has ceased to defeat our hopes. It is spiritualized under our eyes, it vanishes into its Creator, it passes to God like the Sacred Humanity Itself; and finally, it is by this that we pass to God.

CARNAL VALUES

CHAPTER THREE

NOBILITY OF THE BODY

Anima mea non est ego: "my soul is not myself." (ST. THOMAS, *Comment. in I Cor. XV*, lect. 2. in fin.)

THERE ARE FEW SUBJECTS on which so much misapprehension exists, and on which even Christians themselves are more in need of instruction. For we are mysterious to ourselves, and this body of ours is a part of the mystery. It is possible to speak of it in the most contradictory terms: as a help and as a hindrance; as a source of joy and a source of pain; as a means to holiness and an instrument of perversion. Let us try to recover some sense of our bearings by studying, on all their various planes, the nobility and the misery of the body, and by showing that Christ comes to remedy its misery and exalt its nobility.

Let us make it plain at the outset that to speak of the body is to speak also of the soul that informs it, gives it being and builds it up. Body and soul are not to be pictured as two distinct things. We have to think of them as of two aspects, irreducible but implied in each other, of one sole real being, namely the man. It does not in the least alarm us to read in the works of a medical man that "the soul is nothing but the body in activity," or in those of another that science demands "this unicist postulate, to wit that psychic and somatic phenomena are merely two different aspects of one and the same thing." [28]

Provided that we envisage in the soul no more than its vital function—which is to give existence to the body—these formulas are not inaccurate. Since body and soul do not exist as two separate entities, and since one can unite only things that already exist, no problem of their union here arises, but simply the problem of their unity. Man is a composite of soul and body, these being the two principles of his composition, given together, appearing together, and, in a sense, disappearing together. After death no doubt the separated soul subsists; but the human spirit is a soul inasmuch as it gives subsistence to and activates its body, and when this function *vis-à-vis* the body ceases at death it remains a spirit and ceases to be a soul save only in capacity and in desire. Body and soul have disappeared together; so that what we call the body, when once separated from the soul, is no more than a fugitive appearance and a precarious memento. We are speaking here then of the body animated by the spirit which gives it being and life and structure and movement—of the body such as it is made by the living soul.

I

The body is the soul's means of action. That the soul acts only through the body is evident as far as exterior actions are concerned. In order to live we must eat and drink and react on the world around us; to achieve a civilization we must do more than merely think it, we must set about constructing it with our hands. We know the astonishing adaptability of the body for work of this kind, an adaptability of which the plasticity of the hand is the best example: the hand of the mason, horny and hard as the stone in which it works; the hand of the artist, taken to pieces and reconstructed that it may be mathematically exact and inspired; the hand of the surgeon, sensitive, intelligent, keen as a scalpel. Man, from this standpoint, is an animated implement—a spirit that possesses and animates its tool from within, and truly expresses itself in the very action of its tool. Man, as the Ancients said, is *ratio et manus*.

But even for the most spiritual acts themselves the body is still needed. It was made for the spirit and exists but to serve it. This material body is made for the act of thinking. Contemporary science has nothing to say against the following dictum of St. Thomas Aquinas: "The soul is united to the body for the sake of the act of intellection, which is its proper and principal act: wherefore the body that is united to the soul has to be perfectly adapted to serve the soul in everything required for its act of thought." [29] It is precisely this wonderful adaptation that science has enabled us to see more clearly than of old. Let us run over a few traits of this indissoluble association of flesh and spirit in the work of intellection.

No thought is possible at all without a slow education of the whole body. The new-born babe is nothing but a bundle of possibilities, and if they are to be actualized the soul will need to make its flesh supple and controllable, to organize and little by little construct its instrument. Any exact knowledge demands correct perceptions; but the infant has to learn to bring its two eyes into convergence, to fuse into one the two images given by its two hands, and later on to manage, direct and co-ordinate his organs of speech; and to effect all that he has to set up the necessary cerebral co-ordinations, open up the nervous communications, in a word fashion his instrument. Moreover, it is not simply a case of assimilating and perfecting this or that mechanism, but his body in all its entirety, his body as his, has to be discovered and mastered. He constructs, to speak precisely, the image of his body,[30] and it is in the measure in

which he constructs it that he becomes conscious of himself.
Soul and body are here in deeper interaction than ever, and
each contributes to the other's awakening. The infant builds
up this image piecemeal; he brings his tactile, motile and visual
sensations into collaboration; he learns to know his hands before he knows his feet, his right hand before his left; and this
advance is bound up at once with the use he makes of his
members and with the unequal development of the various
brain centres concerned. Towards the ninth month he has
recognized the image of his members taken separately; towards
the second year he knows them as parts of a whole, but some
further years will still be needed to fill out, to organize and to
unify this corporal image. Those parts of the body which are
most frequently brought into play, the best equipped with
strong and precise perceptions—the hands and feet—will be
more individualized and more real than the others, more thoroughly integrated into his total personality: and to such a point
that were they one day amputated they would still survive in
his consciousness, sensitive, troublesome, painful, incredibly
reluctant to disappear.

But all this is merely a preparation. There is no actual thinking without the concurrence of the whole body in all its extraordinary complexity. And first that of the brain, which has been
slowly developed, complicated and specialized in the course of
ages, and presents, in man, a highly developed frontal region—
"this sort of super-brain" [31]—a total surface which, thanks to
the cerebral convolutions, is four times as extensive as in the
anthropoid apes; an extreme degree of organization with different regions of the cortex specialized for movement, for speech
and for the different senses. It is possible to locate the structures
which serve the psychic functions, "the morphological elements where the functional processus is carried on." [32] Such is

the delicacy of these structures that a very limited lesion entails highly specialized troubles: the region adjacent to the fissure of Sylvius being accepted as the centre for speech, an anterior lesion will impede the understanding of the spoken word, and a posterior lesion that of the written word. We may thus realize the wonderful precision and delicacy with which matter can serve the mind. Nevertheless a psychological function is not to be localized, because the whole brain is needed to produce it; and the brain itself, in its turn, is the point where all the organic factors meet and act and react on each other, so that, in the end the whole body will be needed for thought. A bad digestion cripples it; an insufficient flow of thyroid makes the infant dull, incapable of interest or attention, uncomprehending; gestures, conversation, and walking about excite the mind. "When I sit down," said Montaigne, "so do my thoughts." And Claudel has told us how, with him, inspiration depended on a certain state of motor excitation: "The poet is often set going . . . by a kind of rhythmic excitation, of repetition and verbal balancing, of measured recitation somewhat after the manner of the popular rhapsodist of the East. He is seen to rub his hands together, to pace to and fro, he beats time, and mutters something between his teeth; and gradually, under this regular impulsion, between the two poles of imagination and desire, the flood of words and ideas begins to run. All his faculties are at the highest state of awareness and attention . . ." [33] Thus, all sorts of conditions, physical, chemical, motor, the state of the nerves and viscera, the arterial tension, the internal secretions, movement—all are needed to support intellectual activity, and Janet's sally was fully justified: "For fifty years past there has been too much talk about the brain. Thought, it is said, depends on the functions of the brain. They'll laugh at that some day: it is far from accurate. . . . We think with the hands as well as the brain, with the stomach, in fact with all we've got. You can't put these things into water-tight compartments." [34] Carrel put it still more strongly: "Thought is born of the endocrine glands just as much as of the cerebral cortex." [35]

We must go further. There is no thought without an immediate participation of the body in the very act of thinking.[36] It is not the intelligence that thinks but the man; and the body is present to thought not solely as a remote instrument that remains a stranger to the activity it makes possible, but as an associate that provides the intelligence with the essential conditions of its action. A moment ago we glanced at the extraordinary plasticity and complexity of the body. The meaning of these facts should be clear. Soul and body are distinguished from each other by way of their own proper dialogue. The soul forms and trains its body in order to seize itself: the body's activity enables the soul to express itself to itself and achieve self-awareness. Thus the soul is a spirit that attains to self-awareness by constructing its body over against the world. For the new-born babe the world consists at first of what it eats and drinks, and its universe is built up around its digestive tube. Later, its world is what it hears. After three weeks it recognizes the human voice and associates it with its desire for the breast. Little by little the visual sensations are organized, and when it can turn its eyes and its head at the same time it constructs its space. Similarly with the tactile sensations. When it has fingered and felt its body all over it wakes up to the astonishing fact that this body is itself. Let it once get into touch with other persons through ears and eyes and hands, let it observe them and imitate them and play at doing what they do, and it will attain at last to full awareness of itself. Awareness of the world and awareness of self awaken together by means of the body.

And when, in due course, the child, now become man,

develops his spiritual activity with an ease so natural and so perilous, it is always through the body that he does it. There is no perception without collaboration of the body—without movements of adaptation, of utilization, of imitation. No rhythm, whether poetical or musical, can be seized without some nascent rhythmic movement in the body.[37] No voluntary act is possible without "a more or less conscious apprehension of our corporeal personality"; moreover, "abstract or symbolic gestures demand a much more present and living image of the self than do the movements which aim at establishing touch with the outer world"; and, "it is due to this image of the body that we feel, perceive, and put forth our action on ourselves and on the world around us." [38] Finally, if it is true that I exist, that I know that I exist, that I live by this feeling of existence, the matter in which this feeling is clothed is always the body: "Existence has to be achieved; it is a presence, an efficacious presence. The body is the instrument of this presence: which is presence to self because it is presence to the universe." [39]

II

The body is not only a means of action, it is a means of expression. It is through the body that our interior life is expressed, that our souls become open and apprehensible, and that men communicate with each other; and the thing that enables the soul to utter itself, and makes human society a possibility, we shall call the sign. A sign is a corporeal action that carries a meaning, a corporeal attitude that manifests an intention, and, to put it more simply and more profoundly, it is the body expressing the soul.

The body expresses our deeper emotions instinctively. Anguish and joy, anger and love, supplication and triumph, all those affections that shake the whole being—who does not know their visible face? A whole world of signs, unpremeditated, spontaneous, and everywhere the same. St. Augustine already noted this *"natural language common to all peoples, consisting in facial expression, the glance of the eye, gestures of all kinds, and the tones of voice that express the mind's attitude —for example, whether things are to be sought, held fast, thrown away, or avoided."* [40] But the body can also express all that is most personal and premeditated in our inner life. Because it is wholly informed by the spirit the body is wholly a sign; and by the convergence of its movements it is constantly becoming one unique sign struggling to reproduce the motions of the soul. You see it very plainly in children who, when they want to explain themselves, have to resort not only to the voice, but to face and hands and feet; and again in foreigners, who fall back on this primitive mode of speech when at a loss for any other.

The sign *par excellence* however is speech. It will be pertinent here to remark that speech which, like every sign, is spirit embodied, can lean in two different directions. Sometimes it expresses pure thought, and is no more than an instrument in the service of reason; it divests itself of everything that gives out too sensuous a note, of everything too personal and individual; it retains no more of its body than may serve to support a meaning, and tends to disembody itself and to vanish into its significance. At other times it aims at conveying the intimate life and concernment of a person. Then it has to embody itself more fully than ever: it seeks and seizes on the right word, the right intonation and rhythm, on everything that makes the bond between the man and his speech more palpable and helps to make the man himself to appear in his speech; and of all this it makes a body for the revelation of a soul. Pure thought is not the whole of man, and the sign that conveys it tends to thin out its material envelope to let the rational significance more fully appear; it is another side of the same truth that when a man throws himself wholly into his utterance he knits up again the two opposed elements of the sign, intensifies the charge of flesh and of spirit it carries and pushes their tension to its extreme limit, he embodies himself the more that he may manifest himself the more as spirit; and then, and then only, does the word as sign attain to the fullness of its being and its efficacy.

Two extreme cases—opposites of the same genus—will provide a striking illustration of this revelatory power of the word when it puts forth all its power. The first is that of the artist, the actor or reciter, who sets out to create a dramatic character in terms of language. By an effort of voluntary self-embodiment which little by little takes in tone and rhythm and facial play and gesture, the artist strives to conquer his new personality by giving it a body, to express it to himself to seize it the better, and so have power to make it present to his audience. It is enough to have heard Copeau read *Athalie, The Annunciation to Mary,* or *Macbeth,* to have seen rising before one's eyes like presences, the old sinister Queen, or Violaine the saint, or the sanguinary Scottish pair. At the opposite extreme we have the Apostle, whose task it is to bear witness. In Christianity it is by the Word of God that life is transmitted. But this word does not primarily express ideas or abstract theses, but above all the mystery of a Being who is the eternal Word made flesh, who has given Himself in expressing Himself, and who prescribes fidelity to *His* words as the means of bringing about the presence of *the* Word that saves. Only on these terms can the preaching of the Gospel become a divine power to save those that believe. The apostle, then, is one who has to make

God present and active in the world, and, that he may do so, he must incarnate in his words the divine life that quickens his own soul. It cannot be done in the artist's manner, by means of a calculated and laboured technique; it has to be the direct and immediate fruit of his contact with, and assimilation of, the God to be revealed, of a passionate conviction and a vehement love that imperiously drains away all the resources of his being and all its possibilities as sign. His word, when fully incarnated, fully expresses the spirit and becomes Witness—a witness that sometimes has to be sealed in blood.

We have mentioned the artist. Let us add now that the rôle of art is to express through the body the mystery of a soul. Through the body—that is to say by way of all the signs— visual, audible, mobile—skilfully organized, concurrent, often unified and orchestrated. Each of the arts is a synthesis of signs, and they tend to become syntheses of syntheses—poetry sung or lyrical drama for example. Let us note briefly that even the most corporeal of all the arts, the dance, can take on a profoundly human significance. Funeral dances, festal dances, the war-dance, and the sacred dance—has not man always danced his strongest emotions? Doubtless we have degraded and sometimes perverted the dance; but the charge of sensuality it can carry and communicate is itself a sign of its power. Valéry tried in *L'Ame et la Danse* to disentangle the meaning of the classical dance, at once voluptuous and intelligible, full of Socratic virtue and of other elements much less pure. But if we have lost this means of expression, there are other and simpler peoples who possess it still. ". . . in Africa, in primitive Africa, religious feeling finds expression only through the body; hence these magnificent prostrations with forehead bowed to the ground, still to be seen in Dahomey; hence these chants in which the voice dispenses with words—which are left for dealing with men; hence the dance, which is to walking what song is to the spoken word. There must have been a moment in the early history of every people when joy and sorrow and prayer were danced instead of sung. And the usage survives in Africa, where the body, transhumanized by ritual dances, gives back to the divinity the gift bestowed on man in the equilibrium, the harmony, the beauty of the body and the eurhythmy of its movements.

". . . I assisted one day, in a village of the interior, at the ritual dance of a king. Noting the silent and respectful attitude of the crowd, I asked what this profound recollection might mean. "The crowd," they said, "joins in the prayer of the king, who, when he dances thus, is praying for his people." [41]

It is by no means certain that in this matter the European man is the more civilized.

Lastly, the whole body can become, in a way, an image of the soul, a sign conveying something of our personal mystery. I speak of what the body becomes under the influence of our voluntary acts. For the soul moulds its body, little by little it stamps its own history upon it; and in the carriage of the members and the lines of the facial expression, it builds up a certain image of itself. That is true biologically; and if the body acts on the soul, the soul in its turn transforms the tissues, the "humours," the chemical activities of the body, and physiologists are quite prepared to take the popular metaphor literally and to allow that excessive worry for instance "makes bad blood." It is still truer spiritually. A man who surrenders himself to his instincts writes the fact on his flesh, and that is already a punishment; one who strives to master them spiritualizes his flesh, and makes it more and more transparent. We spoke just now of the hand and the brain, but let us speak of the face. The saint's face and the rake's each tell their own story, not to be read by rational analysis but by a kind of intuitive sense that goes deeper than reasoning.[42] These are extreme cases. Between them lies the average countenance, variable, indeterminate, often indeed our own, since we are mostly middling folk who, by the grace of God, are not wholly sunk in vice even when, through human weakness, we fall short of sanctity. And that confirms the law: poor soul, poor face.

Let us add finally that the body does not find it easy to lie. You can twist it more or less into some kind of misleading grimace, but the effort lacks spontaneity. There is discordance in the normal man between the gesture meant to deceive and the natural disposition of the features, and indeed of the whole body; and these latter tell the truth in spite of ourselves. The resultant awkwardness, in fact, is precisely one of the signs of the lie: the child as yet unpractised in the art, the upright man who attempts it one day out of weakness or out of delicacy, invariably give themselves away: and the failure is precisely a sign of the body's nobility, and its transparence to the soul.

III

We come now to the supreme dignity of the body: it is the means by which two persons enter into union and communion with each other. There is nothing very surprising about that, seeing that the body is already our means of establishing touch with the universe. "This body of ours is an admirable instrument, and assuredly the living, who have it still at their disposal, fail to make full use of it. They get some pleasure out of it, and some pain, and a few indispensable activities, such as feeding. Sometimes they identify it with themselves; sometimes they forget that it exists; and now brutes, now pure spirits, they have no feeling for their universal affinities or the prodigious substance of which they are made. By way of the body, how-

ever, they partake of what they touch, they are stones, they are
trees, they exchange contacts and share their breath with all
the matter that surrounds them. They touch and are touched,
they weigh and bear weights, they walk about and carry their
virtues and vices with them; and when they fall into reverie or
dreamy sleep they reproduce the nature of water, they become
sands and clouds. . . ." [43]

So speak the poets, and they are not wrong. But this unifying
function of the body does not take on all its meaning save at the
summit at which we now stand. Spiritual creatures, like the
rest, are incomplete, they are poor and needy and desirous;
and only by partaking with others in community of feeling and
action can they find and realize themselves. Now direct communion of spirit with spirit is not to be had here below. We
enter into communion with all that we are; and because it is
penetrated through and through with soul, because it reflects,
offers and conveys the soul, the body is the medium by which
the mutual presence of souls is brought about. Not by ideas
only, or volitions and conscious gestures, but by the whole man
down to his very flesh; and that is doubtless why human communion is at once so deep and so mysterious.

To come back to words and gestures, they become means of
communion because, over and above their direct and definite
meaning, they are able to convey something of our personal
mystery. When two souls meet after long absence the words
exchanged are often trivial enough, but these two understand
each other and their souls embrace in spite of all the poverty
of speech. When two souls suffer together, a silent look suffices
or a stifled word, or a tear glistening in the eye, and they know
that they share the same grief. There are crucial experiences—at
beginnings and endings—that still more clearly reveal the rôle
of the body. Such is the first dawning smile of the infant on

his mother: it is not simply the prison of the body that is broken through, it is the body itself that has now become means of communion, and thanks to this, mother and child can share in the same joy. Such is the last look of the dying: the body has gradually re-become a prison, the soul is shut up in it before it departs; but this last look is its supreme effort to express its longing, its suffering, or its love. Such, finally, is the case of the blind deaf-mutes. Souls shut up in unavailing windowless bodies—how shall one thus immured be awakened to life? How bring a sign to birth? Eyes are lacking, and ears, and tongue. There remains the hand, the blessed hand, and along with the hand there remains the body's quick docility and the infinite longing of the soul: and that will be enough to ensure that after some struggles, some failures, some lapses into night, a meaning shall awaken at last, a heart shall understand, a soul leap out to the light to commune with its sisters, with humanity, and even with God.[44]

Art will provide us with similar lessons. Art is a means of deep communion which brings all the body into play; in the artist himself on the one hand, who needs a certain tactile refinement or manual skill; and in the spectator, the hearer, or the reader on the other, who responds in his own way and vibrates in unison. A whole education of body and soul is needed to give full right of way in this enchanted land. The case of music is perhaps the most revealing. It can unify a crowd; whether it be a regiment of soldiers marching in step behind a band, or a congregation of thousands of pilgrims chanting the *Credo* in unison, one great physical vibration lays hold on each human being, aggregates him to the mass and sweeps the whole along on its waves. That of course is not the highest flight of art, and is sometimes exceedingly dangerous; but it is a formidable power. When we enter the true realm of music the communion penetrates to deeper levels. An aria of Mozart's, a symphony of Beethoven's, a fugue of Bach's, ushers us into a new universe of feeling, puts us in touch with something intimate and not to be uttered, by which the soul is simultaneously rapt away and freed. We read that Beethoven once paid a visit to a bereaved mother, sat down at the piano without a word, and played for a while, and when he left her she broke down in tears of affection and gratitude.

We are not writing this for a few cultured folk. We conceive that art in some form or other is one of man's essential needs, that in fact it has an enormous influence on human groupings, and that this influence creates some very formidable problems for our modern society—that of the cinema for instance. That the influence of this seventh art is deep and by no means always healthy, is a view that few will contest. An international enquiry set up in 1938 was able to put down some hundreds of murders, burglaries, frauds and adulteries to its account. Such an influence needs explanation, and none will be forthcoming if we look no further than the detailed reports. What has to be said is that man is made for communion and that the child, for instance, finds it at the cinema. Eyes, voice, gestures, the whole soul and body together are thrown on the screen, and the child responds by participating body and soul. He allows the corporeal mechanisms presented to reproduce themselves in his own body, and makes the spiritual attitudes his own. Communion with the sympathetic bandit, with the star or leading lady, charming or immoral, will be translated one day into real life with the results we know. The danger of the cinema comes precisely of its power. It is a means of communion, and through the medium of bodily actions and attitudes it entails an unconscious but very real orientation of persons.

There are images that orientate the soul; there are realities that absorb it altogether; there is a giving, real and substantial, of persons themselves through their bodies; there is love. Its power and nobility come of the unique communion it brings about; so intimate that it absorbs the whole person in all his mystery: wherefore it is one of the gravest acts open to man and woman. Its tragic possibilities are due to the fact that communion is here realized by means of the body. If the union of man and woman is the fruit of a love that is given in purity, generosity and fidelity, then the body itself is spiritualized in the service of a love that ennobles it, and, with God's blessing, sanctifies. Then man remains man, that is to say a flesh sustained by a spirit. If the union is the issue of an instinct devoid of generosity, of a gift made without purity, of an attraction involving no fidelity, then the soul itself is abased, degraded, gradually reduced to the same level of carnality and animality as the love that drags it down: and the man, thus fallen beneath himself, becomes no more than a spirit miserably fettered to the senses. And what, on the contrary, is absence or death if not the separation of bodies and therefore of souls, since either entails the cessation of this presence, at once corporeal and spiritual, which united these two? But it was the body that was the means of union, and the body once disappeared, for a time or for ever, the communion is broken for ever in the form under which it was known. There remains, for those who are Christians, a communion under this spiritual form, sure but obscure, which is found in faith and hope. For others there is nought but a blank. But how well we understand the agonised cry of the mother whose daughter had just been buried: "Surely, I would have torn up her grave with my bare fingers only to recover her body." To recover her *body*, since it was by this body that communion was realized.

* * *

The body is therefore made for the soul, to express it, to open it out and to give it,—*plenitudo animae*. But the soul is made for God, and the body is associated with the soul even to this point: it was made to aid our communion with God. "The body has eyes to behold creation and to recognize in its wonderful order and harmony the hand of the Creator; it has ears to hear the word of God and the law of God; it has hands to perform all needful tasks, and to lift up in prayer to God." [45] Let us dwell on a single point: the rôle of the body in prayer.

The body expresses our gift to God. By the sign of the Cross, the bent knee, the folded hands, the recollected countenance, it expresses the soul's aspiration to God, and it bears witness. It radiates our prayer and our faith around us, and it touches others. . . . The child learns to pray by observing the serious and recollected attitude of its mother by its side. Our prayer in common, our Liturgy, is as it were a poem acted out before God: chant and posture and action are all calculated to express the soul, and bear it away into the spiritual world; and the liturgical year is a representation—joyful, sorrowful, glorious—of the Christian mystery itself.

If the body images forth our prayer, it does so because it is a means to prayer. It sustains it, since it puts it into a recited formula that gives substance and definition to the spiritual impulse, and into a posture of body that emphasizes and supports the interior movement. The body lends added force to prayer: when a man utters his invocation aloud, chants the formula of his faith, kneels in humility, he seeks God with the whole of himself, he draws the soul by way of the body and deepens his supplication. It is even at times the body that realizes the prayer. Distracted, aimless, wandering, despondent, and without hold on divine things, the soul at times would seem to have deserted us and disappeared. Then the body steps in and becomes the effectual means to prayer. Am I distracted? I pick up my rosary, I solicit my will by lips and fingers, and at each *Ave* a prayer goes up to God. Am I weary in soul? I form such words as I can—like Our Lord Himself who repeated the selfsame words: "Let Thy will, not mine, be done," so also I repeat: "Have pity on me, O God"; and this humble iteration is a very perfect act of prayer. Does the soul seem to have disappeared, so that I hardly know whether I believe in God at all? Well, at any rate, here am I; and if no soul at least a body to pray with. I give it to God. I kneel, and keep on kneeling faithfully at God's feet. Through my body my soul bears witness of its presence to God; and God looks down on me and says: "Go in peace, my child." Thus is the body a means to communion with God. That is its highest function: the body is not for sin, it is for the Lord.

CHAPTER FOUR

MISERY OF THE BODY

Here below the light is never without its shadows. Having shown how admirably the body serves the soul, we must now dwell on its misery, and show how heavy, opaque and dangerous it is.

I

The body is an obstacle as well as a help; a limitation as much as a means, a burden that often oppresses the soul.

And first, it hampers effort. It obeys with reluctance, and years are needed to bring it under control. The infant struggling with his mother tongue, the apprentice at his machine, the surgeon with his lancet, the musician with his violin, all have trouble enough to master their trade. Moreover the body's obedience is always limited. Our powers are actualized by every new skill acquired, but specialized at the same time, enriched but narrowed. To speak one language is to set up and co-ordinate a vast number of automatisms, which then prevent us from speaking another correctly. To learn a particular trade is to set up reflexes which exclude others. Time soon robs the muscles of their suppleness, makes them ill-adapted to fresh techniques (nobody learns to play the violin after the age of thirty); and in the form of fatigue it strictly limits our efforts;

59

exercise eventually produces paralysis instead of excitation and we have perforce to stop.

Moreover the body offers special resistance to intellectual effort. Such effort of course is hardly perceptible mechanically and escapes measurement altogether—the slightest muscular contraction, the mere effort of turning a page, registers more strongly than the most active thought. But thought, for all that, is painful and wearing. No harder apprenticeship exists, and the generality of men, apart from rare exceptions, do not take easily to intellectual effort. Children are capable of only the briefest attention; adolescents who work too eagerly run a risk of hindering their bodily growth; adults acquire fixed habits and give no thought to the matter. This poor spiritual creature, man, is faced with constant reminders of his animal condition.

The body can cripple, even suppress, all spiritual activity. It is highly complex and correspondingly delicate. Touch it at one point and you touch the whole, always a dangerous thing to do. A trifling vibration, a sudden noise, a slight stimulus, and the mind for the nonce is out of action, because given over to emotional reaction or to the animal powers. When the body itself is attacked the soul is paralysed. A nervous insufficiency can result in psychological infantilism; a very slight lesion of the brain can throw the whole interior life into confusion; an infection such as *encephalitis lethargica* for example, can change the moral personality and turn a normal child into a monster of anger and aggressiveness. Pain overcomes the soul. All its powers are concentrated on the tortured point and cease to be available for anything else. Few can forget themselves in such a case and think of others,—and who shall blame them for that? If the ill becomes acute nothing is left in the sufferer but an all-absorbing sense of pain; the free spirit seems to have disappeared. Then comes the final struggle. The soul fights desperately to retain its hold on the body. Little by little the latter disintegrates and slips from its grasp, until the moment comes when it no longer provides the soul with the necessary organic conditions, and then the last thread is snapped, and it is death. The body is an instrument—but also an obstacle, a resistance, and a terribly exacting companion.

II

The body is likewise a veil. It is opaque. Never can two souls apprehend each other directly. They embrace only through an intermediary: through eyes or a smile; through words or a pressure of the hand; even through total surrender of the body,—but always *through* something. Here below the naked contact of soul with soul is always a chimaera, and to see a soul in the purity of its being is reserved for Him who created it. We have spoken of the greatness of the sign. There lies its misery.

The body expresses nothing with absolute clarity. We can never utter ourselves fully, and when it comes to deep and intimate confidences, they have to be mainly divined. Words are desperately inadequate. They are social signs, and the trouble is that we never wholly resemble anyone else. They are superficial signs, adapted to concepts, not to the schemata that command the concepts, still less to the living thought that struggles through them for expression. They are abstract signs, powerless to convey the tension, the warmth, the nuance of our desires or loves; ambiguous signs in consequence—the word is a "possibility of judgment"—that have to be analysed and reconstructed. A stroke of genius may occasionally break through these barriers; but strokes of genius are rare, our words too often betray us, and we have to fall back on the humble and despairing resource of a gesture or look to make ourselves partly understood. That is why love alone, love in which all one person's being springs to another's, can bring comprehension without complete betrayal.

The body does worse : it hides the soul, or rather the soul can turn it into a veritable instrument of separation. For the forces of isolation are as active in the human heart as those of communion, and they know how to make use of the complicity of the body. Self-isolation is sometimes a kind of defensive reaction, as in all anonymous crowds brought together by external forces, where the individual feels himself merely a unit and a stranger among his kind. Then he accentuates the separation. He retires behind the protective shell of his body. The mass of bodies may be huddled together and packed tight, souls are more isolated than ever. But isolation becomes a misfortune or a fault when it occurs in the bosom of natural communities. Man is destined to live in community to fulfil his life by giving it. To give himself thus he has to overcome the resistances of soul and body. If he takes the line of least resistance, if he accepts or chooses isolation, soul and body refuse themselves together, and the latter becomes a hostile rampart. No friendly gesture, no gleam of fraternity, no hint of any soul; simply a presence immured and blank walls. Such division can be set up between two workmen toiling at the same bench, between parent and child, between husband and wife: associations made for communion, bodies which touch, collaborate, even intermingle, and souls that turn away in refusal. What wonder then if this lifeless presence of bodies to each other, this real absence in enforced presence, should turn in the end to hate, and shatter every remaining semblance of living community?

If moreover two human beings can never apprehend each

other directly, that is due above all to this: that none has any clear intuition of himself. We touch the soul, we experience its presence, we live by it—but we do not see it. It remains a mystery to ourselves, wrapped in the body's "impenetrable folds." I apprehend it through acts in which the body always has its share, and when I would look on my naked soul, on this "pure ego," this spiritual "I" by which I am constituted, then it has fled already and vanished. Without the me there is no "I," and I cannot seize myself distinctly save by expressing myself to myself and, in other words, through signs. For to seize myself I must stand apart in distinction and distance from myself. This interior distinction and distance are made possible by the sign, which enables me indeed to seize myself, but only under a veil. Moreover this sign is the body. Gesture, image and concept all imply, in varying degrees, an internal relation to this matter which constitutes my body and my "power of signs." Consequently I never seize myself save as engaged with the body, always in the act of doing something or other with it, always therefore made by it both absent and present to myself. Such interior tension and distance are the very condition of the awakening and progress of personal life. But since I apprehend myself through the body, I know *that* I am without knowing *what* I am. An absolute coincidence of presence and mystery, which is as much as to say presence and absence— such is our condition.

It hardly needs to be said that the man who has become aware that he is an embodied spirit will not easily resign himself to this mystery, to this veil dropped between his consciousness and his being. Some few of the best, or the boldest, have tried to tear the veil aside. It would seem that the apprehension of the self in a pure, naked and separated state is the aim of the Hindu Yoga.[46] The terrible ascesis of these mystics is a purely spiritual orientation, and has nothing in common with trickery or imposture. Understanding and experiencing the body as an obstacle, they would overcome it completely in order to shake themselves free of it, to attain to their own pure essence and so emerge into the absolute. It is very difficult to pass a judgment on this matter; [47] in any event, achieved or attempted, the feat remains heroically exceptional, and thus confirms the rule: inasmuch as the spiritual soul, in its normal state, is united to a body, it does not apprehend itself directly and remains a mystery to itself. A psychological mystery since many powers, possibilities, and, on the other hand, deficiencies, thus escape us: a moral mystery, since the state of the soul resulting from its efforts or shrinkings remains unknown to us: and a spiritual mystery, since the relation to God by which the soul is constituted, obscure in its lower term and incognisable in the higher, is given us only as an orientated tension or as a defined call. For the rest, to reveal ourselves in part to ourselves—and without doubt because it deepens this relation—there remains but love: the love of a fraternal *thou* in whom our *I* shall awaken; the love of an infinite *Thou* in Whom our *I* shall find itself because it has ceased to seek itself. But here we touch on another question for which the time has not yet arrived.

III

Resistant and opaque, the body is furthermore a peril. Risk is inherent in life. In man, the risk takes the form of a certain tension—a constitutive tension—between flesh and spirit. For the Christian position is a spiritualism just as far removed from materialism as it is from angelism. To define man as an embodied spirit, is to define him by a structural opposition in the interior of an indissoluble unity. Both body and soul exist; they are made for each other, but each has a consistence of its own and neither is reducible to the other. They are in opposition in that one is a principle of unity and concentration, and the other a principle of dispersion and multiplicity. Their unity is one of tension, of polarized opposition, involving a possibility of conflict, of antagonism and, at the limit, of disaggregation. Their dialogue can issue in single combat.

There is, of course, an internal proportion between soul and body; indeed it is precisely this very definite relation which issues in substantial union and in individuality. But such adaptation to the soul is not the only thing in the body; there is also the inherent law of matter, the *necessitas materiae,* and therefore a possibility of opposition and conflict. The body, says St. Thomas, putting to himself a difficulty, is made for the service of the soul and should therefore be wholly subject to the soul; and yet the flesh resists the spirit, and in virtue of conflicting desires the soul is drawn in opposite directions. He replies: "this conflict coming of opposed desires does not arise exclusively from sin, but also from the necessity of matter. For since man possesses a sensibility he cannot but feel pleasure and desire for pleasurable things, and many of these are contrary to reason." [48] This then is a necessity inherent in the very structure of man. By their own internal law and native orientation the two principles that compose the human essence tend at one and the same time both to complete each other and therefore to unite, and to oppose each other and therefore to start asunder. Their antagonism is no less real than their power to complete each other,[49] so that the two forces can be found either in a more or less marked state of tension, or, on the other hand, of union. If we appeal to experience what do we find? This: that the unity of the human being is an initial unity, it is a starting point, and that on all planes it has to be gradually established;

that in fact it is weak, difficult to realize, and always threatened with dissolution.

Man's unique dignity is bound up with the fact that he has progressively to construct his own being, to become the architect of his own unity. On the basis of a metaphysical personality, which is at once something in itself and a cry for more, he has in the first place to achieve a psychological personality. Now this unity—which is always psycho-organic—is nothing other than a multiplicity in constant process of unification. A unity always *in labour,* since from first to last the elements that go to its composition—organic, emotional, intellectual, volitional— are in constant turmoil; a unity that is highly *complex,* since it integrates a number of activities each of which is itself a synthesis; [50] and lastly a unity always *in danger of dissolution,* precisely because it is always a unity in the making. To keep the discussion within bounds, let us confine ourselves to a few remarks on the affectivity—the realm of feelings and emotional reactions. This is an essential dimension of all psychological phenomena. In man it is two-fold: there is a higher and properly spiritual affectivity, and a lower and psycho-organic. Here we speak only of the latter. It plays an enormous part in the constitution of our psychological personality: there is no self-consciousness, no steady attention, no judgment of reality, without a minimum of affective reaction, of affective *tonus.*[51] Now this indispensable affective groundwork itself depends on the equilibrium of the organic reactions as a whole; through it the whole body, and through the body the whole world, bears in upon the soul. The external milieu with its light and warmth, its pressure and electrical charges, the internal milieu, with the interaction of glands and nerves,[52]—all this forms the deep foundation on which the psychological life is to be built up. But then this life will be exposed to the influence of a world that is unstable, capricious, chaotic in rhythm. Thus, if the affectivity is indispensable in the establishment of psychological unity, it is just as much a danger, a "hostile force" as the psychologists say—a torrent capable indeed of fertilising but also of destroying. To hold the force of a torrent in check you need embankments. To hold the force of the feelings you need the power of the spirit. But sometimes the spirit is worn down by the struggle; sometimes moreover the current is too strong; and the emotional perturbations shake and dislocate the slowly constructed and fragile unity. Mental pathology has abundantly demonstrated the ills that flow from an anarchic emotional life; and the same destructive possibilities lurk in all of us. Here everything starts with the conflict involved in the normal state. If this conflict is not resolved by a solid integration, the affective forces are freed and form autonomous structures of their own. Consciousness of self, power of voluntary attention, sense of reality are all weakened together; and if this state continues, if complexes are set up, then the autonomy results in disintegration. The synthesis is lost, the personality split and unity destroyed—the soul has been beaten by its body.

Moreover this psychological tension spreads further, and transposed on to another plane becomes a spiritual tension, a conflict between flesh and spirit. The very expression should make us reflect. There is here no longer a simple conflict between soul and body. Man is a being with a definite tendency. He is orientated towards an end, that is to say to a spiritual plenitude, expansion in knowledge and love, communion with being—with the Infinite Being. In this field too he has to realize his unity. But the unity in question here is no longer psychological, that is to say the unity of a being whose faculties are all functioning properly and working together harmoniously. We are concerned with the spiritual unity of a being who has to invest himself with a meaning by uniting himself with his end. He can do it only by way of a choice which is at once an act of renunciation and a gift; a renunciation of all that hinders, and a gift of himself to all that goes to realize communion with being. We are no longer on the vital but the spiritual plane. We are no longer concerned with a unity of *functioning,* but with the unity of an *ascension.*

Now tension and conflict are more markedly in evidence here than ever. They are set up, not now between body and soul as such, but between two series of instincts—let us say shortly, between the instincts of egoism and those of generosity. Both pertain to the soul, both are spiritual; though the former, it is true, find a ready-made complicity in the most direct and strongest carnal instincts—self-preservation, combativeness, sexuality. The conflict here is no longer between two component principles, between soul and body, but a conflict within the interior of one and the same "I," between two "selves" of opposing orientation: a carnal self, solidly rooted in the most elementary and violent instincts, and a spiritual self solidly rooted in the deep mystery and radical dynamism of the spirit. There must needs be a choice between the carnal and egoistic self and the generous and spiritual self. And not a calm and quiet choice; not made under windless skies, on a steady deck, but tragic, storm-tossed, a choice between two forces locked in inexpiable warfare. This however is not the place to consider the struggle itself. The thing that chiefly concerns us here is to note that the carnal pull is formidably heavy. It is in fact more potent than the spiritual aspiration. In default of a miracle that only God's grace could perform, man is carnal and sold under sin. From one end of the human scale to the other experience is there to witness it. Even the most exalted souls can recognize their own portrait in the

famous passage of St. Paul, the "typical" description of man
abandoned to himself: *For that which I work, I understand
not. . . . For the good which I will, I do not; but the evil which
I will not, that I do. . . . For I am delighted with the law of
God according to the inward man: but I see another law in my
members fighting against the law of my mind, and captivating
me in the law of sin that is in my members. Unhappy man that
I am* . . . (Rom. VII, 15, 19, 22–24). Here man is brought
face to face with his own hard law: in him the spirit is vanquished. In souls less finely attuned, in consciences more sluggish, in wills but half awakened, there is doubtless less feeling
for the tragedy of their condition, but the weight of carnality
lies all the heavier on them on that account. They yield to it
more easily, they become habituated, they build their unity
on the lower self; and so they fall under the yoke of a law
still harder: in them, the flesh is victorious. Little by little they
become mutilated and disabled, since their spiritual powers
no longer draw them in any effective fashion to their proper
ends; they become earth-bound, since they hold to nothing
but the pleasures of sense; and prisoners, since their world is
now strictly bounded by the demands of instinct. If they still
know peace, it is a dull and leaden peace—the peace of a
satiated body. If they still know love, it is but one distress the
more. For "in any real love," as Nietzsche said, "it is the soul
that envelops the body." With them it is the body that imprisons the soul and enslaves it to its own appetites.

Various social phenomena exhibit, with all the exaggeration
common in such cases, this victory of the flesh over the spirit.
Crowds, like individuals, have their law; and the law is that
the crowd, left to its own devices, is taken in tow by the
elementary instincts. The double charge of affectivity and
carnality we have noted is infinitely stronger than the spiritual

tension. The crowd is given over to the lower affectivity. It is a
centre, not of spiritual communion, but of emotional contagion,
that is to say "the communication from individual to individual of human emotions simply as emotions and independently of their content." [53] The thing that counts above all is
the emotional vibration, the affective thrill, in short the corporeal agitation. And in a crowd already worked up the reaction is released by any chance happening. "A silence, a
trumpet-call, a cry, a gesture, a phrase as vague as you like,
provided only it is emotionally rich, a slight swaying of the
mass, and at once a contagious shiver runs through it and the
atmosphere becomes suddenly tense. At this moment the unconscious and affective get the upper hand, and if only the
basic dispositions are guided into the right channels you can
lead this crowd where you will, to carnage or even to sacrifice.
*For the instinct of self-preservation vanishes in the emotional
storm.*" [54] Then that crowd is thrown to the beasts—to the
beast that each of us carries in his own breast—and is nothing
more henceforth than one huge body convulsed with animal
passions. Cupidity and violence, vengeance and devastation,
such are the powers that seize on these masses and throw them
from time to time into the work of destruction or massacre.
It is the triumph of the carnal and the irrational.

This triumph, under less violent forms, is the aim of all ma-
terialist civilizations. All are characterized by a pagan cult of the
body. For man is made for adoration, and when he refuses it
he falls into idolatry. Not to linger over its feebler forms (bourgeois comfort, fastidiousness, gluttony), let us single out two
of its more acute phases. The first might be characterized as
a pursuit of intoxication, of an exaltation at once physical
and psychical, an inverted quest for happiness and a perverted
paradise. The true paradise is attainable only with effort, in

the pure atmosphere of a soul that masters itself and masters its body. Here, on the contrary, it is sought by renunciation of effort, by abasement of the soul and a violent excitation of the body. Intoxication by alcohol, crude and brutalizing; by drugs, subtler to all appearance, lapping soul and body in unknown beatitude; by sexuality, absorbing the whole being, the commonest, the most animal, the most damaging. Incontinencies and drunkenness, chamberings and impurities—who can fail to recall St. Paul's enumerations, so true and so clearly uttered? [55] And how potent is this miserable concupiscence! Giving way to it with full consent at the start, the soul becomes in the end a prisoner to a practically inexorable determinism. The process is always more or less the same: a kind of oblivion, of euphoria or ecstasy, a need increasingly tyrannical and devouring, and finally a disaggregation of the being, the body becoming a raging beast, the soul foundering in animality, and the whole man going to pieces like an old rag. These artificial paradises open on hell. Yet nothing seems to check the progress to the abyss, and to this day our civilization continues to flounder in sexual intoxication. Witness our morals—the street, the newspapers, the studio or the salon; witness our contemporary art —where man would find his joy!—which exploits, and by that very fact intensifies, the sexual obsession; witness the reports of our official investigators, social workers, doctors, philosophers; [56] everything tells the same tale of a reign of unchained appetite.

The final upshot is an exaltation of the body on principle, a *mystique* of the body. With us it takes on a bourgeois form which has found expression in nudism. This so-called "return to nature," which presupposes an abandonment of all spiritual control and a complete contempt for modesty, is nothing either more or less than a religion of the body, an old pagan dream recalled to life, or, as some are pleased to imagine it, "a return to the Hellenic cult of health and beauty." [57] However, since this new religion throws over the soul, it simply amounts to a dehumanisation of the man. It is by no means clear—we may note in passing—that a certain conception of sport is not obscurely connected with these errors. Development of the body does not, to be sure, imply a cult of the body; but it is easy to slip from the one to the other. When sport is made out to be *the* method for the proper upbringing of youth, and when it indulges in an exhibitionism of which we have examples enough and to spare, it may be suspected that the descent has already begun. There is a logic in things that gets the better of good intentions. Why seek on the sports ground anything other than you would wish to see everywhere?

But faced with this unhappy development we may readily understand the genesis of another and heroic *mystique* of the body, pagan too but with a difference. In the eyes of the Hitlerites, to cite the typical example, man and the universe are sustained by an all-pervading life-force. The body, as bearer of life, is the chiefly important thing: the soul is merely an efflorescence, and its worth is strictly dependent on the structure of the body and the quality of the blood. The biological element thus commands the spiritual dispositions, and accordingly there exist distinct and unequal races of mankind, slave races and master races,—Nietzsche's lesson has not been forgotten. A gigantic effort will therefore be made to protect and develop this body which carries all the dearest hopes of a people. And the first dogma of the new religion will come to expression in the cult of the purity of the blood and the splendour of the body. "The sin against the race and against the blood is the great original sin of the world, and the doom of a people that commits it." Adoration of the blood, therefore of the body; mysticism of the vital forces and a thoroughgoing reaction against those of the spirit; the old pagan dream once more, big with catastrophe; and if we go to the bottom of things, a crude materialism, absorbing all energies, justifying all cruelties: nothing will be too hard, no sacrifice too great, if only the new humanity can be hammered out in the process. In reality, the body becomes at once an idol and a means to the undoing of man. That is the final reckoning.

IV

This tragic situation poses the most urgent of our problems: what, in Christian eyes, is the meaning of this misery of the body?

First, that the body is not an idol, nor an end in itself, nor a god; but an instrument, a simple material instrument. It has all the noble qualities of matter: it is penetrable by the spirit and fit to do it service. It has all the miseries of matter: and it is a limitation, a weight, a force that opposes the spirit; and it seems indeed almost a miracle that it can be overcome, penetrated and ordered by thought and love. That should make us realize how we stand as material creatures. Because he is partly made of matter, man is dull, opaque, subject to suffering and doomed to death—"dust and ashes." If his body enjoys an immense dignity, it owes it all to the soul which makes it the body of a being created to the image of God. Because his bodily being is due to the soul, because in itself it is but a potency which the soul must bring to act, its dignity is that of an instrument wholly defined by its relation to the soul. So that for everyone who considers the body as it is in itself, for the biologist who analyses the living organism, for the physician who takes it in hand in sickness, the body is doubtless a very marvellous machine; but it is still more evidently an ephemeral

affair, carrying the seeds of its own corruption, a frail aggrega-
tion of cells heading straight for dispersion. We must remem-
ber the lesson: the body is a small portion of matter to which
the soul has given life. Why be surprised at its limitations and
miseries? They are normal enough in a creature that bears its
own nothingness about with it, in an animal creature whose
life is simply a promise of death. They should help to keep us
clear of this absurd worship of the body and lead us to the true
wisdom that treats it as a servitor born. They should dispose
us to the adoration of Him who alone is without limitations
and miseries, who knows of what clay we are made, how brief
our days, how humble our paths.

As soon as God is brought into the picture however this
realism about the body raises a most serious difficulty. The body
is a burden too heavy for the soul, an instrument out of tune,
a trial more than a help, a grievous temptation. The philosopher who does not look beyond the pure abstract relations
might deduce a certain misery as involved in the very nature
of the body; but the philosopher who would account for the
concrete condition of man could never, simply from the facts
of the human essence, explain the depth of our misery. For so
acute it is—unhappy man that I am!—that it calls in question the goodness and wisdom of the God who made us, and
anyone with a keen sense of it might well be tempted to revolt
or despair. I think that for this problem, which does not bear
on the essence but on the condition of humanity, none but the
Christian has any genuine solution; and that here again his
first joy—a bitter one—is to know and to understand, while
awaiting the second, which is to be capable of freedom and
to be freed.

The Christian solution hangs in a word: the human body
is not the body that God willed; it is a body that has fallen,

along with the man in his entirety. Something that God did not create has had its way with it; and that something is sin. The human body was made by God, but its actual state is the work of man. Mystery of the fall of man! The body is too much of a burden, too tyrannical, too much fraught with peril, to enable us to think of its state as natural; but then, precisely, it is not natural. God's work has been spoilt, and the lost equilibrium, the body's revolt against the soul, is the sign and the fruit of another revolt: that of the spirit against its God. At the bottom of all our miseries lies human sin, and this it is that has changed our human condition.

God created man in a spiritualized state—we do not say a spiritual state, which would be that of the Resurrection: He gave man a soul spiritualized by a very close and profound contact with Himself, the Father of Spirits, and a body spiritualized by a very full and very strict adaptation to the divinised soul. God had the fullest ascendency over the soul, and the soul in its turn over the body; the soul was wholly given to God, and the body to the soul: a two-fold grace, organic and coherent, of which the central keystone was the soul's own gift of itself to God by adoration and love. A soul fully subject to God, and, consequently, fully master of its body, a plenitude of contemplation, supposing and producing a plenitude of interior harmony—such was man's initial state. His originating sin consisted of a will to be self-sufficient, to be his own master, to determine for himself, in sovereign independence, his own mode of life and his beatitude. The soul thus severed its ties of grace with God, and, by that very fact, it severed its ties of grace with the body. Man then fell into a state which, when compared with the first, must be called a carnal and an animal state: a soul closed on itself by its sinful liberty, and a body henceforth given over to its own law, the law of matter, partly hostile to the spirit. A soul wounded to its depths by its inability to give itself wholly to God, and a body equally wounded by its inability to give itself wholly to the soul—since ties of grace are not within our power. As far as concerns our present problem the point affected by the wound is the relation of body to soul—the tie subsists, but it is weakened.[58] The soul is no longer fully master of its body, and the latter in part escapes it. It is no longer able to make the body live for ever, and so we have death; nor to make it fully available for thought, and so we have its dull opacity; nor to master its instincts, and so we have the violence of concupiscence. To say that the body is partly abandoned to itself, that it has revolted against the soul, is to say, in effect, just one thing: that the soul is no longer able to spiritualize its body, and that the latter, of its own weight, drags it down to animality. Such is the wound that explains its misery, and explains also, not the *existence,* but the tragic *degree* of the three-fold tension, metaphysical, psychological, and spiritual, we have noted above.

But then, as we perceive, though the body fell, the soul fell first. That is why the Christian, even in the midst of all his severities, does not fail to bend with a faithful care over this poor body of his: it is a danger, but it is unhappy. He loves to stress the infinite nobility still retained by the flesh even in the heart of its worst downfall; and from this standpoint St. Bernard was not wrong to emphasize, in a vehement page, the still subsisting grandeur of the body: "It is surely a shameful and monstrous thing that while this vessel of clay, this body formed from the slime of the earth, still lifts its eyes on high, looks freely round on the heavens and contemplates the stars with delight, the rational soul on the contrary, that spiritual and celestial creature, should turn her eyes—her thoughts and inner affections—to the ground; that she, who was made to feed among the lilies, should cleave like a swine to the mire and set her heart on filth. Blush, O my soul, exclaims the body, blush to have thus exchanged the divine for the brutish image. . . . Compare thyself with me and be confounded! Created as thou wert in uprightness, like to thy Creator, thou didst then obtain in me also a helper, upright like thyself. Whithersoever thou dost bend thy gaze thou seest on all sides the reflections of thine own beauty, everywhere to recall thee to thy dignity thou findest familiar reminders that come from the Spirit of wisdom. Whilst I still keep intact this privilege bestowed on me for thy sake, how hast thou not shame for having lost thine own? Why must the Creator behold His image quenched in thee, while thine in me is still faithfully presented and preserved? Thou hast abused my service; and changed from a rational to a brute spirit art worthy no longer to inhabit a human body." [59]

All the same, though the soul corrupts the body, the body oppresses the soul in its turn; and the whole Christian tradition takes up in sad refrain the words of Scripture: *Corpus quod corrumpitur aggravat animam*—the corruptible body weighs like a load on the soul (Wisdom IX, 15). We are fallen once more under the law of *this corruptible* and are ruled by the *sense of the flesh* (Col. II, 18)—of the flesh that lusts against the spirit; and on account of this body of ours we are pilgrims far from the Lord. Since it was the soul that sinned first, the soul must be the first to be freed. Since this body is now our heaviest burden, it remains for us only to lift up our hands to the Liberator of souls and bodies, and to pray God that He would have pity at last on us, poor creatures of clay:

> *Seigneur, qui les avez formés de cette terre,*
> *Ne soyez pas surpris qu'ils soient trouvés informes,*
> *Et bossus et bancals et sournois et difformes,*
> *Et mauvaise nature et mauvais caractère.*

Vous les avez pétris de cette humble matière,
Ne vous étonnez pas qu'ils soient faibles et creux.
Vous les avez pétris de cette humble misère,
Ne soyez pas surpris qu'ils soient des miséreux.

Thou, O Lord, who hast formed these bodies from dust,
Wonder Thou not to find them deformed,
And bent and halting, shambling, misshapen,
Of ill condition and evil temper.

Thou hast moulded them of this lowly matter,
Wonder Thou not that they are weak.
Of miseries Thou hast compacted them,
Wonder Thou not at their misery.

CHAPTER FIVE

REDEMPTION OF THE BODY

The body is for the Lord,
and the Lord for the body.
(I Cor. VI, 13.)

THE SIGNIFICANCE OF EVERYTHING here below is determined by its relation to Christ, for *all things were created by him and in him* (Col. I, 16). The human body—mystery of greatness and misery—finds its last explanation and its total consummation in Christ. The body was created in such wise that the Word of God might lay hold of it and assume it; and because the Word was made flesh the body's condition was thenceforth changed. It is redeemed. It awaits its glorification.

I—THE BODY OF CHRIST

Verbum caro factum est: Christ is a Divine Person who took a soul and a body like ours. Henceforth the body is not simply tied to a spirit, but united in personal intimacy with the Master of Spirits. The Incarnation, in a sense, is God descending even into this material organism, immersed in space and time, caught in the toils of need and pain, subject to wear and tear and to death. An humiliation this, which in the eyes of faith amounts to an annihilation, since the Lord thus took the form and the reality of a *servant* (Phil. II, 7);

79

a thing which, for our clouded intelligence, is simply a scandal. "Simple folk and Christians," wrote Jean Bodin, "but never philosophers, can be brought to believe that the Eternal God should so stoop from the high excellence of His nature as to clothe Himself with a body like ours composed of blood and nerves and bones, and then, in this new figure, should expose Himself to the horror of an ignominious death . . ." [60] In another sense, the Incarnation is God taking the body to Himself. For God does not change, He does not cease to be what He is, and the Word Incarnate, walking humbly in our midst, remains "the only-begotten Son who *is* in the bosom of the Father" (John I, 18). Here then it is the body that ascends—this body which at one and the same instant was created by and united to God, and was assumed by the Word into the living and eternal unity of His being. So that the outlook is now in very truth reversed, since *in Him* (Christ) *dwelleth all the fullness of the Godhead corporeally* (Col. II, 9).[61] Through this humiliation a mystery of glory is inaugurated: *The Word was made flesh and dwelt among us*, but, by that very fact, *we saw his glory, the glory as it were of the only-begotten Son of the Father, full of grace and truth* (John I, 14). Humiliation and glory, the double face of the unique mystery which faith is to embrace in its wholeness.

Christ took a body like ours; and therefore a body *made of a woman* (Gal. IV, 4), *Corpus natum de Maria Virgine*. A human being is formed at the meeting-point of a specific biological process on the one hand, and the creative action of God on the other: two cells unite with each other, and God unites them with a soul; and the outcome is a living man, a person with an eternal destiny, an image of God for ever. When Christ came into existence and entered the world, the Trinity took the biological elements of a human being from the womb of the Virgin and informed this body with a soul. And so "the flesh became flesh" and at the same time the flesh of the Word of God; it was flesh animated by a reasonable soul, and at the same time the flesh of the Word of God; since not in itself, but in Him, it had its existence." [62] But then also at the same time "the Mother of God against all the laws of nature, gave that whereof He might Himself be fashioned to Him who fashions all, and that whereby He might be made man to God the Author of all things, who divinises that with which He enters into union." [63] Thenceforth, Christ's body, like ours, drew nourishment from the flesh and blood of His Mother; it developed and came to maturity like one of ours, with this difference —and this miracle—that His soul was already fully awake and master of its body; it came to the light and was born like one of ours, with this difference—and this miracle—that His Mother's body remained intact and even more virgin than ever—*integritatem non minuit sed sacravit*. It entered at last on its long-drawn history—hunger and thirst, work and sleep, joy and pain, and finally death—so much like ours on our own journey through the world. But it entered on this history only to transform it: and this, its rôle of transformation, is what we have now to study.

* * *

The body is at once a means of expression for the soul and a veil; it reveals it, and it hides; the fall thickened the veil and made it less penetrable by the spirit. By the Incarnation, the human body finds its capacity for expression carried to the infinite, for now it expresses God. The face of Christ was, in all strictness, the human face of God. For Christ is *the image of the invisible God* (Col. I, 15), and, as He said Himself, *he that seeth me, seeth the Father also* (John XIV, 9). If the face

reveals the person, then in this human face is revealed a divine
person—a person whose being and reality is none other than
God's: so that when I contemplate this man I see God Himself. The term "image" should not be allowed to mislead us.
An image, for the Ancients, was not an impoverished or at-
tenuated reality, a mere reflection; it was rather a participation of the very reality itself, it made it present in its substantial essence, and active with its proper efficacy.[64] That is what
has to be read into St. Paul's word: because Christ is the image
of God, he is God Himself, but God as given us and put within
our grasp; wherefore *he that seeth me, seeth him that sent me*
(John XII, 45). Thus the first rôle of Christ is to make God
present to men by way of His body. Faith is doubtless needed
to seize this presence, but faith creates nothing; it is a mode
of vision adapted to divine realities and simply discovers them.
In truth, the body of Christ is the great *Power of Signs,* through
which God Himself is manifested to us: Christ's look meeting
mine, His voice in my ear, His hand on my shoulder, is the
look, the voice and the hand of God made man. And that,
without doubt, is why His look pierces to the bottom of my
heart, why His voice reveals me to myself, and why His hand
is healing; but, above all things, that is why His look and voice
and hand reveal the love, the truth and the power of God.

Christ is the Truth come into this world to give testimony
to the truth. How does He transmit His message? By way of a
corporeal sign, a word. Therefore this word is at once a human
word and a word of God's: *and the word which you have
heard is not mine, but the Father's who sent me* (John XIV,
24). For this word comes from no stranger who himself receives a message from without, but from a Person who is none
other than the living and consubstantial Word of the Father—
the unique Word in whom God utters Himself wholly, the

Word who is identically exhaustive vision; and this Divine Person communicates His own mystery, partially and fragmentarily, but truly, to His soul and to His voice: *I speak that which I have seen with my Father* (John VIII, 38). Christ is the Omnipotent come into this world to authenticate His word, and that is why *a virtue went out from him* (Luke VI, 19)—from His soul incarnated in a body—which cast out devils, healed the sick, calmed the winds, multiplied loaves, and raised the dead. The merest bodily motion sufficed, a word, a gesture, a touch, and at once, by way of the miracle, the divine power was there beneath our eyes. For Christ's own works were His Father's works, the works His Father gave Him to perfect; and He perfects them *that you may know and believe that the Father is in me and I in the Father* (John V, 36 and X, 38). Christ is the Love that gives itself through His witness. His stainless purity, His unstinted generosity, His untroubled holiness in God's sight, His infinite charity— all these rays of divinity shine through His human history. He is *holy, innocent, undefiled, separated from sinners* (Heb. VII, 26); and He is so revealed precisely by His human life. In this Saviour, *the man Christ Jesus, there appeared the goodness and kindness of God our Saviour* (I Tim. II, 5 and Tit. III, 4).

Yet this splendour was not fully shown; it remained veiled. The fall had done its work; and the glory of the Only-begotten Son did not shine out in triumph, it did not instantly exalt the faithful and reduce the faithless to confusion. It was through a body as heavy and lightless as ours, in the likeness of our sinful flesh, that the revelation was made. Once only, for the privileged three, the veil was drawn aside and Christ appeared in all the glory that was His. Death must intervene before Christ can arise and His glory appear, though once again this was to be only for a brief while and to none but the faithful awaiting His ascension to the Father. His glory was normally banished to the summit of His beatified soul, and Christ's body, like ours, was *a humbled body* (Phil. III, 21). And yet this light, tempered as it was for the beholders, adapted to our sick vision and carefully respecting our liberty, was yet glorious enough to leave the minds of the witnesses illuminated by its splendour, so that St. John could speak of *that which we have seen with our eyes, which we have looked upon, and our hands have handled of the word of life . . . that which we have seen and have heard we declare unto you* (I John I, 1–3).

Once entered into His glory Christ was not obliged on that account to fall back on a merely invisible activity. His life is continued in another body, and this too is His own and His permanent means of expression to the world. This body is the Church. Just as our body enables the soul to utter itself and display its virtualities, so that it is literally its "fullness," [65] so the Church, which leaves room for the unfolding and manifestation of all the riches of Christ is *the body of Christ and the fullness of him who is filled all in all* (Eph. I 23). The traits which revealed God in Christ continue to reveal Him in the Church. The Church speaks, and her human word is the very word of God. The Church's path is strewn with miracles, and these signs are always the revelation of God's presence, because *it is God that bears witness by signs and wonders and divers miracles* (Heb. II, 4). The Chuch lives, and communicates the life, the love, and the holiness of God through her own proper life. She too in her turn is thus the great *Power of signs set up in the midst of the nations,* [66] even as was the personal Christ Himself. She is the Bride, already glorious in her Head, *without spot or wrinkle or any such thing, but holy and without blemish* (Eph. V, 27). And because the Bride is the Bridegroom's body (Eph. V, 28) His countenance will be recognisable in hers. Our bodies, gathered into the unity of the Body of Christ, destined in Him to form the Perfect Man in all the fullness of his stature, thus become the means to express to the world, not the life of a created spirit alone, but the life of the Infinite Spirit.[67]

* * *

The body is a means of action. In Christ it finds its potentialities of service carried to the infinite: it became the means of salvation, the instrument of the Redemption. The Epistle to the Hebrews puts it plainly: *in God's will we are sanctified by the oblation of the body of Jesus Christ* (made) *once* (Heb. X, 10). Not that the body is here to be conceived as a distinct dimension, since it was His whole self that Christ offered. But if God became man, this was because He came to save, not the angels, but the human race: the seed of Abraham, father of all believers; so that *it behoved him in all things to be made like unto his brethren,* and *to be made a partaker of flesh and blood* (Heb. II, 17 and 14). That is why St. Paul insists on the rôle of the body. The only way in which God made man could offer Himself, was to offer this body through which His soul expresses itself and acts. This total offering is none other than the sacrifice of Christ, and the three stages of His sacrifice measure the three moments of the Redemption.

The first stage is the complete dedication of His human and corporeal life made at the moment of the Incarnation: *Wherefore, when he cometh into the world, he saith: Sacrifice and oblation thou wouldst not: but a body thou hast fitted to me. ... Then said I: Behold I come, in the head of the book it is written of me that I should do thy will, O God* (Heb. X, 5–9).

This oblation was made in the full light and the full generosity of a soul that saw God; wherefore it is measured not by the merely successive time of a soul that is tied to a body, but by the all-embracing duration of a soul in total union with God; and hence it embraces a whole life, clearly perceived in all its future course, and now having only to be lived out in unfailing daily fidelity: *for I do always the things that please my Father* (John VIII, 29). Here then is thirty years of life in the flesh offered up at a single stroke for the salvation of the world. Henceforth all His bodily activities will be a beginning of the work of Redemption. Carpenter's toil at the bench at Nazareth, in the days of His hidden life. Evangelization of the poor by this humble human preaching that was nevertheless the power of God unto salvation; by innumerable corporeal benefits bestowed, signs of the true life and means to draw us towards it; by forgiveness of sins, in which an all-potent word makes all hearts new. Prayer by the wayside or on the mountain heights, glorifying God, reconciling heaven with earth, but expressed in every motion of the body and so beautiful that it drew from the disciples this exclamation: *Lord, teach us to pray.* Unwearied devotion of this man who wears Himself out with labour, lacks time even to eat, sinks exhausted by the well, and sleeps in a sinking ship. That is the first moment of the Redemption.

And here is the second. The body is not only a means but also an obstacle, a burden and a danger. It is hand in glove with sin and death. It is a *body of sin* (Rom. VI, 6). To deliver it effectively God turns its very wound to account: by the Cross he *condemned sin in the flesh* (Rom. VIII, 3), and Christ re-opens the springs of life by the sacrifice of His body. At the central heart of the Redemption is the Cross and Passion. It was this that He embraced in fullest awareness in the first—

and unique—offering; it was to this that all the rest was
ordered; and now the hour is come to give His life for those
He loves. A formidable reversal! Christ did not suppress suffering and death, but He changed their meaning. Of a means of
destruction He made the very means of life; of a punishment
the means of healing; of an annihilation the means to a resurrection. A mental agony so overpowering that it drew a sweat
of blood, the pain of a lacerated body, sufferings that drew
from Him strong cries and tears and prayers and supplications
(Heb. V, 7); two full-voiced appeals, filled with agony and
trust—*My God, my God, why hast thou forsaken me?* and
this: *Father, into thy hands I commend my spirit*—and lastly
the parting soul severing its bonds with the body: that is the
sacrifice that saves us. At the source of all this suffering and
death there lay a choice: Christ gave His body over to sinful
wills because He had willed it so; He allowed His soul to
wrench itself away from His body because He had positively
willed this thing to be. And, at the source of this choice, there
lay a measureless love, a love that never hesitated, never drew
back, never murmured; a love on the contrary that accepted
and desired and bore with everything. "In the true love, it is
soul that envelops body"—we have cited the phrase above.
Here the soul envelops and surrenders its body with such fullness that we are saved by the oblation of the body of Jesus
Christ.

But this is still only a stage. This death is not a goal but a
way, the tomb is not an end but a resting-place; the body
entombed not a corpse but a seed. Because He offered and
willed His death, Christ has a right to His reward; because
He gave His life He had a right to take it up again, and, moreover, in that state which was its due. Because He was crucified
the Lord of Glory merits thereafter to be exalted. His soul

took back its body, it penetrated it through and through, and made it spiritual. Instead of the *body of our lowliness,* Christ now has *the body of his glory* (Phil. III, 21) ; a spiritual body, transparent, obedient to the spirit, unconstrained and lightsome, an apt and natural instrument for the soul of the Divine Saviour. He died that we might die to sin. He rose again that we might live in Him, and rise again one day with Him. The body sacrificed has become the body glorified. The final touch is put to the redemption of man.

Let us rather say that now that all is acquired in Christ, the work of redemption will be continued in the bosom of humanity. In this Body which He gathers up daily into Himself, Christ will manifest his *power of an indissoluble life* (Heb. VII, 16). His Passion and Resurrection will be continued in the Church. In her, since she is His "fullness," will be consummated those sufferings and that glory that shall render His unique Redemption present to all ages, and shall crown it at the Last Day. But in the Church, as in Christ Himself, the thing that predominates is the Cross, and the hours of transfiguration are only passing gleams. If glory is real in this Church which Christ would have glorious, it is none the less normally veiled and mingled with humiliation—it is much less a sign for unbelievers than a reward for the faithful. That is why, while yet proclaiming that the New Covenant, as compared with the Old, is a Covenant of glory (II Cor. III, 7-11), and that, while veiled for unbelievers, the light of the Gospel is the light of the glory of Christ (*Ibid.* IV, 4), St. Paul nevertheless declares, *I fill up those things that are wanting of the sufferings of Christ in my flesh for his body which is the Church* (Col. I, 24). And the sacred act which makes of each of us a new man in Christ is of all acts the humblest, and its glory invisible—this baptism which signifies and reproduces in us the death and resurrection of Christ, and thereby aggregates another member to His Body.

* * *

We reach the final marvel and the supreme glory of the body. It is a means of communion, and now we find that the body of Christ is the appointed means of union with God. Thanks to His body and to mine, man and God enter into communion. Here again, it is a union through the sacramental signs, the real appearances of bread and wine; through the sacramental reality, the body and blood of Christ; through the veil of signs and through the veil of flesh and blood. All this because the economy of the Incarnation continues, and because we are always in the realm of faith, in the domain of signs which simultaneously give and hide. But it is indeed Him who came down from heaven and is always in heaven that we receive. The whole redemptive mystery is present in the Eucharist: here is the flesh surrendered and the blood poured out—here is the whole Passion; here is the body risen again and ascended into heaven—here is all the glory; here is the living bread that gives life to the world—here is everlasting life.

Thus we may realize that this union, in spite of the double veil that is not to be torn, is of all unions the most tangible, the surest, the most transforming. The most tangible, because it is by His body that we lay hold on God; the surest, because the body of Christ is an objective reality, independent of our feelings, affections or thoughts; and the most transforming, because the man who eats the flesh of Christ partakes of the very life of God. This transformation is noted in the Gospel, and thrice in its triple depth. Man is a solidly subsistent being, a personal centre of life, and capable of assimilating the universe. But he is unachieved, incomplete, and in point of fact mutilated, in so far as he has not yet recovered the grace of God. By the Eucharist, *he has eternal life* (John VI, 55)—he has it as a power assimilated, become His own, but one which nevertheless transforms him, and in which he finds the principle of a solidity that is definitive because divine. Moreover, man is open on all the real and on all being, and he must enter into union with it if he is to fulfil his potentialities. By way of the Eucharist *he abides in Christ, and Christ in him* (John VI, 57) : the two-fold bond of love, once knitted up, realizes this full community which is strictly called communion; and because man is *called by God into the fellowship of His Son, Jesus Christ* (I Cor. I, 9), he fulfils his vocation, and so also his own being, by way of his relation with his Saviour. Finally, since Christ receives all from His Father, and returns it to the Father in an outpouring of adoration, love and praise, the Christian communicant *lives by Christ as Christ lives by the Father* (John VI, 58) ; he is gathered up into this beatifying movement and takes his place in the trinitarian life; he finds his fulfilment in the Triune God who made him to His own image and likeness, and who now, through the body of Christ, restores the disfigured image to its proper life and beauty. Thus the body of Christ becomes, in the strictest sense of the word, our spiritual principle of life; it is, despite the conflict of terms, the soul of our soul,[68] and it endows the human person with the fullness of his being, conformed to the creative will.

But the Eucharist is not primarily the life-principle of the individual Christian; it is, first and foremost, the life-principle of the Church. By the Eucharist is built up—in silence, suffering and hope—the mystical body of Christ; and, in the words of Pius X, it is "the symbol, the root and the principle of

Catholic unity." For if *there is one body,* it is because *there is one Bread* (I Cor. X, 17). The Body of Christ is not multiplied in the multiplication of Hosts; Its presence alone is multiplied. But the sacrament is unique, "subsisting from the birth of Christianity to the end of the world, outside me in itself, integral and complete"; and consequently there is but a sole Eucharistic Bread and Chalice, from the Cenacle to the end of the world, partaken so many millions of times over by priests and faithful, and drawing the whole Church throughout all ages and nations into the unity of Christ, so that these two, Christ and the Church, form but a single mystical person.[69] In Christ and the Church, as in each of us, body and person go together; and we may apply to the Eucharist what St. Paul said of Christ as the Head: that by It *the whole body being compacted and fitly joined together, by what every joint supplieth, according to the operation in the measure of every part, maketh increase of the body unto the edifying of itself in charity* (Eph. IV, 16). And that increase will continue till the day when the body having attained its fullness, and the glory of God its consummation, the Church will cease to proclaim the death of the Lord because He will come Himself; and when the communion of our earthly pilgrimage shall give place to communion in glory, in which all shadows shall flee away along with all the veils and all the signs, and the very Eucharist Itself.

II—THE CHRISTIAN'S BODY

We must now return to the state of our own bodies in so far as we are still pilgrims far from the Lord. Note first that the Christian's body is a redeemed body. It has been transferred to another master; it has passed from evil to good, it has returned to God's ownership, it is no longer a thing profane, but sacred; and this change of ownership is precisely a consecration.

Since the whole man is to become a member of Christ, in baptism Christ takes possession of soul and body together, snatching the body from the corruption of the old Adam and from the power of the devil. The ancient exorcisms strongly insist on this point; but the formulas, for all their emphasis, do not signify that the still pagan flesh is really possessed by the devil, but simply that the flesh, not yet belonging to God, is normally the prey of sin, and, through sin, of the devil. By baptism, all is changed: cleansed henceforth, anointed, signed with the cross, the body is consecrated to God as a holy house, as a worthy instrument, as the fraternal companion of the soul, evangelized and converted in principle. Some ancient rituals spoke out here with joyous and triumphant precision: "I sign thy forehead that thou mayst be Christian, I sign thine eyes that they may behold the light of God, I sign thine ears that thou mayst hear the voice of the Lord, thy nostrils that thou mayst breathe the sweetness of Christ, thy lips that thou mayst utter the words of life; I sign thee on the breast that thou mayst believe in the undivided Trinity; I sign thee wholly, in the name of the Father and the Son and the Holy Spirit, that thou mayst come to life eternal and live for ever and ever. . . ." [70] So real is this consecration that to sully the body in a direct manner by impurity is a special profanation: he who commits it sins against his own body—this body of his which is *not for fornication, but for the Lord,* because he is a member of Christ (I Cor. VI, 13–20).[71]

The Christian has to bear witness; and that he may be capable of so doing he receives the sacrament of Confirmation. But the body is necessarily engaged in this task. The Christian

ought to be proud of his faith, and so needs an "unblushing
front." He should radiate his faith by the candour of his look
and the ring of conviction in his voice. He should spend himself, and toil and suffer, and die if need be, for Christ. The last
witness is given in persecution unto blood and in martyrdom;
but short of this is the unending effort that wears out a life
in God's service, the trial borne without flinching, sickness
endured in patience, resignation and hope—so many signs
of this steadfastness in the faith, or this bold confession of
Christ, which is the grace of Confirmation. Thereby the body
is fully restored to its proper rôle as image of the soul, and it
bears witness of its virtue, of its love, of the presence of Christ
within it. To such a point is this at times the fact that, obtain-
ing from Christ a share in His sufferings, and giving way under
the violent stress of faith and of love, it receives the imprint
of the Five Wounds, and bearing these stigmata becomes a
living image of the Crucified.

Then, to complete the baptismal consecration, comes the
Eucharist. In it, Christ once more lays hold on the body to heal
it, and so restore it to its proper function as the soul's instrument. The body subjects us to temptation, and it is the instrument of sin. Even when redeemed it still remains profoundly
sensible to pleasure, and shamefully weak in the face of its
seductions. The Eucharist sweetly appeases and heals it; not by
any abrupt miracle, but by way of a contact infinitely hidden,
deep and efficacious.[72] Little by little it brings the body back
under the governance of the soul, it helps the spirit to master
the perpetually resurgent force of desire; it prevents those
sudden and overpowering revolts which can destroy the purity
of the heart at a blow; it puts new tastes into the newly flowering flesh; it "purifies the springs," and of all these fleshly
members once given up to iniquity it makes, by a slow re-ap-

propriation, so many instruments of holiness. Progressive re-
possession of the body by the sanctified soul, thanks to the
progressive spiritualization of the flesh, leading to an ever more
and more real consecration of the body to God, and, in short,
to an ever closer affinity of our body with the Body of Christ—
such is the first effect of the Eucharist.[73] The Liturgy begs this
grace of healing with its customary simplicity: "May this
Host, O Lord, we beseech thee, cleanse us from our sins: and,
by the celebration of this sacrifice, may it sanctify the bodies
and souls of thy servants"—"O Lord, our helper and our pro-
tector, succour us by making our flesh and our hearts to blos-
som forth anew in modesty and chastity." [74] And again, in
the prayer of St. Thomas Aquinas, so humble and so true, to
be found in the Missal for thanksgiving after Mass: "May this
holy communion . . . root out all my carnal desires . . . and
may it serve for quiet ordering of all my impulses, whether of
the spirit or of the body."

The body's wound, involving sickness and suffering as it
does, hampers also the normal activities of the soul. For the
Christian, to be sure, sickness and suffering are means to service; and health, if a good, is always a subordinated good. It
remains a real and normal good; it aids the work of building
the Kingdom of God, and the lack of it is often so formidable
an obstacle that St. Paul thrice besought the Lord to remove
from him this *sting of the flesh*. When this good is needed—
and it is so always, at least in a measure, and for a time—God
Himself preserves or restores health. And here again the Eucharist has its part to play. It brings our flesh into contact with
Him who healed the sick, and has lost neither His power nor
His mercy because He is the Saviour and the God who gives
life. In a measure which He alone determines, because it is
bound up with the mystery of our vocation, and therefore with

the form of our service in the world, in a real but commonly
indefinable fashion, the Eucharist keeps the body in health.
We have only to open our Missals and we may see the Church
asking for health as one of the normal graces that flow from
the Body of Christ: "Defend us, O Lord, from all perils of
mind or body"—"Grant unto thy servants, O Lord our God,
at all times to enjoy health of soul and body"—"May our
reception of this most holy sacrament . . . profit us, O Lord
our God, to health both of soul and body"—"We beseech
thee, O God, that our sins may be blotted out by these sacrifices,
because then thou dost accord us true health of soul and
body." [75] And finally every day in the Canon of the Mass:
*Let not the partaking of thy Body, O Lord Jesus Christ, which
I, all unworthy, presume to receive, turn to my judgment and
condemnation; but do thou, in thy loving-kindness, make it
avail to my healing and safeguarding in body and soul.*

Lastly the body is wounded so deeply that one day it will
slip altogether from the soul's grasp, and that means death.
For the Christian however this death is not final; he knows
that his body will rise again. The Eucharist is directly concerned with this resurrection: *He that eateth my flesh and
drinketh my blood hath everlasting life, and I will raise him
up at the last day* (John VI, 55). Thus the Eucharist is the
seed of immortality; it enhances and develops the affinity of our
bodies with Christ the Head of the Body, with Christ who
rose from the dead, *the first-fruits of them that sleep* (I Cor.
XV, 20). Therefore Christ's path will be ours. He knew death
and we shall know it, He passed through it and we shall follow.
The Eucharist does not give the soul back its power to make
the body live for ever. But it enables the man as a whole to be
touched, incorporated, assimilated in still deeper fashion by
Christ. When the union of soul and body is dissolved, the soul

does not cease to be apt to animate its body, the glorified soul calls for the glorification of its body; and the Eucharist has given it an exigence, a principle, a radical power of resurrection: "Our bodies which have received the Eucharist," said St. Irenaeus, "are no longer corruptible, because they bear within them the hope of resurrection." [76] Thanks to this contact with the risen body of the Saviour, we too shall rise one day with Him and by Him. And that is why the priest, when he places the Viaticum on the lips of the dying, offers up to God this prayer: "We pray thee, holy Father, Almighty and Eternal God, that the body of the Lord Jesus Christ, Thy Son, for this our brother who receives it, may be an eternal remedy as well for the body as the soul."

This body consecrated to God must serve, and its immediate duty is to *glorify God in our bodies* (I Cor. VI, 20). Henceforth none of its activities is profane, all, as of right, are sacred, and ought to be freely devoted to the service of God. As regards our strictly religious activity no question arises; it is clear, for example, that our prayer offers up to God the sacrifice of praise, that is to say *the fruit of lips confessing to his name* (Heb. XIII, 15). But the same should be true of all our bodily activities whatsoever, since our very bodies are the *temple of the Holy Spirit* (I Cor. VI, 19). "The Holy Spirit dwells chiefly in man's heart, into which He pours the love of God; but next also in all the members of the body, inasmuch as they perform acts of charity." [77] Thus all our bodily actions not excluding the humblest such as eating and drinking, are to be consecrated to the service of God. Why should necessary things be pagan? Thanksgiving goes up already from the whole creation because God refreshes it and nourishes it:

Thou sendest forth springs in the vales: between the midst of the hills the waters shall pass.

All the beasts of the field shall drink: the wild asses shall expect in their thirst.

Over them the birds of the air shall dwell: from the midst of the rocks they shall give forth their voices. . . .

May the glory of the Lord endure for ever. . . .
(Psalm CIII, 10–12, 31.)

But the creation exists for man that he may daily quench his hunger and thirst in it, and that his earthly sustenance may avail him not to blaspheme but to praise his God: *Therefore, whether you eat or drink, or whatsoever else you do, do all to the glory of God* (I Cor. X, 31). All: the hardest activities, the sweat of toil, the daily accumulating fatigue, sufferings which have to be stiffly and interminably borne, the exhaustion of bodies broken by labour, by anxiety, by all the calls of life—in all this the Christian is *assured that Christ shall be magnified in his body, whether it be by life or by death* (Phil. I, 20). The most intimate activities, those by which man and woman unite to become one flesh, by which their life is handed on to others, by which is fulfilled a mystery of union and fruitfulness imaging the mystery of the union of Christ and His Church—in all this the body is a means to the service of God, as the Church teaches us in her prayer: "Protect us, O Lord, the servants of thy mysteries; that ever cleaving to divine things, *we may render acceptable service to thee with body and soul.*" [78]

This will help us to understand the magnificent—and primary—significance of Christian chastity. It is in no wise a shrinking from life. It is an essentially voluntary consecration of the body to the glory of God. First, because it is homage offered to God by way of the imitation of Christ. The first ascetics vowed themselves to virginity so that, in the admirable phrase of Ignatius of Antioch, they might "honour the flesh of the Lord." [79] His flesh was human and passible, but attuned to the spirit and joyously responsive to its calls. St. John seems to have this in mind when he writes: "The Word was made flesh and set His tent among us"—that is He dwelt not in the massive house that encumbers us and drew groans from St. Paul: but as it were in a light tent pitched on the surface of our earth, which a breath of the Spirit will suffice to carry away into paradise. That is the Christian's ideal. For he knows that "the body was not created to live in shame and debauchery but to follow Christ as its head and to be ruled by the Lord." In his baptized flesh he sees the likeness of a maiden given over to a libertine—the devil—redeemed by the King, who is Christ, and henceforth to be treated as a "royal betrothed." [80] Holy reverence for the body thus comes of an outlook wholly religious and wholly Christian, and chastity is the homage of the flesh to Christ our Model, and an act of adoration to the God who is Spirit.

Moreover, and by this very fact, chastity is a spiritualization of the body. It subdues the flesh, it gives it an orientation, it makes it readily obedient to the spirit, a loyal servant of the soul, and so also of God. From this standpoint, chastity is the most admirable of sacrifices, because it removes the body from the sway of debasing instincts; the most beautiful of testimonies, because it shows that the grace of Christ has power to free us from the tyranny of carnal desires; and the glory of God once more, because it restores that order within the human being that was set up by the creative will. The dream of the early Christians—of the Greeks especially—was to recover, at the end of their efforts, the subdued and transfigured body that God had bestowed on the first man; and this *apatheia,* for which the whole Greek spirituality exhibits a yearning, was

perhaps simply, in its deepest reality, the name they gave to
the old Christian dream realized, or at any rate, unweariedly
pursued: the complete victory—willed by God—of the spirit
over the body.[81] And we may well believe that they would
have enthusiastically endorsed the formula of St. John Chrysostom: the man united to Christ by total chastity "becomes in
some sort a spirit, even while yet in the body. For when nothing
corporeal, nor gross, nor earthly, holds him any longer, then
he is simply enveloped by a body; and when he is governed
wholly by the soul and the spirit, then is God glorified." [82]

The full subjection of flesh to spirit is, for the Christian, an
ideal to be unweariedly pursued, but not a state that is normally
realized. His body remains carnal, and has to be spiritualized.
That is a datum of faith as well as a fact of experience. Even
redeemed, the body resists the spirit; it subjects it to grievous
temptation, it brings suffering and death. All the misery we
have described above still hangs around it even when the body
becomes Christian. What means this enigma? And what is
meant by a body that is still described as carnal even when
redeemed?

Let us observe in the first place that if the body's misery
remains, its sign is changed; it is now on the way to be sub-
jugated and headed towards a nobler destiny. The grace of
God by Jesus Christ, Our Lord, has delivered us from this
flesh which so incessantly gets the better of the soul, and from
the tyrannical yoke of the law of sin that is in our members.
Henceforth we are spiritual men, indwelt and quickened by the
Spirit of God, subject to the law of the Spirit, a law of liberation, and so become capable of overcoming the solicitations
of the flesh. The current is therefore reversed, the air is purified, hope returns—hope, with clear eyes, helmeted, hope
that confoundeth not (I Thess. V, 8 and Rom. V, 5). St. Paul

summed it all up when he said: *We are saved by hope* (Rom. VIII, 24). For here below the redemption is effected only in germ; this world of time, of crises, of progress, of first-fruits and of expectation, exists simply to give it scope for development; it will not come to full fruition until the day when days shall be no more. The Christian is therefore a man who, *forgetting the things that are behind, stretches forward to the things that are before* (Phil. III, 13), who is ceaselessly beckoned on from the thing that he is, to the thing that he is to be; he is one who does not attain, but hopes. And the meaning of this tension, essential to hope, is the thing we have now to consider.[83]

The body is redeemed in hope alone; that is to say it remains unsubmissive, a trial, a temptation; and under one of its aspects the wound inflicted by original sin is always open. The soul's hold on the body has been weakened by original sin, and not re-knit by baptism. The grace of Christ has healed the soul as regards its relation to God, but not, in any direct manner, as regards its relation to the body: its original mastery is not restored, and the interior distance that separates soul and body remains intact. Whatever efforts the person may make to recover his nature and knit up his unity, this distance will never be wholly abolished, and the body will always be a material mass against which the spirit will beat in vain. Never perhaps has the soul a more acute perception of this than at the moment when, after the most drastic purifications, it seems about to tear away the last veil and look upon its God. "Break the web of this sweet encounter," it can but cry; but the web does not break, for it is the body itself inasmuch as it is not yet glorified. Here it would seem we hold the root of the spirit's sorrowful longing: inasmuch as it is tied to this flesh, it is still as one who seeks and can never fully find either its own being or its God.

If now we ask the meaning of this tragic tension, we shall have to say first that it is a call to our liberty. The body is given us back redeemed in hope, that we should redeem it in reality. We are faced with a choice: *Let not sin therefore reign in your mortal body, so as to obey the lusts thereof, neither yield ye your members as instruments of iniquity unto sin: but present yourselves to God as those that are alive* (risen) *from the dead, and your members as instruments of justice unto God* (Rom. VI, 12–13). Instruments of sin or of sanctity—that is the sole real alternative for the body, and through the body for the spirit. But, by that very fact, God takes us into partnership with Himself to re-fashion our total being; and this effort of spiritualization is what we call chastity. Not now simply a consecration, but a virtue armed at all points, virile, playing the man. The body has to be restored, subdued, chastised—a slow process since it has to do with matter, and hard, since this matter is rebellious. At the first stage, if we may venture so to schematize, the will to chastity is frequently overcome by "the evil that I will not." At the second, the virtue takes root but commonly has to fight; the flesh is simultaneously rebellious and held in check. This state the Ancients called *continence,* and certain saints have known it to the day of their death. At the third, the body is tamed and reconciled to the soul, which rules it now in peace; and that is *temperance.* But this peace remains an armed peace; its first law is an evangelical vigilance, and its only security lies in ceaselessly renewed conquest—*castigo corpus meum et in servitutem redigo.* For the rest, this strife remains fraternal. The Christian never forgets that his body by nature is the good and faithful companion—*bonus plane fidusque comes caro spiritui bono* [84] —; that it is a burden not on account of its presence simply, but its corruption—*gravati corporis necessitate, non socie-*

tate [85]—; and that henceforth it is redeemed and becomes a temple of the Spirit. *No man ever hateth his own flesh* (Eph. V, 29), and the Christian least of all since his flesh is the flesh of a member of Christ. Severe as he may seem to be on his body, the severity is always enveloped in love; it does not aim at a separation but a closer embrace; he chastises the body to make it a better companion, and not in view of any impossible divorce. If extreme cases arise, if ever we have to pluck out an eye or cut off a hand, that is only in so far as these members may have become pure instruments of sin, and for the integral salvation of the body itself as well as the soul. It is our duty, for the rest, to nourish and cherish our own flesh (Eph. V, 29), no less than to clothe the naked and to give drink to the thirsty, and to succour him who lies bleeding by the roadside.

The strangest mistake in fact is made about the Christian attitude to bodily suffering. It is supposed that the Christian is bound to regard it as primarily a direct benefit and to accept it as a pure blessing. If that were so, Christianity would be simply inhuman. The truth of the matter is that suffering, for the Christian, is at once a trial and a call. It is a trial, and thus an evil. It was not made by God but by sin; and that is precisely why it bears on man so hardly. It unmans, unnerves, and tempts—who does not know the frenzy of blasphemy and despair that so many pains bring along with them? Consequently, the first duty of the Christian is to combat suffering, to restore integrity and strength to the body that God has given us; to save the suffering flesh so that it can once more serve the soul, and serve God. Such an effort is truly religious and truly Catholic. In very consciously acting thus the Christian cooperates with God the Creator who gave the body its life, with God the Redeemer who heals it with the touch of His own flesh, and with our Mother the Church, so full of active compassion and suppliant prayer for her suffering children. There is a Mass for the sick in which we may read: "Almighty and everlasting God, the abiding health of all who believe in thee, graciously hear our prayer for thy servants who are sick ... that being restored to health, they may come with thanksgiving to praise thee in thy Church." There is a sacrament for the sick, of normal effect on the health of the body as well as of the soul, as witness this prayer from Extreme Unction: "O our Redeemer, by the grace of thy Holy Spirit, heal the ills of this sick man, close his wounds, forgive his sins, banish all sorrows of body or soul, and give him back to health within and without; so that, restored by thy mercy, he may be able once more to go about his daily tasks." An admirable supplication, humble, holy and tender. She who speaks there is indeed a Mother. She loves this poor body mingled with soul and longs to save them both.

But pain is no mere brutal, useless, unintelligible trial: it has its purpose, it serves. For him who suffers as for him who sees another suffer, it is a call to redemptive charity—to the charity that is imitation of Christ and by which the Christian saves his fellow in the act of saving himself. When he stands in the presence of suffering the Christian is to imitate the Serving Christ, who stoops to distress; and must tender his hope, his prayer and his efforts to help the sufferer. That is one of the essential traits of Christian charity. If we would understand it aright, we have but to consider the parable of the Good Samaritan. It is nothing less than a concrete definition of the essence of the relation of charity, which consists in looking on my fellow man as a neighbour, and in making him another self. Now this relation obtains between the man who suffers and the man who stoops to help him: it is a relation of compassion. Suffering is thus the essential call that brings these two men together, and which will prompt the Samaritan to fulfil himself by forgetting himself in the other. Its first service then is to compel us to open ourselves. For man remains hard and egoistic even when redeemed. He readily isolates himself in his own body as in a shell—which protects—and as in a prison—which confines.[86] Both shell and prison have to be broken open before he can truly commune with others; and it is precisely the acceptance of suffering that breaks it and opens his heart to love. The Levite and the priest pass by on the other side and do not stop; they have not seen the suffering because they have not accepted it, unfaithful alike to its call and their own duty. The Samaritan accepts it; he allows it to make its way into himself; through his flesh it moves his spirit and awakens him to his true vocation; it reveals to him— since it puts it in act—this relation of compassion that links him of right with others, and which is one of the essential dimensions of charity. It would be a complete mistake to see only a movement of the sensibility in the action of the Samaritan; it was the act of one who, by way of a corporeal emotion, discovers, accepts and realizes his vocation. Misery is, once more, a call to our liberty, but so that liberty should give itself to charity and open itself thus to a grace that comes to save (and save together—by making them neighbours) both him who stoops to show mercy and him who receives it.

For in the sufferer also pain is a call to redemptive charity, but by imitation of the Suffering Christ, as the medievals had it. It was not God who made suffering, and yet Christ has taken it on Himself and sanctified it and made it a direct means to redemption. And henceforth what we have to welcome in it is the call of the Love that strips itself of all things—*Nudus Nudum Jesum sequi*—the love that consumes and consummates at once, which nails to the cross, because the work of redemption continues, and so that each shall make his personal contribution to the consummation of the Church by giving to the Passion of the Head its saving radiance through his own flesh. An act of liberty, an act of free acceptance and welcome, is needed to transform suffering, to invest it with its divine meaning, to make it a communion with the sufferings of Christ. But here again, this act saves others only in saving ourselves. For Christ—the perfect Image of the invisible God —came to save us by re-creating us in His image; and henceforth we can attain neither the consistence of our being, nor the full extent of our influence, save by imitation of the Crucified. All the misery of the body—its weight, temptation and pain—is thus a call of the love that consummates all. The ways of love are always mysterious, and its action is devouring, because it is the last reality, and because it reaches the centre of the person to re-make him in its image. The way of the Passion was opened through quivering human flesh by love. It is the call of the infinite love to our own love; and when we set our feet on this path we respond to the deepest call— God is love, and there is nothing beyond that; we are in touch with the supremely "formative" energy—for without love I am nothing; simultaneously with the salvation of the other we accomplish our own, by attaining the truth, the efficacy, the fullness of our redeemed being—and therein precisely is the glory of God. But as we perceive, the definitive measure of all our values lies in the reference to Christ. *"I love the Cross,"* said Charles de Foucauld, *"because Christ Jesus loved it."* In Christ once more, through this body of misery, by grace and liberty we are drawn to life eternal: in suffering in union with His lies the the hidden source, and the mysterious seed, of everlasting Joy.

Such is the law of the being who is saved in hope, and who

waits for the (full) *redemption of his body* (Rom. VIII, 23).
With Christ and by Christ, the Christian should say to his
God: "A body thou hast fitted to me; behold I come to do
thy will." In its final significance therefore the body of the
wayfarer far from the Lord is essentially *a means to sacrifice,*
and all is summed up in St. Paul's exhortation: *"I beseech
you therefore, brethren, by the mercy of God, that you present
your bodies a living sacrifice, holy, pleasing unto God, your
reasonable service"* (Rom. XII, 1).

* * *

There comes a day when the body's days of service are
done, and it is now no more than a corpse—

L'âme est partie, on rend le corps à la nature.
La vie a disparu sous cette créature:
    Mort, où sont tes appuis?
Le voilà hors du temps, de l'essence et du nombre.
On le descend avec une corde dans l'ombre
    Comme un seau dans un puits.[87]

The soul has fled, they give back the body to nature.
From beneath this creature life has ebbed away:
    O Death, canst thou sustain it?
Nay, it has passed beyond time, beyond essence and number,
And now they lower it on a rope into the shadows
    Like a bucket into a well.

St. Paul said: the body is sown in weakness, in dishonour,
in corruption (I Cor. XV, 42–43); unresisting flesh, soon
dissolved, divided from its soul; and thus, with all its nobility
gone, given over to the law of nature, and falling back into a
nameless existence which is but a form of nothingness.

A last hope however, and the most radiant, is present in the
heart of this supreme misery. The body, says the Apostle, is

sown—a word that transfigures all. The body is not a vanishing mass, but a grain sown, and some day to come up. This earth is no mere tomb, but a mighty field that nurses the scattered seed, whence bodies shall spring again for an eternal harvesting. "As the sprig of the vine, set in the earth, fructifies in its season, as the grain of wheat fallen into the earth and dissolved, rises again in manifold increase thanks to the Spirit of God who sustains all things; and as these elements come at last to the hand of man, and, having received the word of God, become the Eucharist: so also our bodies, nourished on this Eucharist, buried in earth and decomposed, shall rise again at the time appointed, because the resurrection of the Word of God shall do them this grace for the glory of God the Father, who freely endows this mortal body with immortality, and this corruptible with incorruption. For the power of God is made manifest in weakness." [88] Thus the proper cause of this unexampled marvel is the sole power of God, and it is altogether vain to speculate on its mode of action. We may nevertheless usefully reflect on the meaning of this resurrection, and on the state of the risen and glorified body.

Our resurrection, in the first place, is a prolongation of the resurrection of Christ. We are members of the Risen Christ, and we shall rise again with Him; for the power of His glory, *the power of his resurrection* (Phil. III, 10), must be made manifest. That will be brought about when this power shall unite all the members with the Head, *by reforming the body of our lowness, made like to the body of his glory* (Phil. III, 21). Those who see only the outside of things see nothing in this corpse but dust. When Christ appears in His glory then also this dust will open all its beauty to the light, appearing as part of this divine light, sinking into the sun of His glory and shining with the same rays. . . . In that day the just will shine in one splendour and one glory with Christ, filled with gladness, they to receive it from Him, as He to communicate it. . . . When the Head shall come in the clouds of heaven, He will gather His members from every part, God among the divinised, glorious Leader of a glorious choir. And as bodies suspended in the air fall to the ground when support is withdrawn and tend directly to the earth's centre, so, when the hour of deliverance shall sound, the bodies of the just, bound down to the earth under the empire and tyranny of corruption, will fly up towards Christ their centre of gravity with irresistible force. To mark the impetuosity of this flight, St. Paul likens it to a ravishment: *Then those who are alive shall be taken up with them in the clouds to meet Christ, into the air, and so we shall be always with the Lord* (I Thess. IV, 16). Thus shall our bodies hymn the glory of Christ, and, with His, the glory of God.

This resurrection is a pure grace; and yet it is a kind of justice to the body. The soul has worked and suffered in its body and with it; it has used it as its natural instrument for good or for ill, and man will be judged *according as he hath done in the body, whether it be good or evil* (II Cor. V, 10). Reward or punishment are therefore dealt out to the whole man, including his body—to some a resurrection of life, to others, of judgment (John V, 29). Such justice moreover answers a desire that is deeply rooted in man's nature. The soul is still attached to its lost body, it is still definable by its relation to its body: to speak of the soul is to speak of the act that once gave life to this body; and consequently it still longs for its body with a purely natural impulse of love. "Until death is swallowed up in victory, and the perennial light so invade and take possession of the boundaries of night on every side that the heavenly glory shines forth even in the bodies, the souls cannot utterly disencumber themselves and pass over to God, because even yet they are bound to their bodies, not indeed by life or sense but by natural affection, so that they have neither will nor power to be consummated without them. . . . O, how truly did he speak who said: All things work together for good to them that love God. To the soul that loves God, her body avails in its infirmity, avails in its death, avails too in its resurrection: first indeed for the fruit of penitence, secondly for repose, thirdly for consummation. . . . Those who have now received the second robe—their bodies invested with glory—are borne to the love of God all the more freely and swiftly as nothing now is left of their own which can in any wise stir or hold them back." [89] The resurrection is therefore God's response to the soul's aspiration, and thus it completes our beatitude. It adds nothing to its essence: the soul as spirit rejoices in fullness of happiness in the vision of God. But it lacks the normal complement of this happiness, and the normal participant. When the body is also caught up into the soul's glory then this joy will be full because now fully communicated, and because the whole man has entered into everlasting life.

If now we try to form an idea of this new state we find ourselves face to face with mystery. Two words contain the mystery: the resurrection body is a spiritual body. If our bodies are a clogging weight and a grievous temptation, it is not because they are united, but because they are not sufficiently united to the soul, and so partially escape its control. That comes of the further fact that the soul does not fully possess itself, and has to seek itself, overcome itself and lose itself to find itself. Now the spirit is made for God, and its most deep-seated capacity is to be divinisable. By the beatific vision it is divinised, and the glorified soul finds itself fully in

finding its God. It was called in Christ, it is now consummated in Christ; it knows as it is known, it loves as it is loved;
it realizes the full perfection of that image which God eternally
meant it to bear. When therefore God gives it power to take
up its body once more, it is enabled, by grace, to transform
it and adapt it to its own new life: it possesses itself in so
total a manner that now it can possess its body totally. Matter
exists for spirit, and its deepest capacity is to be spiritualizable.
Because the spirit is divinised, it is able to spiritualize its body
—as far as the body can be spiritualized without ceasing to be
itself and ceasing to play its part as body. Soul and body are
henceforth united in unexampled intimacy, the former not
crippled or impeded by matter, but, on the contrary, as St.
Paul says, swallowing up in life all the impurities of mortal-
ity.[90] The interior distance that separated soul and body is
now suppressed, all possibility of interior conflict has vanished,
the war is over and perfect peace has taken its place. The
body is spiritual "because it obeys the behest of the spirit. For
thee, no further contradiction coming from thyself; in thee,
no further revolt against thyself." [91] The glorified soul penetrates its body with such power that it obliterates all its carnal
characteristics and makes it partake of its own. It gives the
body its being; it gives it such fullness of being that this very
being itself is spiritual,[92] that is to say it becomes a pure instrument of the soul's expression, action and communion.
Henceforth no more resistance, no more opacity, no more
passibility! Still less will any touch of animality survive. The
purely animal activities—nutrition, generation—which imply
the imperfection at once of the body and the human species
itself, are sublimated or absorbed in the incorruptibility proper
to the glorified spirit; and, in this sense, the elect will be as
the angels of God in heaven (Matt. XXII, 30). They will

still be men; and the body, far from being itself a spirit, will become more thoroughly body than ever, because it will be fully mastered, fully assumed, and brought into full conformity with its eternal Type—the glorified body of Christ.

St. Paul's formulas now become clear. The body is spiritual, that is to say *incorruptible* (I Cor. XV, 42–44), like the spirit that gives it life; *glorious,* like the spirit bathed in the divine light; *potent,* like the spirit that participates in the triumphal creative liberty. All this in Christ, whose power of life is incorruptible, glorious, and all-potent. In such total appropriation by Christ, man will attain his consummation: *and then will be the end, when Christ shall have delivered up the kingdom to God and the Father* (I Cor. XV, 24) ; and when "all the members, united as one, shall break into a never-ending hymn of triumph, glorifying Him who raised them from the dead, and bestowed upon them life eternal." [93]

SPIRITUAL VALUES

CHAPTER SIX

THE HUMAN PERSON

THE NOTION OF THE PERSON is at the centre of all our human problems. Every philosophy, every religion, every culture has to take up some position here. Conflicting views have not been lacking recently: enthusiastic essays, impassioned debates, sharp critiques—who can fail to recall the effervescence of the pre-war years? We have no wish to add yet another theory to all the others. We shall simply try in these pages to bring out the essential antinomy that makes the human person the most paradoxical of all realities: a being who is simultaneously spirit and body, closed and open, existent and yet to be achieved; or, if you prefer it, the paradox of a being in a state of tension between the two principles of his composition, between himself and his fellows, between himself and his God.[94]

I

The human person is an embodied spirit, and therefore we shall have to say of him what has been said already of the two worlds, that of bodies and that of spirits.

The human person is a body, and, as such, he is subject to all the laws of matter. Spatiality confines him to one small corner of the universe; temporality makes him emerge and fall back at defined points of the cosmic movement; opacity makes him resistant, impenetrable, divided off from others; plurality denies him inner unity, and makes him a precarious and unstable assemblage of forces only momentarily composed; and finally the synergy of relations compels us to call him a meeting-place for passing forces, a medium of co-existence, a knot of contacts and reactions. But the human person is also a spirit, that is to say a reality primarily defined by opposition to the body, and one who escapes its laws. There is nothing spatial about him, or temporal; he is not shut up in a place nor held within the limits of a movement; he comprehends space and surpasses time; he is made for eternity, and when he thinks eternity he is no longer of this world.[95] He is made, moreover, for understanding, and in the very act of understanding he is disengaged from sensible conditions and escapes from time; and finally as spiritual substance, he is not measured by the flux of time, but by the duration proper to created spirits, the duration which comes of their permanence and takes them out of the movement of pure succession.[96] He is transparent; for he is neither a mass, nor resistant, nor a screen, but wholly definable in terms of intelligibility, perfection and actuality. He is simple, not to be defined by any plurality or co-existence of parts, but rather by an absence of parts and plurality: as a pure presence to self, linked up, beyond number and enumeration, with other immaterial presences; and as a totality [97] able to unify and concentrate within himself the whole infinite materiality of a universe.

And yet this spirit and this body are one being. That is the first paradox of the human person: he is the unity of this spirit and this body. A spirit becomes the "act" (that is, the actuating principle) of a body, communicates its own being to this body, makes this body exist as body; it informs, unifies, possesses and develops it. And therefore, with and in the body, it enters into space and time, it becomes subject to all the variations of the appetitive feelings,[98] it acquires a whole biological, psychological, and social individuality—things which for a pure spirit would have no meaning. But it becomes the act of a body in the only way in which a spirit can do so—that is to say while still remaining spirit, and so knowing, surpassing, and infinitely transcending its body. At his pure point the person surpasses and escapes all definite proportion with the body, so dominating it as to remain in himself immaterial, intemporal, breathing his own native air, and, so to speak, infinite with respect to it.[99] The person is thus a spirit at once immersed and emergent, immanent in the body and yet transcendent. That is the full significance we have to see in St. Thomas' figure: "the human race stands at the confines of corporeal substance, and is, as it were, an horizon between time and eternity." [100] This composite being, man, is neither animal nor angel, but partakes of both; and in him are accumulated all the paradoxes of an essence composed of contrary principles, of a being situated outside place and time, and developing in place and time.

Moreover, when spirit appears it rules, wherefore man is much more spirit than body. He belongs to the world by his body, but only to bring into it a hitherto unknown greatness and a royal dignity. Man indeed is the miracle of the world because in him is realized the epiphany of the spirit; and this spirit brings radically new values into the universe—thought and love, choice and commitment, communion. And further, this spirit is not simply polarized downwards towards matter but still more upwards, towards the Infinite Spirit, towards God. At the root of the spirit lies its power of knowing and of loving God, and it has to be defined as an image of God, an image in which God appears in the world in a manner hitherto unknown. Consequently, the human person is not fully comprehensible save when viewed from above, in the light of his relation of likeness to God; and that is as much as to say that he is strictly mysterious, that he escapes all definition, or can only be defined as indefinable. What can be strictly defined in him is the relation to the body, the soul as form of the body; what is not strictly definable is the relation to God, the soul as spirit.[101] Hence the formidable deepening of man in Christian doctrine: as soon as he is thought of as the express image of God, subsistent and indestructible, "man infinitely surpasses man." He bears in himself a mystery he will never exhaust: an ontological mystery, since his own being can never become transparent to himself save only by another who is God: to see himself he must see himself in God; a psychological mystery which echoes the former, since the embodied spirit can never apprehend himself save only through his body, the *I* only through his *me*; and this interior tension, this ceaseless pursuit that never ends in a capture, expresses the mystery of a spirit too great for its matter—the mystery of the spiritual individual.

II

If now we set out to explore the structure of the person, we encounter a new paradox. He is at once subsistent and open.

The person is of all beings the most firmly and perfectly existent. Stones, plants, even animals, really exist, but their existence is provisional, precarious, and finally not very emphatically differentiated; whereas the human person exists in himself, by himself, and for himself. This supreme mode of

existence we shall here call subsistence.[102] A thing that exists
in itself is one that exists without having to inhere in another
subject, with no merely borrowed being, but one that suffices
to itself because centered on itself. A thing that exists *by*
itself is one that exists as being its own source, as positing
itself in being by its own internal and unfailing power, and
as possessing its own being in a substantial and exclusive
manner. A thing that exists *for* itself is one that has a meaning
and a value of its own, which is ordered to itself, which is an
end, with an absolute, definitive and unique character in the
universe. The spirit, and the spirit alone, is the principle of
this full subsistence, because it is simple, wholly identical with
itself, wholly given to itself, and constituting a totality and a
universe in its own sole self. So true is this, that thus to subsist by itself, in virtue of itself is "to return to its own essence,"
or in other words, to coincide with itself, to be present to itself,
and therefore to be capable of knowing itself by way of reflection.[103] Subsistence by itself, return on self, consciousness of
self—three terms of necessity linked with each other because
they define the structure of the spirit.

We could doubtless carry this further by saying that spiritual
subsistence implies both a power of *possession* and a power of
exclusion. To subsist is to possess one's own being—yes; but
then in how absolute a fashion! In a fashion so deep, and so
deeply rooted in the essence itself, that the person is necessarily unique, irreplaceable, different from all others. In a
fashion so complete and constitutive, that it makes the person
wholly distinct, inviolable, closed on himself, and consequently
not to be absorbed as a part in a whole, as an element in a
synthesis—not definable in terms of anything external to
self. In a fashion so strict that it excludes all possibility of participation in this possession, all possible communication of this

being; so that self-communication on this plane would amount to destruction.[104] Possession and exclusion, affirmation and negation, go hand in hand, and here more than anywhere. In virtue of his subsistence each person so firmly negates and excludes the others that he stands over against them as a being that is absolutely distinct and necessarily incommunicable.

He is therefore in himself, and by reason of his own depths, an inviolable mystery. He belongs to none but himself, and therefore enjoys a liberty no less inviolable, autonomous, closed on its own intimacy. He is truly the master and measure of his own acts. And that is not only the transparent and dominative element of his liberty (since it is consciousness and possession of self) but also its perilous element, its great temptation (since it can will to shut out even God). In any case no created person can penetrate this intimacy which the Creator Himself has closed. And if God can penetrate it He does so in His own sovereign manner, respecting this dominative independence and this inviolable intimacy, of which He is Himself the Source, the Model and the End.

* * *

But all is not yet said. An analysis that went no further than that would stop too soon. It is correct enough on its own plane, but incomplete; for the person exists for an end, and is not to be fully accounted for if this datum is neglected. Moreover it falls short in itself, for if the person really exists in, by, and for himself, this has to be taken in an altogether relative sense. He subsists, but he is open; and that in a twofold direction.

In the first place his subsistence is borrowed; it is continuously communicated, wholly participated. It may be said then to be a relation to the First Subsistence in which it participates, to the Pure Act who communicates Himself, to the being who gives and loses nothing because He is pure Existence. If then the person is resistant, absolute and closed on himself, he is all this in virtue of another; and in all that makes him what he is—subsistent, distinct, incommunicable— he bears a relation to God. An internal relation, because it links up the person with God as with the permanent principle of his total being; a constitutive relation, because it expresses nothing alien but his very being as participated; and an immediate relation, because no intermediary is here possible or even conceivable, and because nothing can be at all without directly drawing on the unique source of all being. Thus the person is necessarily a subsistent relation to God.[105] In the case of man we can even put a finger on the precise point at which the relation is inserted. Not in the composite of soul and body as such, since it is not through matter, or anything that follows from matter, that God touches the human being; but only through the spiritual principle, through the soul itself, by giving the soul this *esse* which is the act of every subsistent form and so also the unique act of the man in his entirety.[106] It is in virtue of this actuality, immediately, totally and enduringly participated, that the person appears as a spiritual and subsistent relation to God.

His ties with God are so much the closer inasmuch as he is His express image, and may be said once more on this account to be a unique relation to God. True, the soul was created to inform a body, and is therefore individuated, not indeed by matter as is too often said, but by its relation to matter, *secundum habitudinem ad materiam in qua est.*[107] That is possible because, in our hierarchised universe, the soul is a point of junction; it stands on the lowest rung of the scale of spirits, and on the highest of that of natural forms. Yet its place in the universe is determined, not by the relation to matter, but by the relation to God.[108] The human soul is indeed the last of spiritual substances, but the important thing here is not that it is last, but that it is spiritual, and that its subsistence is that of a spiritual substance. Now if the order of material substances is determined by their relation to matter, that of spiritual substances is taken from their relation to God; the plenitude and perfection of their being is measured by their proximity and likeness to God; and it is this therefore that defines the spiritual species. Subsistence in an intellectual nature—there we have the relation to God which makes the human being a spirit, a person, an express image of God. If man exists in himself, by himself, and for himself, it is because he participates in a certain plenitude and concentration of being which are proper to God; and because he imitates, miserably enough no doubt, the simple perfection of God. Far from being something that isolates the person and shuts him up in himself, this possession of self by self, this return of self on self, is on the contrary, something that links him up the closer with, and brings him more and more under the sway of, Subsistent Being Itself, since it is a divine mark ceaselessly participated from God. The more the person exists in himself, incommunicable and perfect, so much the more he receives from, so much the more he depends on, God. His spiritual subsistence does not close him down, but opens him and suspends him from God.

* * *

The person subsists in a spiritual nature. Now this nature is at once individual and specific: individual as belonging to a given person; specific because open on the whole species. The person subsists in *a* nature which is in relationship with

the nature. The nature here in question is not to be envisaged either as a subsistent idea—such a realism of essences
becomes superfluous as soon as a Creator is admitted—nor
yet as a pure object of thought—for so we should retain
the concept only, and not the *res* of human nature—nor yet
again as a reality purely individualized in a human person,
since in this sense it is closed and incommunicable (*natura in
persona considerata includitur intra fines personae*):[109] but
as a reality present in all the individuals of the human species:
prout est in omnibus individuis ejusdem speciei.[110] In this
sense, the nature surpasses, englobes and unifies all the individuals; and this is the standpoint we shall have to adopt if
we want to understand the real history of humanity, and, to
begin with, the real meaning of the human person.[111] *Through*
this nature, *in* which he subsists, the person is in contact with
the entire human species; he is immanent in the species, and
the species is immanent in him.

In a sense, what is here first is the species, the human race
envisaged as an organic whole. This whole alone corresponds
to the creative idea which posited humanity in being, and
which multiplies men in space and time to bring humanity
to realization. We know the classical comparisons indicative
of the way in which a man belongs to his species. He is as a
part in a whole which exceeds him, and for which he is made;
as a member in a natural body, finding there his organic unity
and fulfilling a certain proper function; as a moment in the
growth of a unique man. For humanity develops through
persons, and does so only by communicating itself to this person and to that, and through this person to that. In virtue of
their unity in the species, all men form but a single man—*omnes
homines, unus homo.* And human nature here appears as a
force that propagates itself from man to man, from the first

man to the last, until the human idea shall be fully achieved, until humanity shall be consummated, until the divine likeness, which is the final goal of every species,[112] and the immediate end of humanity, shall be fully unfolded for ever.

Thus the spiritual individual is englobed in a wider unity, which gives him his meaning; and we shall have to say that he is defined by his ties. *Expressional ties* in the first place, since he is an individualized image, a unique participation, of the specific nature, and therefore a true expression, albeit limited and relative to all the others, of this same nature. *Positional ties* next, since he is as a part integrated into a whole. On this account he finds himself placed at a certain point of space and time in the process of the development of the human species, and he stands in a certain relation, not now spatio-temporal but intelligible and ontological, to the whole body of thinking members which constitutes humanity. *Functional ties* finally, since he is a particular member of an organic and progressive whole. As a unique and specified image each man has to realize some hitherto unknown aspect of humanity by way of the development of his own personal resources and values. He can do it only by entering into union with others, and by thus setting up this community, extended across space, charged with life and meaning, nourishing and expressive, which we call society. Because he is a moment in a development he is a partial embodiment, at once provisional and necessary, of the total power of humanity; and it will be his task to assure the development in which he has his place, and to prolong humanity in time. This he does in the act of generation, whereby he communicates that very humanity in which he participates.

The person therefore subsists to unfold the content of humanity, to carry it on and perfect it. Whenever he falls back into himself he feels his ties with the human community, he discovers there the call of the whole species, and that is why his essential power is the natural love of the Whole.[113] He is a member and a part; he is defined by his significance for, and his position and rôle in, the species; he is a relation to the Whole in virtue of his very being, and he is thus open on the totality of persons—in a way that invests him with a kind of infinity; and, consequently, his own profound and necessary inclination incessantly urges him to overstep his individual limits, and to tend to the good of the specific community. In this being, who is defined by his ties of participation and communion, the love of the Whole is at the centre of the structure, at the base of the spiritual impulse, at the heart of his historical condition and of all his concrete problems. In virtue of his being, as of his radical tendency, each person partakes of this One who is none other than the species itself : *omnes homines, unus homo;* [114] and in this sense it is strictly true to say: "The Whole is the pole of the person." [115]

But this, inevitable and evident as it is, conceals a yet deeper truth. The man is not simply immanent in the species as a part in a whole and a member in a body. The Whole, in its turn, is found in the part, the species in the member, *the* nature in *each* nature, humanity in each man. There we have an even more radical immanence which brings us, this time, into the very heart of the person, and compels us to balance our formula: *omnes homines, unus homo,* by this other one: *unus homo, omnes homines.* There is a double reason for this.

In the first place man is a form united to matter. Now every form is an act, a principle of perfection; it does not carry with it, in its own line as form, any internal principle of limitation; it can be contracted only from without,—in point of fact by its matter. In its own line as form and act it retains its internal illimitation, a kind of infinity which equates it *in potency* and *in desire* with the species itself. It carries "the illimitable idea of the entire species." Contracted by the matter in which it is individualized, it is not actually infinite; but is so in potency because there is nothing to limit from within its capacity for extension and development; and it is so in desire because it is an active form tending to achieve itself, and thus to overstep its limitation and communicate itself to attain to its full actualization.[116] Thus, in potency and in desire, all the *values* of humanity are latent in the individual person; all the *riches* that lie within the capacity of the form are prefigured in the man; and all the *states* in which a real human possibility can be expressed and embodied are present to the person, in a radical tendency and dynamism that is practically infinite. And since these values, riches and states cannot exist in fact except in distinct individuals, we shall have to say that each person carries in himself, in potency and in desire, the whole sum of the individuated persons who will in fact be needed for the total and exhaustive expression of the species itself.

But man is more than a form that animates a matter. He is a spirit, and therefore "a form wholly spiritual," [117] subsisting in itself and by itself. This form is not immersed in its matter, it exceeds its body, it contains and commands it as a potency to which it gives actual existence by communicating, partially and imperfectly, its own actuality. But immediate consequences follow. To command *its* matter is to command *matter,* since all this last is simply potency in the face of the actuating principle which is spirit. To contain *a body* is to contain *bodies,* since the relation here is not quantitative but a relation of being to being, involved in the very essence of the spirit.[118] And further, since it subsists in itself the spirit, as such, is above time, and essentially transcends the whole temporal progression of the species. It gathers up and unifies the species from within, whereas its own progress is effected only by the extrapolation of the individuals. The species is maintained only by way of a perpetual passage from individual to individual, whereas the spirit maintains itself by its *act*.[119] But to command matter and bodies and time is, in consequence, to command the species in so far as this appears as a numerical multiplication of individuals each referred to a matter, and expressing an imperfect and non-subsistent reality. For the human person subsists by himself, by this spirit which possesses and confers subsistence; it does not subsist by the species, but the species subsists by it and is ceaselessly being enriched by the definitive integration of persons in whom it is expressed (hence their dependence), and for whom it is made (and hence their autonomy). For this being, the person, has an absolute value in himself; and the species cannot *absorb* him, it can but *integrate by fulfilling*.

Moreover, and precisely because it subsists in its own right, the spirit is a totality; consequently it is in affinity with the Whole and is a power of totalization. It is, in a certain way, all things, because its power of understanding is limitless. Ideas may be accumulated to infinity, universals extended to infinity, individuals multiplied to infinity,[120] but the spirit can know them all and contain them all. And just as its subsistence in its own right lifts it above the whole material progression of the species, so its capacity for comprehension, and therefore of unification, enables it to embrace and surpass the specific multiplicity of the individuals. It must even be said that the spirit exists only for the sake of this unification. The world is a finite image of the divine Goodness, and God contains it all in the unity of an infinitely simple and purely spiritual act.

Now the spirit was created to imitate God precisely by its function of unification, and to be an image of His power "by containing the corporeal world, not in the grasp of a superior quantity, but in the purity of an intelligible act." [121] Thus, by its act as by its subsistence, the embodied spirit commands the materiality of the species itself which is referred to him. Finally —and this we have already indicated—the spiritual person finds his consistence and intelligible order only in his direct relation to God. He may well be engaged in a matter, but he is not immersed in it—as spirit, he is not exhausted in his body but turns away from it towards God; his very being involves a relation—vertical—to God which takes him out of the line of development—horizontal—of the species. And all the more so since all his activity orientates him immediately to God; and since, made as he is to know God and to love Him, he can thus double his ontological relation by a free relation which constitutes his "dignity" and perfects in him the image of God.

All this goes to show that the human person has an absolute value of his own and is willed for his own sake; [122] that he is the most perfect of creatures and the one for whom all the others are willed; that he is the principal part of the universe, supreme, fraternal with the whole, capable of gathering it all up in himself and therefore himself indispensably necessary in order that the Whole may exist. He is a free creature, capable of participation in the divine government of the universe, and so a cause willed for itself. He is immortal as an individual, and not simply in virtue of participating in a species; his spiritual acts have therefore an eternal value, and it is under their strictly personal aspect that God wills their performance here below. He carries the image of God, substantial, unique, ineradicable, but perfectible, and the whole universe is there to help him to perfect it. He is willed "according to his proper individuality," [123] and he is therefore never a means, either to the species or to the universe: he is an end.

We may now perceive how deep is the immanence of the species in the person. In virtue of his subsistence which is strictly personal and owes nothing of its permanence to the species as such; in virtue of his power of totalisation which enables him to contain the species; in virtue of his immediate relation to God whereby he is willed for his own sake within the bosom of the species,—the person is so to speak the pole of the Whole and the end of the species.

When he returns on himself he finds the whole species there within him, but as something that was made for himself. And that is why, if the deepest impulse of his being is a natural love of the Whole, he loves it not as something that englobes him and absorbs, but as something that perfects and personalizes. And therefore once more the two specific phenomena which mark him so profoundly—society and generation—are not at all in him as they are in other creatures, simply for the benefit of the species, but equally for the benefit of the person. For generation is normally implicated in a state of life in which the person, as subsistent, finds the fulfilment of his being in a love shared; and, as open, by communication of self. And society is willed as a whole of communities in which the communion, and therefore the fulfilment, of persons is prepared and brought about.

This brings us to the essential paradox of the person considered in relation to humanity at large. In so far as he is a spirit informing a body, he is drawn towards the conditions of material substance; he is a member of the species and exists for the sake of the species. In so far as he is a spirit transcending the body, he shares the condition of the spiritual creature;

he is marked by direct relation to God, and surpasses a species made for his sake. He is defined on the one side by his multiple ties with, and integration in, the species; and, on the other, by his simplicity and capacity for interiorization. He is at once a member and a whole, an excentric point and a centre. He is a living tension between himself and the Whole, and neither can come to fulfilment save *in* the other and *by* the other. The paradox is resumed in Pascal's famous phrase: mankind is *un corps de membres pensants.* Because it is a *body* the members come to fulfilment only in the body,—in its progressive unity; because the members are *thinking,* the body comes to fulfilment only in them,—in their free movements of interiority and communion. And if there is to be a full solution of the paradox it will demand that the species itself shall be gathered up into a personal unity and become a single man: an absolute paradox, pushing both the tension and the unity to its limit, and realized only in Christ.

III

When he first sees the light man is only a vague hope. He exists but in germ, and must come to his full development of himself. Not in the least in accordance with his own mere fancy and anarchically, but in accordance with the law of his being. Now a spiritual being is nothing other than the term— personal and conscious—of a personal will of God. He is therefore a being divinely *called,* and he has to *respond* to this call.

His deepest reality is to be called, that is to say posited in being: not simply to endure as posited but to achieve his being for himself. He is open on the world, on humanity, and on God; and that means that his first and fundamental impulse will be to augment, to surpass, and to, fulfil his being by entering into union with all three. In the very heart of the human being therefore there lies a radical and ineradicable exigency to expansion, and this is no abstract and anonymous law but a personal invitation from God. Man is thus called to *enrich himself* in body and in spirit by every kind of cultural activity, and by gradually establishing his dominion over the world; to *possess himself* by way of an infinitely more intimate activity of mind and will, leading to full self-awareness and self-mastery; and to *give himself* in an unforced generosity which shall carry him over his own frontiers and introduce him to the blessed world of communion and love. This call, and the energies it calls forth, commands the structure of the human being, constitutes his abiding worth, and defines the radical law of his action.

For man, thus called, has to respond; and in the response is implied the whole of his struggle for liberty, since what is in question here is a self-conquest. A difficult conquest, slow and never completed, but nevertheless the tragic stake and the splendid prize of every life. To enrich himself, a man must be constantly re-climbing the slippery slope of habit, he must keep his powers in lively tension and all his capacity for reaction intact. To possess himself, he must learn to look himself in the face with perfect candour thanks to a deep-seated humility (often bitter enough), and to strive for self-mastery through an inexorable purification of his animal powers. To give himself, he has to break down the interior barriers, to overcome all the obstacles that lurk in the dark places of his soul, to renounce all egoistic possession of self, so that he may find himself at last by ceasing to seek.

Thus man is always a call and a response intermingled, or better, the embrace of call and response. He cannot choose but

respond, but he chooses his response. Sometimes he welcomes
the call, cleaves to it with all his might, and so closely that he
seems to make it one with himself: a pure and joyous response
wholly coinciding with an ever more and more potent and
triumphant call. Sometimes he rejects the call, shuts his ears
to it deliberately, and this refusal invests the call itself with
destructive power, a force of negation that obstructs his deepest impulse, divides, disaggregates, and prepares to torture.
Sometimes a man offers himself and turns away, gives and
takes back. The capricious response, it may be, of a heedless
and timorous soul, shrinking from risk, devoid of courage to
choose between aye and no: or perhaps the painful and contradictory response of a soul divided between good and evil,
tossed about by the violence of its ayes and its noes, a soul
that through the night pierced by fitful gleams, writes a history of sorrows and joys, ambiguous, tragic, indecipherable by
any eye but God's. The inexorable embrace of this call and
this response constitutes the whole drama of human vocation,
and indeed of the person himself: an unending drama which
has always a meaning—however mysterious—at any given
moment, but is always ready to take on another. It is indeed
a terrible choice, whereby a man is to invest himself with his
own meaning, his own validity, and if not exactly his own
being pure and simple, at least with his moral and spiritual
being, his destiny to election or damnation. A terrible wrestle
between divine love and human liberty, in which God Himself
is not assured of victory.

Two important consequences follow from this. The first is
that the person is fragile. If he would make a success of himself he has to maintain his coherence through all the risks that
time may bring. This demands a permanent integration of
all the elements corporeal, psychical, social, spiritual, which

are given and needed from time to time. Now these elements offer resistance, their interconnections are always provisional, and the integrity of the person may easily founder in the difficult attempt to maintain his unity. This creature, who has to conquer himself and all things else, seems to be always himself in need of protection—"a reed, the feeblest in nature." . . . Moreover, by his very response each person acquires a value that leaves him in ever varying inequality with others. Considered in their common essence and their common vocation all human persons are equal, since all belong to the same world of embodied spirits and all are destined to the same end in union with the Infinite Spirit. Considered in their several and distinct vocations they differ and are non-comparable, because their functions in the bosom of humanity are different and complementary. Considered as realizing these vocations concretely they are unequal,—unequal in original endowment, in self-mastery, in development, in short in completeness as persons. This concrete inequality of persons is evident enough, and the common-sense of mankind is not wrong to make distinctions between criminals and respectable men and heroes. But nothing is more difficult to evaluate precisely: not to speak of the inviolable secret that each man carries in his heart, human worth is apt to change its sign, and our judgments are always in danger of going astray. If we may venture to remove a celebrated expression from its context we might perhaps say that the true sphere of creative evolution is not in the world of living things, but in the world of persons. For man, as by definition, is the creature who can bring himself to birth as he wills,[124] always able to take himself in hand, to affirm or deny himself, until at last he shall come to wear his eternal face "as his liberty at last would have it be." Quite as much as a definite reality, man is always here below a mysterious hope.

IV

This philosophical analysis still fails to touch the human person in his concrete condition: in point of fact [125] it is in Christ that the person is called to being.

The bond with God essential to the person is, in fact, a bond of grace with Christ. It is therefore doubly divine. First, because it is supernatural in the strict sense of the term, and makes the person capable of participation in the divine nature—this source of activity by which God knows Himself, loves Himself, and creates all things in order to communicate His goodness—capable therefore of seeing God as He sees Himself, of loving Him as He loves Himself and of spending himself for His glory; capable thus in his very essence, of assimilation to and participation in the divine Being.[126] Secondly, because this immense divine benediction, eternal and beatifying, is realized in Christ. It is in Christ as in the cause, the model and the end of our total being that we are called to supernatural existence; or, as St. Paul puts it, it is in Christ that we are eternally loved, chosen, predestinated, called, and become, from the day of our creation, creatures of grace: *gratificavit nos in Dilecto Filio Suo.* We are therefore called to be partakers of the divine nature (II Peter I, 4); but called in Christ and consequently called by the Father to the fellowship of His Son, Jesus Christ our Lord (I Cor. I, 9).

Thus the total term of the creative action, according to God's plan, is not simply a natural being, but a divinised being and a "Christic" being. The human person was willed as an image of God, but an image transfigured in Christ; as a spiritual relation to God, but divinised and subsistent in Christ. Just as natural creation endows man with a being which is a certain likeness of the divine Goodness, so his filial adoption endows him with a being which is a likeness to the natural filiation of the Word in God.[127] Now the full being that God would bestow on us is both one of creation and one of adoption,—a being of creative adoption. In fact, the subsistence of the personal being of man—both natural and supernatural—is based on a direct relation to *this* person who is Christ.[128] *Omnia in ipso constant*: Christ is the Whole of which all other persons are but a participation.[129]

Nevertheless, this supernatural relation to God in Christ is in fact broken in the person that God brings to existence. Adam's sin entailed on the race a disjunction between creation and adoption. God always gives life, but no longer *His* life. When a man is born into the world he is not all that God would have him be. He is separated from Christ, in whom alone he would find the fullness of his being, the efficacy of his action, and the reality of his communion with his brothers and with his God. He remains destined to life in God through Christ, and he is deprived of it in fact. This ontological deficiency, this aching void, offensive to God and disastrous to man, this uprooting of the divine life from his soul,—this precisely is original sin.[130] If the essence of man remains intact his being is henceforth wounded. He lacks the efficacious power to reach his end; he has neither eyes to see nor hands to lay hold on this divine presence in which lies nevertheless his true sustenance and his true happiness; he is without strength for the act of union with God that would bring him life, and he can but fall back helpless into himself, impotent and captive to self, closed to his brothers and to his God. In a word, he has kept his *natural being* and lost his *deiform being*. In the heart of the former there remains only the call to the latter,—a call no longer actually divinising, but one which puts all purely human self-fulfilment out of the question with-

out yet fulfilling him in God. Thus the person suffers from
a void in his heart that is more tragic than any grief; he is
affected by a kind of co-efficient of emptiness, of unreality, of
nothingness, in comparison with the real fullness to which he
is called. He is given up therefore to vanity, to the flesh, to sin,
to enmity towards God and towards man. This active governance of the spirit, this vital openness on God and on humanity,
this exigent vocation to union with God, all that we have
recalled and emphasized above, is now but a germ that lacks
reality, a power devoid of strength, an impulse strangled at
birth. And the sole reason is that the person comes into being
in a state of separation from Christ, and is therefore deprived
of this grace which would give him his true and completed
being by efficaciously knitting up his ties with his God and
with his brothers. Without Christ, and in comparison with
the thing that God would have him be, the human being is
no longer anything but a kind of matter that lacks its form; [131]
he has become "a stranger to the unifying matrix, and wandering from the womb in which he was formed." [132]

For anyone who rightly reflects, the concrete condition of
the human person is explicable by a double relation. He is
born in a fallen *state,* while all the time retaining his place in
the supernatural *order.* It is not as a singular person, taken
in his individual subsistence, that his being is thus impaired,
but as a human person bound up with the whole species, and
very particularly with the principle and head of the species. If
the person is indeed a moment in an organic development,
he draws his meaning and reality in the first place from him
who sets this development in train, its source and its starting-
point. He cannot therefore exist save as positing himself as a
relation to the first father of the race, from whom he derives
his nature and the conditions of his existence. He is a living

relation to the old Adam, and he is fallen because Adam fell.[133]
All his misery comes of this only too real and efficacious relation which robs him of all his supernatural reality and life.
Inasmuch as he is a living relation to the first Adam, he cannot
be a living relation to Christ; and that is why he is deprived
of his supernatural being and dead in the sight of God. But
in the actual order of Providence he cannot be without relation to Christ. Quite the contrary. For if he is linked with the
principle of the species, he is still more closely linked with Him
who is its end. He is willed for Christ, "for whom are all
things"; his last significance and reality come from Him who
is the completion of the Whole; and the whole dynamic movement of his being is due to the call of Christ. In short, he
exists *by* Adam, but exists *for* Christ; and the relation of origin
can in no wise suppress the relation of finality. The person
therefore is subject at once to the *weight* of the first Adam
and to the *attraction* of the Second. And we must go still
further. Behind Adam, the principle of the race, the figure of
Christ is once more discernible, for Christ is He "by whom
all things were made." Thus he holds Adam also in His grasp;
the latter's fault and fall does not exempt him from the will
of God, nor prevent him remaining, in spite of his sin, and by
that very same reversed causality that made him the source of
sin, *the figure of the Adam who was to come* (Rom. V, 14).

The human race, comprised in Adam, remains interior to
Christ in its first forthspringing as in its last call—and how
should the final cause fail to respond to the efficient? So much
the more so since Christ is not simply the source and the term,
but also the Centre of all, and because the human being exists
in Him permanently, as in a principle that communicates itself
and in an end that envelops him in its attraction. We see how
concretely we have to take our formula: the human person is

subject at once to the weight of the first Adam and the attraction of the Second. The phenomenon of "pressure" is certainly the easier to fix and define, but that of "aspiration," less
tangible, more subtle, is still deeper: the person remains called
to communion with Christ; he is reached by the Redemption
in principle and in right, in the eyes of God and by the will
of Christ; and this appears in his orientation, real albeit in-
efficacious, towards life with Christ in God.[134] The person,
when he enters the world, is thus torn between two influences,
he is subject from the first to the weight of the old Adam and
to the attraction of the New. We are not told that the influence
that lies on us the heaviest is therefore also the strongest. We
are told, on the contrary, that there, where sin abounded,
grace did the more abound—to overrun and envelop it and
to conquer it in the end. Sin *holds* the person when he comes
to birth, but Christ already *contains* him, and prepares his
release; even while he remains in the grip of the old Adam he
is polarized by the call towards the New; and the living relation to the old Adam cannot smother this relation to Christ,
tenuous no doubt, but involved in his very being, indestructible
here below, and a pathway open to salvation. Only this relation is as yet neither living nor really established; it exists only
as a call and in hope, it is thwarted by the relation to the old
Adam. The latter will have to be destroyed before the former
can be realized, and man must be rooted up from the first
Adam and grafted into the Second, if he is truly to be and to
live. This uprooting and transplantation is nothing other than
the Redemption itself, and it is in Christ that it is brought
about (Col. I, 13–14).

The person thus recovers his deiform being, and consequently his full being, when he becomes a living relation to
Christ—"a new creature in Christ"—and when the latter

"divinises all and each at the source of their personality." [135]
By faith and baptism, which efficaciously unite him to Christ
and organically aggregate him to His Body, the new man is
created and efficaciously established in justice and holiness.
The element of error, of emptiness, of unreality—the root of
the old man—is henceforth exorcised. The person is dead to
sin, to the law, to the flesh, that he may belong to Christ (Rom.
VII, 4) ; and because he belongs to Christ, because he is in
the true Son, Jesus Christ (I John V, 20), he is restored in
the truth of his being—of his being as it was loved, chosen,
and called in Christ from all eternity. But by that very fact
the paradox of the human person is pushed to its limit. He is
no longer simply a spirit and a body: he is a man divinised.
He is indwelt by the Spirit, transfigured by the Spirit; he possesses henceforth a *pneuma* which in him is a participation of
the divine Pneuma, a divine seed, the principle of a new birth,
and so of a new creature. All is brought about in Christ by
whom the Spirit is given us, and who is the Unity of all believers taken together, just as He is also the internal unity of
their several personalities renewed in time conformably with
a choice that was made in eternity.

The person is now subsistent and open in an unheard-of
fashion. He is more thoroughly subsistent than ever before
because he receives the whole of the creative influx in all its
fullness and without deficiency, and because he is already in
mysterious contact with his End, and thereby mysteriously
sealed and consolidated in his being. In Christ, by whom and
for whom he was made, he finds in reality and in truth his
full consistence and subsistence, because in Him he is (efficaciously) *called,* and (really) *is,* a son of God (I John III, 1).
Because he is a living relation to Christ,[136] he is subsistence
perfected in truth. By that very fact he becomes profoundly

united with his God and with his brothers; in Christ he is a true son of God, living with His life, and a true member organically bound up with all the others. His expressional, positional, and functional ties with the species are drawn infinitely closer because they are knotted up *in the interior of a Person,*[137] and because they come to expression within the bosom of this Body which is His fullness. All are one in Christ (Gal. III, 28), and in Him are to form this Unique Man, who is Christ in all the fullness of His stature (Eph. IV, 13). And the person is so much the more emphatically a person, as he is the more strictly a member. For in becoming a member it is precisely the person whose vocation is fulfilled, who is renewed in his divine part, and who becomes a unique and indispensable image of the personal Christ within the collective Christ.[138]

But we have not yet seized all the complexity of the human paradox. The Christ who redeems us is the *Christ crucified.* The centre of the Christian mystery, and therefore of the mystery of man, is the Cross. It was on the Cross that Christ brought us from death to life: it is on the cross that the Christian, for his part, ceaselessly passes from life begun to life perfected, from life crucified to life re-arisen. There lies the last paradox: man is not at once a *sinner* and *redeemed,* for that would be a contradiction; but he is at once *fallen* and *redeemed,* and that is the very essence of his cross.[139] The fact is that the embodiment of the person is far from perfect, since his body is only partially penetrated by his spirit. This imperfection is due to a certain lack of being,—of that being which God gave by grace to the first man and does not give us back with our redemption. The spirit has not recovered that power of spiritualizing its body which alone would enable it to embody itself fully; and the body's autonomy, still far-reaching and tenacious, albeit partial, is the great peril and the great

anxiety of the embodied spirit. While he still remains here
below the person awaits in anxiety, in distress and in tears *the*
(full) *redemption of his body* (Rom. VIII, 23). Moreover
the spiritualization of the person is also incomplete. The unruli-
ness of the emotions is not the only thing to threaten and en-
slave him: there is division and temptation within the very
spirit itself. The forces of egoism and pride are always active,
always menace the fragile likeness to God that was sealed on
his being by Christ, they can always call his fundamental orientation into question and compromise his free response to the
eternal love; [140] the wrestle between the old man and the new
will go on to the end. Now here again the root of the conflict
is a lack of being. The spirit is not sufficiently penetrated by
God, not united to Christ to the whole extent of its capacity,
not yet entirely saturated by grace; and that is why—even
after its effective redemption and prior to all personal sin—it
still harbours virulent seeds of conflict. The history of the
person begins at this point, and it will be written by this spiritual
liberty which, by making him either sinful or righteous, will
either make him more and more captive and empty, or more
and more freed and enriched with the true life (I Tim. VI, 19).

Thus the person redeemed still suffers from a double lack:
of spirit to cope with his body, and of spirit to attain to his
God. A two-fold deficiency, issuing in difficulties of every kind
and entailing on the person himself a kind of crucified state. It
is in the very act that brought him to new birth—in baptism—
that he finds himself nailed to the cross, and henceforth, to be
fully himself he must needs freely carry this cross which is
simply himself,—renounce himself to affirm himself, lose himself to save. He shares the sufferings of Christ that he may
have a part, and each day a greater part, in the virtue of *His*
resurrection, that is to say that his spiritual stature may receive

increase and attain to its fullness in Christ. As long as he remains here below he is not yet completely born,[141] he is a
new creature indeed, but only in the state of first-fruits,—a
blade that pushes above the ground, a harvest in prospect.
If every human person is made up of hope, how much more
so is the Christian! [142] He awaits the fullness of life, the full
consummation of his being, the plenary fulfilment of his eternal
vocation; and he will reach this pure perfection when he shall
attain to absolute communion with Christ, when Christ shall
be *All in him* as He is *All in all*, when perfect unity shall be
realized in the bosom of perfect distinction: one sole Image
in a profusion of images; and each of these images, each of
these members, each of these sons, fully achieved in their being
by their full relation to the Father and to the Spirit in the Son,
as the Son Himself is eternally achieved in His absolute relation
to the Father and to the Spirit. Because then they will all be one
in Christ, and Christ in them, and the Father and the Spirit in
Christ—men will be one in the Three; and not absorbed but
consummated, in and by the very act that unites them and
makes them a body: *Consummati in unum* (John XVII,
21–23).

CHAPTER SEVEN

SPIRITUAL LIBERTY

F REEDOM PRESENTS TWO PROBLEMS which might be called, in Augustinian terms, the problem of free-will and the problem of liberty. The first is a problem of mechanism, and it concerns the power of choosing, essential to every spiritual creature, making him master of his own acts, of his own objects, and of his own judgments. The second is a problem of meaning or purpose, and it concerns the power of self-realization which characterizes the person, and enables him to respond to his vocation and to achieve his destiny. The two problems are implied in each other as a partial problem and a total, as a problem of structure and a problem of dynamism, as a problem of the means and a problem of the end. For free-will is a means to liberty, and the power of choosing is there to serve a power to self-achievement.

The whole problem of Christian liberty lies in the dialogue between these two necessarily connected powers. And it is not difficult to see how this problem reflects and prolongs the problem of the person, as we have just set it out. The person is subsistent and open: and liberty likewise is a power of autonomy and a power of gift. The person is a reality given and a reality still to be achieved: and liberty likewise is a power of choice, inherent and indestructible, and a power to self-fulfilment, which is something that has to be conquered. The person is wounded and in need of healing, and liberty likewise is captive and has to be freed. In this sense, the history of the person is the history of his liberty; the problem of personalization is the problem of liberation; and the essential components of this history and this problem have now to be considered.

I

And first, the free act is the act of the spirit in its entirety. Necessary as it is to identify the respective parts played by intelligence and will in the interior of the free act—a thing already repeatedly and sufficiently done—it is altogether vain to attempt to separate them. An explanation of free-will can be neither exclusively intellectualist nor exclusively voluntarist without falsifying the problem. To be free is to be master of one's judgment—*libere judicare*,[143] and the free act therefore always implies a "judgment willed" and a "will judged"; hence we find St. Thomas saying, that the subject of liberty is neither the intelligence nor the will, but the will considered in its relation to the intelligence.[144] In other words, the free act is the act of the whole spirit, and so also of the whole person; and from this standpoint already this act should be defined as the act of the person as such,[145] and it is just that fact that makes it so grave. In the old battles that raged around this subject the Church always understood free-will as the power essential to the religious man, as the spiritual energy that enables him to believe, to will, to love, and to act.[146] And that is why any attack on the intelligence or the will is so serious a matter: it strikes at the two-fold root of free-will, and transforms the very exercise of liberty.

The free act is essentially a choice. The spirit is the power of the universal, and never attains to any but particular objects; it is open on the infinite and never meets with any but finite things; it is made for the act that would give it the Absolute Spirit as object of knowledge and love and never falls in with any but limited and individualized spirits which it can neither fully know nor unreservedly love. Because of all this there is always an abyss between its desire and its possible objects, its capacity and its realizations, between what it would have and what is offered it. This breach, open within the spirit itself, the spirit cannot close. It translates its desire for an absolute end into a ceaselessly renewed desire for particularized ends; these it seizes by way of ideas which, however universal they may be, are always ideas of some particular thing; and these apprehended ends themselves are realized by individualizing and restrictive actions. Neither the action, nor the idea, nor the end, will ever be able of themselves wholly to satisfy the spirit and leave it no choice; and if they are to attract it, the spirit itself will have to give them the power to do so. By an act of its own the spirit leaps the gap, makes sufficing what was not so, particularizes its infinite longing, makes this object rather than that to be fully attractive and fully delectable. This act is what we call choice. Such an act is the mark of a spirit that is still seeking itself, and does not wholly coincide with itself because it does not yet possess the end that would saturate its desire. It is therefore the act of a spirit in quest of its end. It is essential to the created spirit to have thus to discern its orientation towards its end, to measure the distance that divides it from it, and to determine its movement. It could not be created in possession of its end because this end, unchosen and unmerited, would not be truly its own, and because such possession would forestall the act in which lies all its greatness and all its significance. This tragic greatness goes with the human creature all through his history: as long as he does not yet see God, as long as his desire is not yet satisfied, he must leap the gap, he must choose, and so must exclude in the very act of accepting; he must opt for this or for that, that is to say he must sacrifice one advantage for another, one good for another, one joy for another. Renunciation is thus installed in the very heart of human activity, and involved of necessity in every attitude, in the most disillusioned as in the most grasping, in the most calculated as in the most indifferent—a refusal to choose being itself the worst of choices. Man is simply master of the significance of his detachment, according as, renouncing a lower value for a higher, or a higher for a lower, he makes of his option either a sacrifice or an abdication.

Moreover the power of choice cannot possibly be indifferent as to its objects; like the spirit itself, it is orientated. Were it not so it would have no end and its choices would be without meaning. In reality, if free-will is the essential power of the person, it partakes of the nature of the person: now the person is made for self-fulfilment in communion with the Absolute, and free-will is properly the power possessed by the person to fulfil himself by communing with the Absolute. Consequently, it is not a power to choose good or evil indifferently; it is a power to choose the good by following out the tendency of the nature, and a power to choose evil by falling away and deviation from the tendency of the nature. It is therefore essentially an orientated power,[147] and this is where all our problems begin. And to start with, it is wholly orientated towards God, it is a spontaneous love of the Absolute Good, and it exists only to make the person capable of entering fully into union with his end. This it can do only by coinciding with the tendency that is given it, by welcoming and falling in with the happy movement that urges it on from within, by simultaneously ratifying both the dependence and the call that constitute it, that is to say by expressing itself in a radical humility and generosity. Thus our freedom is there to serve; it is the power we possess to realize ourselves in obedience to our own interior law, or better, to our constitutive call; and since the end of the person is communion with God, the proper task of freedom is to bring about this communion by an act that is both an act of obedience and an act of self-giving.

But this freedom, orientated as it is, remains fallible. It tends to its end—a sure sign that it does not possess it. It possesses it in the movement which the end awakens in it, in the desire for the end experienced; but it does not possess the end in itself, it does not "precontain it in act"; and the interior distance between itself and its end involves a possibility of missing it. The will is *capable* of the infinite, but it *is* not the infinite. Because its being is only partial, it is a principle that is only partially good and contains a possibility of failure. Because it is not attached of necessity to the Absolute Good it can detach itself therefrom. Because it is infinite not by its positive perfection but only in the sense that all choices are open to it, it can still deceive itself, fall short of itself in falling short of its end, and sin. It was made from nothing, and the permanent congenital poverty thus arising sets a capacity for illusion at the source of all its thoughts, a capacity for emptiness at the heart of all its strivings, a power for nothingness in the bosom of all its acts. If we recollect that the human being is necessarily a being in tension—metaphysical, psychological, moral—we shall have to conclude that a latent conflict is installed in the heart of his freedom. It is *orientated* towards the good, and not towards evil; but it is *capable* of good and of evil, and the forces that are brought to bear on it draw it both to good and to evil at once, but very often more to evil than to good. Such is the source of the conflict in human action, and such also the knot of our problem. The free act that bears on the end itself, which ratifies or refuses the essential orientation of the will, is the capital act of the person. This act, and the whole series of attitudes it draws in its train, delimits the field of spiritual liberty; and this is the field we have now to explore.

II

The first problem that arises is that of the meaning and purpose of our freedom. It is not given us for its own sake, or for any end we please, but quite definitely that we may realize ourselves. There we have a starting-point to which every reflecting man will assent. To develop all our capacities and aptitudes, our physical and spiritual powers, to fulfil our human task and play our part in the world, and thus to construct and create ourselves—to bring ourselves to birth as we would be—that is assuredly man's true greatness and the essence of spiritual liberty. But here we stand at the parting of the ways. We are faced with the choice: are we going to realize our being in accordance with the dictates of our own will, or by responding to our vocation? That is the tragic and decisive choice that divides mankind into two opposing camps: those who refuse and those who consent to give their allegiance to something higher than themselves—let them name this "something" as best they can, whether duty, or ideal, or God. For the former, liberty consists in refusing, not indeed all constraints (one can choose one's constraints), but at any rate all obligations: it is a power to realize one's being in strict independence of any transcendent call. For the latter, liberty is found in giving oneself to the service of something greater and better than self, it is a power to realize self by self-dedication to the Good, and by opening oneself to God. The liberty that refuses is essentially anarchic and destructive; the liberty that gives is essentially committed and constructive. The two are mutually exclusive, and mark the deepest line of division between men.

The first takes many different forms. Sometimes the will takes its own sheer power of choice for its end. Mastery of its acts, objects and ends, which is meant to enable it to attain to its good, is here entirely isolated from its Last End, and cherished with a devouring love for its own sake.[148] Not to commit oneself, not to be dependent, not to give, to make a point of refusing to do anything more than lend what can always be taken back at a moment's notice,—there we have the lesson of the *Nourritures Terrestres,* and all this passionate recitative is sufficiently familiar. Gide himself has fixed its meaning in a penetrating phrase: "I have always found the need for choosing intolerable; the choice, to me, seems to be much less an election than a rejection of what I do not elect." Since he refuses to be committed, the choice is no longer referred to an End that would give it an infinite value, but simply to another choice which it excludes. It can therefore be thought of only as an exclusion, a void, very nothingness itself. And then life simply crumbles away into ever smaller and smaller pieces, until liberty itself vanishes like smoke in a shapeless dissipation, without meaning,[149] without efficacy, without value—and without beauty. Instead of a strong spring gathering itself together and pouring itself out in fertilizing streams, we have nothing but a fountain idly jetting up and falling back, while everything around it dies of thirst.

But the liberty that refuses can take the form of an option

in place of mere dispersion; an option for some definite human value, but still involved in refusal of every transcendent value. Here then is a deliberate commitment and a refusal still more deliberate; wherefore this attitude is doubtless worse than the first. Because it bears on an authentic value, because it calls for devotion to that value to the point of sacrifice, it is capable of enlisting enthusiasm and of sustaining generosity. Because at the same time it severs this value from its superhuman and divine orientation and confines the spirit within the limits of the human, it results in the end in a radical slavery and a monstrous stifling of the spiritual energies. Whether the object chosen be thought, or love, or beauty, or power, whether the human type to be realized is that of the sage, the lover, the artist or the conqueror, it is always a type and an object which the man determines for himself and achieves by himself, and of which he remains the sovereign master. It is the call to become properly a creator in his own right,[150] and to refuse to have anything to do with anything that transcends and obliges him. Even supposing that "man is something to be surpassed," it will still be man that surpasses man: "Life itself has confided to me this secret: *I am the being who must always surpass himself.*" [151] At the limit, with the logic of insanity, the supreme manifestation of this terrible liberty and will to aseity, will be found in self-destruction,—witness the Kirilov of Dostoievsky: "For three years I've been looking for the attribute of my divinity, and at last I've found it. The attribute of my divinity is my independence. That is all I can do to prove to the utmost my autonomy and my new and terrible freedom. For terrible it is. I shall kill myself to prove my independence and my terrible new liberty." Here, since there is mingling of engagement and refusal—engagement to the human, refusal of the superhuman—the balance may be struck at very different points. Among the unreflective the refusal may pass almost unperceived, and give rise to enormous exploitations of man by man. It can, on the contrary, be perfectly conscious,—accepted calmly or rebelliously but either way in full awareness. Once this attitude is understood and willed, it vitiates all engagements, all disciplines, all sacrifices, since these are conditioned by a fundamental refusal which suffices to void or pervert them.

So then, instead of men who refuse to admit obligation to anything higher than self, let us have men who give themselves to its service. According to the object to which it is addressed the form of the gift will vary. Some devote themselves to duty taken as an absolute value,—and they find their dignity in following conscience in performing the human task, in doing good. Others devote themselves to an ideal, not scientifically thought out, but divined, glimpsed, slowly discovered, very high and remote, an eager pursuit investing their life with all its meaning; whether it be the pursuit of beauty, as with Flaubert, of truth, as with the Curies, or of justice, as with Proudhon. "Whence comes this consuming passion for justice which so stirs me to my depths . . . I can't account for it. It is my God, my religion, my all; but try as I will to justify it philosophically, I can't do it." [152] Others, finally, will give themselves to God as distinctly known—to Him in whom alone is found the ultimate foundation of duty and the realization of the absolute ideal. They solve the problem at a blow. They know that man is orientated to God and that this orientation commands his growth; that he is called of God, and that his liberty is precisely the power to respond to the call and to realize his greatness in union with God. The forms of the gift are here very different, but the spiritual impulse that lies behind them all is of the same nature: in each case there is a gift to something surpassing, to something that liberates and fulfils, and liberty is conceived as the power of serving it. What components enter into this magnificent act? Adoration in the first place, since there is recognition and acceptance of a radical dependence; faith next, since there is confidence in the reality of the call, a setting aside of risk, and an expectation of the future; and lastly love, since there is an offering of the whole being to this mysterious and splendid reality in which all desire shall be satisfied. This triple outpouring is so much the more marked, so much the more limpid and deep, as the true meaning of our human vocation is the more clearly perceived. It is the more vigorous as the human person, as person, enters into closer union with the Infinite Person, in that "self-surpassing" that alone can fulfil his being. We might call the act thus specified an engagement, and say that spiritual liberty is the engagement by which a man enters into full possession of himself, expands and fulfils his own being by giving himself to God.

Such liberty has its conditions, and its genesis is always a conquest, slow, difficult, dangerous, involving a three-fold effort. The root of liberty is the reason. Man is free because he is intelligent, capable therefore of judging between good and evil, of apprehending ends and means as such, and so of deciding his own destiny. A certain effort after mental lucidity is therefore at the root of liberty; and all ignorance or error about the conduct of human life will be an obstacle in its way, and a danger. The child who does not know that lying is bad, that certain physical habits are bad; the man who does not know that the soul is more important than the body, or that our temporal life is a preparation for an eternal; the man who has never looked into his own soul, never noted his own desires or aspirations or propensities,—such as these are already imprisoned in views, habits, automatisms, errors, which impede or deform the springs of liberty; they can neither judge nor choose with full knowledge of what they do, and they cannot be truly free. In this sense a certain amount of precise moral knowledge is needed by the human being, in default of which he regards his error as natural and is already a prisoner. That is the element of truth contained in the saying: "To open a school is to close a prison." The master who dispenses a sound moral doctrine—whether by explicit teaching or by force of example —is already a liberator; and in this sense it is equally true to say: "A child taught is a man saved." Thus to grasp the meaning of human life, to be alive to its demands and duties and conscious of how we meet them, to do one's best to arrive at a sound judgment on these matters,—all that is the starting-point and the necessary condition of liberty.

This initial effort will be insufficient and effect nothing unless another is added: an effort at self-mastery. The proper cause of liberty is, in fact, the will. Merely to know is not enough: we must be willing and able. Now man, in point of fact, is torn between the flesh and the spirit, solicited by good and by evil, weakened moreover for the good by a mysterious wound, by his actual faults and falls, and a certain acquired taste for sin. Under what weight do we labour all our days! The man who yields to his senses, even with regret, who shrinks from his task even with self-reproach, who falls foul of others in spite of all his resolutions,—all are divided against themselves, prisoners of pleasure, of cowardice or of pride. They cannot command themselves, or rule their instincts, or bring their gestures, words or actions to the issue they themselves have proposed. They are not free. They are slaves of their passions, of their affectivity, and, in the end, of their bodies. They will not achieve freedom save at the end of a bitter struggle, when at last they shall have made themselves capable of resisting temptation, of overcoming it, and of realizing, by the spirit, the unity of their being.

There is a subtler and more terrible prison for liberty than error or passion: the prison erected by the spirit itself when it deviates in its own higher regions where the essential drama of gift or refusal is played out. A penetrating intelligence and a will of iron, when put to the service of egoism or spiritual pride, can lead to the most fearful evils. Then we have men of appalling and pitiless wickedness, the great criminals of history, enslaved by the most consuming of passions: to succeed at all costs, to dominate the world around them and mould it to their will. Pride that conceals and serves an egoism emptied of every trace of charity; slavery the most subtle, the most enduring, the most complete, since the man has become to himself his own proper end, since he has rejected his vocation, severed himself from the source of his own being and shut himself out from love; the closest prison of all since it joins an absolute responsibility to the most radical servitude. For these are they who have refused to understand that the deepest root of liberty is neither intelligence nor energy, but love. The man who loves what God works in him, what God would have of him—his duty, his vocation, and the Good which is their basis—breaks through the barriers of error, passion and pride; he turns his mind and his energy to answering the call of duty, to serving God and his brothers, to fulfilling his vocation, that is to say his personality itself. He enters the realm of communion where liberty gains strength and spreads and integrates all things and fulfils them. He interiorizes all laws, all commandments, all obligations. He loves to give the thing that is asked of him; and this coincidence of will and commandment, of desire and end, of love and duty, of the creature and the Creator, this is liberty itself. *Dilige, et fac quod vis!* That is now the supreme law.

Only *love* your duty, and your God, and your brothers, and then you can do what you will! For then you will loyalty, purity, justice, generosity, and, in a word, all good. And if a man could love thus in an absolute fashion, that man would be wholly free, because it would be altogether one and the same thing for him to do his own will and to do what he should. But we know too well that this is to be achieved only on the final heights, and that a long and bitter struggle will be needed before we attain them.

III

Thus spiritual liberty is reached at the end of a long effort of integration—the corporeal, affective, and spiritual powers being re-grouped, unified, and orientated towards the gift of oneself which shall perfect the person. Spiritual servitude represents a like integration in the opposite direction,—the same powers are unified for that self-refusal which makes men "carnal." If we take due note of the tension between flesh and spirit which characterizes man, of the conflict between his egoistic and generous self within the same ego which is his essential tragedy, we shall realize that he cannot be neutral; that he is constrained to choose and give his acts a determinate direction; that he must give in an essential adhesion either to flesh or to spirit; that this adhesion will be ever at work, by its force and its inclination, through the whole range of his concrete activities; and that thus our liberty is always surrounded by a concrete complex, which it helps to form and maintain, but which gives it an orientation in its turn and limits and fixes it.

Here we touch on one of the capital data of our problem. Man is never stripped naked, never neutral; he can never amount to a mere disintegrated dust of impulses, choices and decisions; and if he pretends to a "naïve incohesion of appetites and desires" this superficial incohesion and laboured naïveté conceal a clear-eyed, decided and pitiless will to refusal, and therefore to unification on the basis of the egoist self. But every option for an essential end does to some extent unify the ego around itself. Motor habits, spiritual habits, physical automatisms, feelings and inclinations, voluntary choices—all become organized little by little around the end pursued. This organization, which spreads and becomes stabilized, subjects the man in the end to a dominant inclination. Not to any necessity or any determinism in the strict sense of the term, because the adhesion to the end can always be reversed. It is none the less an habitual inclination which tends spontaneously to canalize our choices; for all that accords with the habitual end attracts attention, awakens desire, promises pleasure, seduces the will, and seems to call out to be chosen. It must even be said that all that accords with the end adopted is perceived and experienced as satisfying the appetite, and so is chosen on the spot. This inclination is strengthened by every convergent element, the torrent is swollen by every trickle that comes from the hill-side, and the man ends by entering into a state defined by his concrete dominant inclination. Every human life is thus like a river which in spite of all pauses, hesitations, backwaters, very surely follows the course appointed. According as he tends to good or to evil, the man takes his place in the ranks of the spiritual or of the carnal. His free-will is prisoner to no necessity, but more and more led by an inclination. There is this difference however between the two cases, for if a man has chosen to follow his lusts the corporeal and affective elements tend to become dominant until they materialize the spirit and hold it in the grip of a practical determinism which rapidly hardens and proves mortal; whereas if a man follows his aspirations, then the stirrings of his spiritual affectivity and his generous decisions will gradually get the better of his materiality, will loosen its bonds, and reinforce the spiritual movement of liberty from within.

There are therefore certain states of liberty, the extreme forms being respectively a state of captivity—that of the carnal man—and a state of deliverance—that of the spiritual. It would be a grave error to take them for states involving opposite determinisms to good and to evil; for the infinite amplitude of the will can never be ontologically suppressed, the possibility of recovery is always real, and even if a man bears on him for the time being all the marks of enslavement, the only determinism that holds him is one that has been *willed and constructed,* and is therefore capable of being *refused and destroyed.* But it would be an error no less grave to speak of liberty as a power always identical with itself, with an efficacy essentially inviolable, always ready to give and take back *ad nutum,* in total independence and serene "indifference." This untenable rationalism neglects alike the most evident facts of experience and the most unquestionable demands of analysis. Man shapes his own being daily by the exercise of his freedom, but yesterday's freedom lies heavy on to-day's, and the latter already casts its shadow over to-morrow's. The human being is too obscure to himself, too deeply involved in matter, too much immersed in habit, too easily carried along on the current of life, to be able at a moment's notice, to put everything in question again. He chooses, he follows up his choice, he follows his bent; and that is why, according to the concrete complexes of their liberty—captive or freed—there exist two races of mankind, the carnal and the spiritual.

Consequently again we shall have to distinguish two types

of the free act: those that simply follow up and prolong, and those that create. The former move to an end already accepted and ratified within an adhesion already firmly established. They respect, develop and strengthen the concrete complex within which they came to birth. The miser, the libertine, the man of ambition—Grandet, Don Juan, Caesar—in so far as they adhere to their lusts; the wise, the generous, the heroic, in so far as they follow their aspirations,—all simply ratify a decision already taken; and whatever their object or aim, their choice proceeds from the starting-point of a liberty already adherent and committed. All these free acts are simply acts that prolong; they are, in this sense, secondary and partial because they do not go back upon the whole orientation of the person and the essential trend of his life. The shape of that life may change, it may undergo adaptation to circumstance, enter on another course, but its deep significance remains intact. The roots of liberty are not touched. However varied, divergent, tragic, or chaotic the choices made, they differ only in their points of application.

But then, precisely, there are acts that put the end itself in question, which touch the roots of liberty, the whole trend of a life, the spiritual being of the person. These are acts of conversion, whether involving a total break—on the plane of willing—with the past, or a decisive deepening, a radical purification or perversion, carried out in accordance with the habitual inclination but through an option that puts a whole destiny in question. Such acts are creative. They constitute the most splendid proof of the abiding liberty of man; and from that standpoint the apostate is as good an example as the convert. Such acts are always possible since the essential core of the will remains inviolate, and its infinite capacity will never be satisfied with the finite. They are difficult, because they demand a total resumption of the self, an absolute putting-in-question, the *tanta deliberatio* of St. Thomas. They are rare, because no one can repeatedly make a clean sweep of the whole orientation and mechanism of his life, the equilibrium and play of his powers: the human fabric simply would not stand it. But such acts are the deepest expression of a personality, they are acts of the person as such, that is to say as self-constructive. Whenever they appear they initiate or resolve a crisis of growth or collapse in the history of the man, and mark him for time and eternity.

CHAPTER VIII

CHRISTIAN LIBERTY

CHRISTIAN LIBERTY should be studied within the outlook just defined. It is nothing else than the real and concrete liberty of a creature fallen and redeemed. That is why the whole question centres round these two affirmations: without the grace of Christ our liberty is captive; and this same grace alone can set it free. Enslavement and liberation,—these are the two points we have to establish.

I

Enslavement in the first place is a fact of experience: man is conscious of an aspiration to liberty, and of its frustration. He would be freed from all constraints of every kind: whether those of the body which cripple his powers; those imposed by others which limit their range; those arising from the brute resistance of things; and those that come from within the soul in disaccord with itself. An aspiration to be freed, which is the means and the negative face of the aspiration to fulfil himself by mastering the world, by building the human community, by discerning and realizing his happiness. This is the aspiration that always haunts the mind of man, sustains him, urges him on, and gives him power at times to brush all obstacles out of his path. When a man—or a people—is too much oppressed and too miserable, then he revolts and smashes everything. Youth throws off the beliefs that hamper it, woman breaks up the home whence love has fled, the worker breaks through the social conditions that have become too hard to be put up with any longer, a people casts off the yoke or perishes in the attempt. All of them revolt in order to live and breathe freely. This freedom from constraint, this spontaneous and untrammelled play of heart and soul, of gesture and action, this urge of the whole being towards activity, life, joy—this is the liberty men would have, and for which they still know how to die.

Now we are bound to note—and it is one of the saddest things in the world—the check imposed on all this measureless aspiration. Society exists to help man to develop his powers, and man maintains it to be more fully man, to be greater and freer. Straightaway it begins to secrete obstacles to liberty. Economic oppression breeds wholesale misery, a kind of "temporal damnation" that robs a whole people of the elementary conditions of freedom; political oppression unleashes a welter of rivalries, hatreds and wars, and suppresses the liberty to be so much as a man; spiritual oppression poisons the very air we breathe, debases the masses, falsifies youth, and deprives all, the atrophied and the enraged alike, of the very taste of liberty. We must go further and say that everything that man invents as a means to liberation ends up by enslaving him. A miserable law, and all too easily verified. He invents the machine. At once his power is increased ten-fold, his heaviest burdens are lightened or removed, his mastery of the universe triumphantly asserted, and liberation appears to be at hand. But in fact the machine only makes his work more inhuman than ever; mechanical progress brings unexampled scourges in its train, and a nameless slavery. He creates the trade union. He wins the right to protect himself against exploitation, to lead a more human life, to free himself from economic and social constraints. But in fact the union leads to open war between employer and employee, to the destruction of the liberty of the operative in

the name of unity, to every kind of regimentation and tyranny.
He invents the cinema, the starting-point, it would seem, of
a revolution in collective life. Now he can re-create the universe before his eyes. Unrivalled opportunities for culture,
education, relaxation, communion with beauty, seem to lie
within his grasp. What in fact happens? Abandoned to the
sway of his nerves and his senses, dazed by portrayals of
violence and immorality, he undergoes a collective drugging
which effectually stifles any remaining aspiration to interior
liberty. Each attempt at liberation issues in a new slavery,[153]
and testifies once more, as Jacques Rivière said, to the presence
of this *"fidèle malheur"* which seems to dog his steps.

But this is only the outside of the picture. The source of the
evil does not lie in things, but in the soul; not primarily in
society, but in the person; in this terrible division of man
between good and evil,[154] in the complicity with evil that still
predominates even when he seeks the good, in his inexplicable
penchant for sin even while he savours the good: *for I am
delighted with the law of God according to the inward man*
(= the spiritual aspiration), *but I see another law in my
members fighting against the law of my mind, and captivating
me in the law of sin that is in my members. Unhappy man that
I am! Who shall deliver me from the body of this death?*
(Rom. VII, 23–24). Aspiration to liberty and captivity to the
flesh—with that we get to the bottom of the wound. We must
try to become fully conscious of this captive liberty; and let
us therefore look first at the sources of the captivity.

* * *

As long as he is still unregenerate the person is deprived of
his bonds of grace with Christ, and so of his supernatural
being and "true life." The wound goes deep. It touches the

natural springs of liberty. First, because the natural movement of the will, when left to itself, is without any real aim. It can no longer tend to God as known and possessed in Christ, but is capable only of "natural" ends, that is to say of ends that are voided of their essential value and inner substance. A liberty orientated to a saturating but unattainable end, and thrown back on attainable but unsatisfying ends, and so a liberty without efficacious orientation—that is the starting-point. But further, the dynamism of liberty has no better basis to rest upon than a being whose powers are in disaccord with themselves. The divine virtue that bound the energies of the soul together and brought them into convergence on their real end, has disappeared. Since they are no longer unified by the efficacious call of their end, the spiritual and sensitive powers are out of joint; each has resumed what I may venture to call its own unhappy liberty, each tends independently to its own end, and this entails a quasi-autonomy of the sensitive powers, and a dangerous and indefatigable assault on their part on an impoverished and enfeebled spirit. Clamouring with wanton violence, raising its head in moments of revolt, asserting itself with a force not easily quelled, the sensitive appetite has become a concupiscence "passing the bounds of the spirit," tending to its object in defiance of all rational restraint, and therefore against nature in the very bosom of nature.[155] The human being is no longer unified nor in accord with itself; it is rent by the war of spirit and flesh, thrown as a prey to the most brutal instincts of passions in revolt; and this incoherent pluralism—*dissolutio harmoniae* [156]—threatens all the efforts of a fledgling liberty with disaster.

The wound goes deeper still. It touches not only the relation between spirit and flesh, but the very spirit itself. We can never sufficiently insist that original sin brought no new principle of evil into the structure of the human being, and that from this standpoint such words as "stain" and "corruption" have to be handled with the greatest care. But neither can we sufficiently emphasize the wound it inflicts on the whole human being, and on the spirit in particular. At the root of free-will lies the intelligence, and the intelligence of fallen man is wounded. He was created to know God in Christ, and it is in this line that the wound takes effect.[157] He can know that God is, since he still has a reason; and the Church has solemnly affirmed that this power of knowing God is fundamental and ineradicable, always inherently capable of reaching its end whatever difficulties may impede its exercise. But she still insists on the wound of ignorance which is so disabling in the realm of religious truth—the realm of the true knowledge of the true God, in which knowledge and adoration, contemplation and thanksgiving, light and humility, are so inseparably bound up with each other. Acute, vigorous, wholly admirable when temporal realities are in question, the intelligence is mysteriously weak before its proper object, the spiritual. And the wound can be expressed in three words, of which the first is *obscurity*.

It is difficult for the wounded intelligence to seize the idea of God in any full or lucid manner, since it labours under the spell of the senses and has very little hold on the pure intelligible, especially on God, the highest of all. The difficulty was fully appreciated by St. Thomas: on the one side, it was manifest in his eyes in even the greatest of the pagan philosophers: they knew nothing of divine Providence, of God's omnipotence, of the supreme worship due to Him, "and other such matters"; [158] and on the other side, it is still present in faith, which attains to God only through the medium of obscure ideas, and has to grope for Him as for one absent.[159]

This obscurity, which is not natural but the outcome and punishment of sin, is moreover coupled with a sort of intellectual *inertia* when God is in question.[160] Man is a creature; but his wounded intelligence tells him nothing spontaneously of his absolute dependence on God: if it does so, it is by way of ideas without warmth or life, without power to awaken an aspiration to God or to take effect on his actions; while on the other hand, to make matters worse, he is given over to an absorbing awareness of self, and a very direct enjoyment of his own activity and his own being. After that it is only a step to habitual nescience of God, to an utter inertia and blank imperviousness of soul in the face of religious truth,[161] to pride in its common form, unconscious, "settled" and sterilizing.

Finally, and without involving anything out of the way or "satanic," the mind can proceed to a positive *refusal* to yield to the exigencies of truth, and so an outright rejection of God. When we have once caught a glimpse of God, the natural movement of the mind leads us on to adoration, we have to acknowledge our creaturely state and recognize our dependence; and this exigence witnesses to the active power of truth in our souls. But the mind, shut out from the true God, can refuse to acknowledge it, can close its eyes to the call of the truth, reject the homage it demands as a sacrifice, and seek its own norm and its own end within itself. Then it holds the truth in captivity,[162] it commits the sin of pride in the strictest sense of the term, it falls into a state of ignorance that leads to idolatry (for we must needs adore something).

If we add up all these factors—obscurity, inertia, tendency to refusal—we may form some idea of the wound of ignorance of which theology speaks, and of the inclination to paganism that lurks in every human mind. It is understandable enough that when it treats God as a merely abstract object, impersonal, devoid of living interest, or, contrariwise, as intrusive and disturbing, the mind will easily fall into false ideas of Him, into received and socially accredited errors; and that we shall see whole peoples given up to error and adoring idols.[163] If we add to this inner weakness the terrible weight of social structures and mass mentalities, we may appreciate the tragic condition of human reason—intact no doubt, in its essence, but wounded in its state; and how, apart from the institutional transmission of the truth effected by Christ through His Church, there can be no sure, stable, and integral hold on even natural religious truth. In the full tide of the nineteenth century Pius IX was obliged to recall, in the face of rationalistic attempts, the "grave wound" inflicted by original sin on the human reason itself, and to insist once more that it is "full of obscurities, weaknesses, uncertainties"—*ratio qua nihil incertius*—and crying out to be "freed from its errors by faith." [164] But then we shall also appreciate the grave danger that threatens liberty from this enfeebled reason, deprived of its supernatural light, incapacitated for its proper work, incapable of seizing its own true end, and tempted in consequence by mere appearances, by "vanity," and by empty dreams.

Moreover the will also is wounded, and here the wound is more sensibly felt. Just as the reason is stricken in its movement to truth (especially moral and religious truth), so is the will in its movement to the good. It is deprived of all real contact and all real union with its end: "man in the state of original sin no longer has his heart united to God by charity." [165] The wound touches that love in which is the very motive power of the will and the ultimate source of liberty. He is incapable by himself of directing himself really to communion with God in Christ, incapable even of really and freely loving God above all things. Thus deprived of all efficacious orientation to God, he is the prey of a whole world of animal forces, strongly unified, vigorously orientated, at once subtle and brutal. He suffers accordingly from what theology calls the *"wound of malice,"* that is to say, "a certain proneness of the will to evil." [166] This slackened hold on good, this dissolvent of pleasure and self-interest, lays him open to and produces a grievous debility in well-doing and a shameful complicity with evil. The outcome of it is that the fallen creature is morally incapable—without grace—of any full and steady performance of his human duty.

Combine these two wounds—in mind and will—and consider how liberty fares in consequence. Liberty demands self-mastery: and in man the starting-point for this is a state of acute division and chronic conflict, with all the weight of the flesh oppressing the spirit. Liberty demands enlightenment: and man no longer knows his own true end, nor his true objects, nor his own genuine nature; his starting-point is a kind of dull unconsciousness both of his lost greatness and actual misery. Liberty demands a generous gift of self: and man detached from God is thrown back on himself, incapable of a fully generous love; and his starting-point is a spontaneous leaning to egoistic love of self. Thus the free-will is wounded in its power for good, therefore in its spiritual liberty; far from being able to fulfil all its vocation, it cannot even push its natural effort to its proper conclusion. Were it not for the gratuitous grace of God the case would be desperate. But grace is there and calls to all, or rather Christ is there who by His grace would have all men saved. If man accepts this grace, the history of his deliverance begins. If he refuses it, captivity awaits him. His will adheres to evil, his intelligence to error, his choice to egoism and cupidity. Personal sin takes a hand, with all its formidable consequences: *Whosoever committeth sin is the servant of sin* (John VIII, 34). The capacity for evil that lurks in every fallen creature is now actualized. The man is no longer simply attracted to sin, he commits it. He "walks according to the flesh"; he "fulfils the lusts of the flesh"; he becomes carnal,—and this word, in Catholic doctrine, defines a well-marked state of liberty, namely a captive liberty. To understand this state we have only to resume and apply the foregoing analyses.

* * *

The captive liberty in question is nothing other than a concrete complex of liberty. At the root, a voluntary adhesion (voluntary, though of course under pressure) to error and to evil; a submission of the spirit to the flesh accepted by the will; a gradual organization of thoughts and volitions, of impressions and feelings, of acts and reactions and habits, around the purposes of a proud or sensual egoism; the impregnation and unification of the whole being by a dominant inclination, a dominant love, a dominant delectation,—these three words marking different aspects of one and the same reality. A choice, a taste, an inclination, a unity lived,—there we have the major elements of the complex. When all this, coming from the flesh and tending to the flesh, becomes active in a more or less habitual way, then we have become carnal,[167] that is to say in no wise prisoners to necessity, but led by an inclination or a dominant delectation.[168] Psychologically, the subject is no longer empty, nor virgin, but impregnated and charged. Morally, he is no longer undecided or neutral; he has taken his stand and is now drawn by choices that all look the same way, that reinforce each other and call for each other and lead to an adhesion, that daily becomes more complete, to the life of the flesh. But at the source of this captive liberty lies a creative act, the act of a will which, in one way or another, by open revolt or tacit withdrawal, prefers itself to God and goes over to the flesh. From this decisive option there flows a whole series of acts which follow it up without further question. Every new choice made in accord with the fundamental adhesion swells and strengthens the torrent. Then it begins to imprison itself in its own matter, in an accumulation of corporeal and psychical habits all tending spontaneously, joyously, in one direction and hollowing out a bed with high imperious banks down which the current of the will is to run henceforth. The trend of that life then becomes clear and the *fruits* of this liberty *are manifest* (Gal. V, 19)—the evil fruits of an evil tree. The man is given over alive to his lusts like a *prisoner of war* (Rom. VII, 23), and slavery holds him, a slavery chosen and accepted (even were it with shame); a slavery bound up on the one hand with this preferential attention to evil, with views spontaneously partial and carnal, and, on the other, with this profound absorption in pleasure, the mortal delights, the terrible hunger and thirst to which the soul is abandoned; a slavery which, by daily choices, draws ever tightening bonds around his unhappy liberty.[169]

And nevertheless this slavery is no determinism. The two terms belong to different worlds. Only a person can be a slave; and only a thing without reason can be determined. In the sense in which we can speak of a will enslaved to its pleasures, meaning thereby to exclude liberty, there is no such determinism here, and that for a double reason. First, because however carnal the subject may have become, he is always performing particular acts which, as such, do not prolong the dominant adhesion. The sinner, observed St. Thomas, following St. Augustine, may very well plant vines or build houses, and do many similar things which are all good. Let us add that he can work conscientiously, devote himself to his family, and even give his life for his country. Slavery to the flesh will not put a stop to that, and such acts, though intermingled with the carnal complex, do not draw thcir sap from it but come from deeper regions of the soul. They testify to untouched resources and uncorrupted powers. For the human being is never fully one, and contradictions can get along very well together within him. Neither reason nor will can be totally absorbed by evil; the generous instincts, enslaved as they may be, are never wholly extinguished by the egoistic, concupiscence can never exterminate aspiration, and sin, finally, may very well bring about a certain unification of man, but never his unity. Evil obstructs and seduces, it does not "compose." It disaggregates, because it proceeds from a refusal.[170] It can unify only tyrannically and from without, like a torrent that scores the mountain-side with a trail of scattered rocks, uprooted trees, and dead cattle. In spite of all appearances and all connivances unity is not achieved, the deep springs of the will are seduced and captured but not deflected from within; the fruits of sin are in mutual conflict rather than union; and such unity as may be effected is not a unity of life but of violence, of disorder and not of harmony. Many living forces therefore escape the infection, many acts flow from still untainted sources;[171] so much so that within the carnal complex itself, side by side with *acts that confirm* the central adhesion, there are always *acts that escape it,* and doubtless tend to contradict it implicitly.

Furthermore, it is always possible for a man to go back on his carnal adhesion. However deep, however strong, however much ingrained it may be, it remains always a finite determination of an infinite tendency, a particular orientation of a universal tendency, or, in technical terms, "a *habitus* which freewill can always ratify or reject." [172] For the infinite desire of the will subsists in the face of each of its concrete realizations; there is always an abyss between what it wills and what it is capable of willing; it can therefore restrain its habitual tendency, resume control of its attention, set once more in the mind's eye those aspects of reality it has been accustomed to neglect, and make a thoroughgoing re-examination of the whole trend of its life. A man who lies under the spell of the flesh is still called by Christ, and stirred by Christ. His vocation in Christ is still present at the bottom of his consciousness. The grace of the Lord in its "infinite variety," and subtler in its pure simplicity than all the wiles of the flesh, will not fail to awaken him in its own good time, to shake his frail and clumsy defences, and recall him, sweetly and strongly, to his eternal destiny. It is to the innermost sources of liberty that grace is addressed, to the infinity of a desire that sin can never satisfy, to a vocation it can never wholly extinguish. And so it is always really possible for a man to shake off even the deepest torpor, to regain the mastery of his judgment, and put everything in question again. He can, if he wills it, by an act of creative liberty, springing at once from the depths of his own soul and from the power of God, break away from his fundamental adhesion, change the whole trend of his life, and achieve a new birth.

These considerations explain the attitude of the Church in this matter, an attitude which some find contradictory. Let us suppose a doctrine with no conception of a liberty rooted in a nature, of a liberty which would therefore be both orientated to the good and exposed to the influence of the states of this nature. Then we should have a liberty which would be a pure power of choice, essentially indifferent to good and evil, endowed with a native and unalterable equilibrium, incapable of receiving an interior inclination, and one, consequently, which nothing could ever *wound* or anything *heal*. Against such a position—Pelagianism in point of fact—the Church affirms a wound in the heart of free-will and its absolute need of healing: as a consequence of the first sin our free-will has become incapable of understanding, loving, or fulfilling the evangelical commandments (Council of Carthage, can. 5); incapable of loving, believing and acting supernaturally (Council of Orange, c. 5–8); incapable, in short, of "compassing the mystery of salvation" (Ibid. c. 8). Suppose, on the other hand, a doctrine interested solely in the spiritual or religious aspect of free-will, a doctrine affirming that sin has finally destroyed our moral liberty, that man in consequence can no longer perform a morally good act, nor even collaborate interiorly with grace. Against such a position—Protestantism in point of fact—the Church will react by affirming the abiding reality of free-will. Man has lost the power of producing supernatural acts, and so of assuring his own salvation, without the grace of Christ—so much is evident. But he retains the power of choosing, of welcoming or refusing the awakening call of God, the power—with grace—of really choosing the good and of thus preparing himself for justification, and the power of growth in holiness (Council of Trent, Sess. VI, chap I–4, and can. 2, 4, 5). Free-will is therefore neither lost nor destroyed; it is a real and active power, though powerless in respect to life in Christ, and enfeebled and enticed by the flesh. Consequently it is capable of producing, of its own sole power, not only bad acts but many acts that are not sins, and do not merit the wrath of God (*Ibid,* can. 6 and 7); and capable finally, with the aid of grace, of performing supernatural acts which spring from its renewed energies, which are truly its own, and which impel it from within to bring forth fruit in God and for God.[173]

The position of the Church is perfectly coherent. She maintains, with equal insistence, both the enduring permanence of
free-will and the vanishing of its liberty. She does not trespass
on the philosophical field, and confines herself to affirming
the data of the faith; but she lays down principles which oblige
the theologians to push their enquiries in a certain direction.
When she maintains, against Pelagius, that man has lost his
supernatural power of action—his "original liberty"—she
implicitly opposes every rationalist and closed conception of
liberty, and she calls for the philosophic establishment of the
possibility of captive or liberated states of free-will. When
she affirms, against the Protestants, against Baius and Jansen-
ius, that free-will persists in fallen man, that he is not necessitated to sin in all his acts, that he can collaborate with grace,
she rejects all strict determinism on the religious plane, and
calls for the elaboration of a doctrine of the states of liberty,
which shall define a *dominant inclination* precisely to exclude a
determining necessity. At every attempt to forestall or eliminate
the possibility of a wounded liberty in the name of free-will, or
contrariwise, to eliminate the possibility of genuine choice in
the name of a wounded liberty, the Church will react with
vigour that she may remain faithful to the deposit of revealed
truth. Here then, once more, a double affirmation will be
needed to keep the truth intact: carnal liberty is very really
captive under the weight of its adhesion, of its repeated choices,
of its rooted habits, of a pleasure to which body and soul are
both abandoned, compromised together in joint complicity,
silently sold under sin. Such a man *walks according to the flesh*
and there we have the principle of his acts; he *minds the things
that are of the flesh,* and there we have the aim to which his
choices tend; he *is in the flesh* (Rom. VIII, 4–8), and there
we have, so to speak, the spiritual substance he has voluntarily

bestowed on himself. So strong is this inclination that for St. Paul it is a law. But then, precisely, this captivity is the captivity of a liberty. The captivity is willed and chosen at its point of origin, consented to and welcomed all along the line. It does not exclude acts that escape it, and contradict it. And what is more, it harbours that within itself which is still able to negate it and to liberate: these tranquillizing views, this humble love, this faithful desire for the good, this nostalgia for the law of God still indelibly present at the apex of the spirit, and asserting itself at times in the midst of the worst abandonments—a window left permanently open on infinite Goodness and Purity. Mysteriously, by ways that remain untraceable, the prison walls are broken through by the grace of Christ, never absent, never refused, and superabounding where sin abounds. This captivity therefore can always be dissolved, the law destroyed and replaced. Our unhappy liberty is a slave that is always ready for enfranchisement by an act that is always difficult but always possible, springing from its own depths and from the pure mercy of the Saviour.

St. Augustine was undoubtedly the first among theologians to work out the solution of the problem: and perhaps it was St. Bernard who gave it the most striking expression, no less precise than dramatic. From the many texts that offer themselves let us single out this admirable analysis of liberty in bonds: "Man alone among mortals can resist the constraining power of nature, and he alone among earthly creatures is therefore free. But even he becomes subject to coercion when he falls into sin. This coercion is not from nature, but from his own will, so that not even then is he deprived of his native liberty; because whatever is voluntary is free. And it is altogether owing to sin that 'the corruptible body weigheth down the soul,' and not at all by the weight of its mass, but by the force of its concupiscence. For the fact that the soul is now incapable of rising of herself from sin, although indeed she was able of herself to fall, is due to the will, which, weakened and prostrated by the depraved and vicious love of a corrupted body, cannot simultaneously admit the love of justice. And so, I know not in what wicked yet wonderful way, the will, when turned towards evil by sin, imposes a constraint on itself; so that on the one hand such constraint, since it is voluntary, cannot avail to excuse the will, and, on the other hand, the will, being drawn away and allured, is unable to resist the constraint. This constraint, I repeat, is in some sense voluntary. . . . Thus, my brethren, in a certain evil yet marvellous way, the soul is held captive under this voluntary and sinfully free necessity, at one and the same time bond and free. She is a bond-slave by reason of her servitude; she is free on account of the voluntary character of this servitude. And what is stranger still and still more pitiful, she is guilty because of her freedom, and she is a bond-slave because of her guilt; that is to say she is a bond-slave because of her freedom. Unhappy man that I am, who shall deliver me from the shame of this servitude? I am unhappy, yet free. I am free because I am a man; unhappy because I am a slave. I am free because of my likeness to God; unhappy, because opposed to God. . . . It is I who have set myself in opposition both to Thee, O God, and to myself; and I find in my members that which is equally at variance both with my mind and with Thy law. Who shall deliver me out of my own hands?" [174]

II

If liberty is to be freed, man must be transformed. Nothing less will suffice, because the very roots of liberty are attacked,

and the remedy must reach the point of the disease. Now Christianity, which is the Good News of deliverance, proclaims the
liberation of liberty: *Qua libertate Christus nos liberavit!* For
it amounts to a total re-making of the human being by Christ,
the creation of the new man in Christ, an absolute re-birth in
the Holy Spirit, true entry into the "true life." There is therefore here an ontological transformation of the entire person
into his spiritual being, which carries with it, as we hardly
need to add, a radical transformation of his action. The deliverance of liberty from its bonds is consequently a liberation
on the plane of being—which is a *gift*—to be followed up by
a liberation on the plane of action—which is a *conquest*.

*   *   *

The first way in which grace delivers man is by transforming
the roots of his liberty. To be free, he must see clearly. Now in
the man who is converted, who enters the world of faith, and
who changes his life, the grace that acts in the first place is a
grace that opens his eyes. Grace is light, and through the familiar shape of things it brings unknown and divine realities
into view; it is a principle of vision, and it transforms the power
of the mind from within; it is the mind of Christ, grafted on
our own, and giving it power to seize, in Him, a two-fold
and unique mystery: that of God, who gives Himself and "calls
us to things eternal," and that of man, fallen, redeemed, and
introduced by the Cross into the very life of God. By the grace
of faith the mind is literally re-created and born a second time;
it becomes capable of "knowing in truth," and it can read in
its own life and in the world what God Himself there sees and
would bring to realization. Throwing off the errors and illusions of the night which sealed his eyes, man now discovers
the divine aspect of his being, his vocation as a spiritual crea-

ture, made that he may give himself, in Christ, for the redemption of the world and for the glory of God; and thus at a single blow he finds once more his dignity, his self-respect and his liberty in the face of the universe. In the heart of this vocation he recaptures the deep significance of his effort, of the life of struggle and slow re-conquest by which Christ unites us here below with His sufferings and with the power of His resurrection, that He may transform us hereafter into His glory. A realist and magnificent outlook which makes of the Christian a man armed, resolute, generous. And finally grace reveals God Himself: the God of Benediction, God of Redemption, God of Beatitude, God of Charity, in whom we are called to everlasting life. Consequently for the Christian there is an *evil,* which consists in separating himself from God to follow his own instincts or his own wills; and there is a *good,* which consists in giving himself to God that he may love and serve Him. Henceforth his path is clear and his steps assured. The Christian is a man who knows, a man set free by this Truth who is Christ Himself. He can measure with precision the genuine worth of things, the true exigencies of his destiny, the true implications of his acts. He is capable henceforth of a lucid judgment, and it is in the full light of day, cleared of illusions and of lies, that he makes his choices: *Blessed be thou, O God, who hast delivered me from idols!*

Man, to be free, must be master of himself, and therefore establish the rule of the spirit over the flesh. Now grace is a true energy, which comes to strengthen the vanquished will from within. The will is weak, first because it is divided from its end; by turning it away from sin grace unites it with the God of Benediction, *whose power is exceeding great towards us who believe* (Eph. I, 19). The presence of faith in a soul suffices to reveal *the operation of the might of his power*

(*Ibid.*). And this is that same power *which he wrought in Christ, raising him up from the dead* (*Ibid.*, 20). Grace is therefore a power which dominates the body and the flesh, and their corruption and revolt; a power that can master this "mortal body," at once the instrument and the victim of the powers that tend to death; a power that heals and divinises the spirit by quickening it from within by the Holy Spirit, and which therefore reverses the pagan equilibrium in man at a blow. Over the carnal powers, still ready for revolt, the thing that now watches is a will strengthened by the Spirit, brought once more into touch with its Source and its End, endowed with efficacious energy, firm of grasp, and terrible to the devils as Christ Himself. Now that the power of Christ dwells within her the will is freed from her radical impotence; she can fight against the flesh, she can overcome it; she can *possess her vessel in sanctification and honour: not in the passion of lust like the gentiles who know not God* (I Thess. IV, 4–5) ; she sees, rising before her eyes, the dawn of Liberty.

To be free, finally, man must love and give himself. Love, which took the deepest wound, receives the most radical healing. For grace is a love that gives itself, and invades the soul to stir up another love unit; grace is *the love of God poured forth in our hearts by the Holy Ghost who is given to us* (Rom. V, 5). At the heart of the will, at the source of its energy, there is henceforth the power of divine charity, merited by Christ and given by the Spirit; a gracious "drawing" that manifests the presence of the Father; a profound call, and so sweetly accordant with the natural movement that even while rectifying and passing beyond it, it does but carry it on; the outpouring of a desire, of a gift, of a joy, springing up to life eternal— "living water" as St. Ignatius of Antioch said, "springing within me and murmuring: 'Come to the Father' " (*Ad Rom.* 7).

By changing this man's love grace has changed all his powers, and because his will is now really turned towards his end, its impotence has gone, its deviation is rectified, its egoism is dissolved. It has become an efficacious generosity, and to those thus liberated this counsel can be given: *You, brethren, have been called unto liberty: only make not liberty an occasion to the flesh, but by charity of the spirit serve one another* (Gal. V, 13). Love that comes to birth, frail as a new-born babe, enwrapped in all manner of weakness—*infantem pannis involutum*—but destined to grow, and to subdue and transform the entire personality. For indeed the Christian who is animated by charity loves God more than himself; he is freed from the egoism that mews him up within himself, from the crippling hardness of heart, the freezing isolation. His heart has become as the heart of a child, open to the evangelical "sweetness," to the compassion that makes all one; he enters into communion with the Father, with his Saviour, with his brothers; he is ready for fellowship, friendship and service. Love that breaks all fetters has set him free. Because it participates in this new love, which is the love of God Himself, the will now knows another inclination, another joy, another hope; it is capable of a new impulsion, a new choice, a new engagement, in short of a new liberty—the liberty of the children of God.

The roots of liberty are therefore transformed by the grace of Christ, the "Word of liberty." [175] Judgment, self-mastery, and generosity are now deposited in germ in the womb of the soul. But this ontological transformation is no more than a starting-point. The new birth calls for a new growth. The ascendency of the spirit which changes a man's condition and makes him spiritual on the plane of being, asks that he should become such on the plane of voluntary action. Become what

thou art! It was no part of Christ's plan, even supposing the
thing were intelligible in itself, to give us a liberty ready-made;
but rather by way of deliverance begun to make us capable of
full liberation; to enable us by the *gift* of a radical liberty to
effect the *conquest* of our personal liberty. All is transformed;
and nevertheless all remains to be done. We have now to indicate the essential stages of the work of liberation, of the slow
ascent to a plenary liberty.

* * *

The starting-point for the effort is sufficiently humble. The
ontological liberation is still so far from amounting to a psychological and moral one, that St. Paul does not hesitate to call
this state a slavery. The unbeliever who embraces the faith, the
libertine who changes his life, the baptized sluggard who
awakes at last to his duty, the youth arrived at the critical age
who realizes that to be a Christian is to be a hero—all those
who are *freed from sin* discover that they have been made
servants of justice (Rom. VI, 18), and, at bottom, *servants to
God* (*Ibid.* 22). Quite literally, they have exchanged one captivity for another. They have known, without doubt, the vague
peace of a sluggish soul, or the heavy sleep of a vanquished
soul; but now the struggle is on them again! Christ dwells in
them, the Spirit stirs them, and nevertheless (Gal. V, 17–19)
the *flesh*—which means the proud egoism as well as the sensual
—the flesh lusteth against the *spirit,* and does not fail to give
battle. The old instincts, the old hungers, the old greedy desires
awake, protest, and revolt. *The spirit,* on its side, steeped in
another light, another love, with a pure and trembling joy—
the spirit *lusteth against the flesh,* and its shameful delights:
for these are contrary to each other; and now they confront
each other on the narrow field of the Christian's soul, so that

he *does not the things that he would*. And what is that but slavery? At this first moment of the Christian life the root of the soul alone is Christian, nothing else; and because he feels that to be a Christian is to obey courageously, to offer resistance to all concupiscences, to serve God like a soldier who shall *yield his members not as instruments of iniquity unto sin, but as instruments of justice unto God* (Rom. VI, 13), and who fights, suffers, and puts all to the hazard—"the spiritual combat is as brutal as any human war"—because he is thus torn between his concupiscences and his aspirations, the Christian beginner feels his fledgling liberty as another kind of servitude. He is delivered because he is no longer dominated by a force that is alien to the natural order of his will, because he no longer strives against this order,[176] and because he has rediscovered the law of his being; but he remains a prisoner to a part of himself, he submits to God's law against the grain of his carnal tendencies, in the act of giving himself he tears himself asunder, and his all too feeble love knows nothing yet of the easy, joyous and unfailing spontaneity of the free soul. He is the servant of justice.

Nevertheless, the Christian daily loosens his bonds, for the divine power which has renewed his inner being tends more and more to overrun his spiritual activity. Slave as he is still on the plane of conscience and of action, he knows himself freed in the depths of the spirit; and that conviction is the source of a hope that is ever re-born. Moreover, the more he battles with his concupiscences the more he knows himself to be freed. Whenever his carnal being follows its law he is materialized and imprisoned; whenever his spirit follows its own he is opened to God, plunged in the Spirit, unfettered and spiritualized. His act is the fruit of the sap of Christ rising in the veins of his personal effort, and under that quickening influence his budding liberty slowly grows and ripens. If it is true that the Christian lives by faith that works by charity, this faith is the source and the measure at once of life and of liberty. When it is a question of resisting temptation, of supporting a trial, of shouldering a daily burden, at the heart of all is an act of faith quickened by love; and this is what we shall have to look at if we are to understand the growth of Christian liberty.

* * *

To start with, every time that a man makes an act of faith, he makes an act of liberty, and allows his spiritual liberty to strike deeper roots. The object of faith is the Beatitude proposed to us by God in Christ. Since this Beatitude is the Last End, and since to affirm it fully is to accept it for oneself; since it is supernatural, and since in it God freely gives Himself; since it is proposed by way of the Cross and demands renunciation and sacrifice; since it is offered us through the medium of a testimony that veils it as much as it reveals, and fastens the yoke of obedience on a wounded intelligence—for all these reasons it throws the spirit back on a capital option, and it is not to be welcomed, accepted, affirmed, save by the full act of a total liberty.

Moreover, to affirm this truth which is its End, the spirit must be proportioned to this end and has to be impregnated therefore with the principle of an efficacious desire for the end. Now this principle God gives: His grace awakens a profound movement in the soul which leads it to welcome and cleave to the truth, to cry out "Lord, I believe"; but whatever its form, the essential thing here is the orientation to the Beatitude proposed, the inclination to faith—*pius credulitatis affectus*—the birth in the depths of the soul of a love awakened there by

God Himself. Now this humble and dawning love draws us to a Good that is obligatory, to an End imposed in absolute fashion, to an adhesion which is the most essential of our duties: to love, is here to obey. This divinely infused inclination is a new call to our liberty because it is a grace, because grace is never determinism and can always be resisted, because it is a nascent love which the will is master to accept or refuse, because it is an invitation to the sacrifice of a closed autonomy, and because this sacrifice is the heroic act of a will that is master of itself. Thus to draw us to the faith and to keep us in it, God has infused in us a love that sweetly invites and inclines us to believe,—*suavitatem in consentiendo;* which at the same time demands obedience and renunciation—*inspirationem corrigentem voluntatem nostram de incredulitate ad fidem;* and which lastly invites us to the capital act of our liberty. This act is at once consent to the call of grace, choice of obedience to duty, and love of the God who offers Himself through His testimony; and this act, under these three aspects, is nothing other than the act of faith in its voluntary element: a love that chooses by consenting to grace. The first act of faith is therefore, in the strict sense, an act of creative liberty, an act that changes a man and makes him *pass from death to life* (John V, 24), and makes him a son of God. The acts that follow carry on and strengthen the first and root it deeper; when the act of faith is renewed the choice and option is consolidated, they incline the spirit and master the flesh. The presence of Christ goes deeper, the action of the Spirit becomes more efficacious, the inner tendency of the will more tense. Thus the believer *mortifies by the spirit the deeds of the flesh* (Rom. VIII, 13). To be free demands that we should be masters of ourselves. Living faith affirms this mastery and effects it, because it is the refusal, the rejection, the passing

over of the "flesh" and of the "world" that tyrannize over
man—because it is, as St. John says, *the victory that over-
cometh the world* (I John V, 4).

Faith moreover is destined to progress immeasurably; and
because it is the "proper act" that God expects of us, it brings
growth to the whole being, and thus to the very roots of liberty.
Faith is an obscure mode of knowledge, and so it will always
be in the sense that it will never know God save through His
testimony to Himself; but it becomes more and more luminous
in the sense that the testimony becomes more and more transparent, and that the soul in a state of grace is always learning
more and more of God and of itself. The Christian soul moves
on from light to light; Christ, the light of the soul, reveals
Himself more fully; and, in Him, the divine truths, the personal vocation, the Blessed Trinity, the whole of our life in
short, are ever more fully illuminated (I Cor. II, 10–16).
Whereas the sensual man does not perceive those things that are
of the Spirit of God and cannot judge them, he who has received the Spirit of God, who has the mind of Christ and becomes increasingly spiritual, knows the things that are given
us from God and judges all things. He acquires a sense of
spiritual realities, a penetration of divine things, a feeling for
life in Christ which endows him with a wonderful discernment,
and so makes for the full deliverance of his liberty.

Faith is based on love and lives by it. Thanks to this love
it becomes more and more a contact: God is no longer far
away and felt for gropingly and blindly, but near at hand,
touched, held and possessed. Faith becomes communion; no
mere passing encounter or distant glimpse, but God and the
soul revealed to each other, given to each other, embraced by
each other. It becomes an eager and infinite aspiration, for its
partial knowledge and possession of God is as nothing to its

hunger. It does not know as it is known, nor love as it is loved, it remains weak, and miserable and impure. Ah, might all that vanish,—all stains, all miseries, all faltering joys, all veils— the lightest is still so heavy!—and may there come the hour when I shall see thee, O my God! In the meantime one thing only counts—the will of the Beloved, and sacrifice without reserve in His service. Such a love is henceforth so rooted in the soul that she is but one in spirit with what He wills. She seeks that will, she tastes it, desires it, embraces it, wills it beyond recall, even were this will to crucify her; and thus, to her, the law of God becomes fraternal, interiorized, "natural." Because the spiritual man realizes his obedience as an act of communion, his liberty is delivered from its bonds, and "he is a law unto himself because love inclines him in the manner of a law and makes him act as a man who is free." [177]

By that very fact this faith is nourished by generosity, by sacrifice, and, if need be, by heroism. It fructifies like the grain of wheat, that gives a hundred-fold for one. Yet it bears but a single fruit, the fruit of the spirit which is love; but this is the living source of all the other fruits, and it makes the soul bloom like a marvellous garden. Such faith bears witness, and stirs up faith and love around itself. The infused and active aspects of the Christian life are so closely interwoven in the soul that they can hardly be distinguished; altogether surrendered, altogether activated, altogether active in *bringing forth fruit to God* (Rom. VII, 4). This allied docility and generosity nourish understanding and love in their turn, and therefore liberty. And so, strengthened by its own efforts, quickened by grace, led by a love that is full of light, the timid liberty of early days becomes little by little the full liberty of the children of God. If the person is called to fulfil his own being by entering into union with God, now at last he fully responds to his vocation;

his liberty, which is this response itself—living, ardent, potent —increases along with the fulfilment of the person, and the liberation is the measure of the personalization. *Dilige, et quod vis, fac:* to do the thing that he wills is to do the thing that he ought; and he is free, not because his inner duality is suppressed (that is impossible here below), but because it is surmounted, because the intestine war of flesh and spirit has given place to their "peaceful concord and consent," [178] because he has found his unity in God, and because against such there is no law.

* * *

Such then is the spiritual liberty of the Christian, a liberty, in other words, delivered from its bonds. It is the complex opposed to that of a captive liberty, and it is easy to see why: the elements are the same, but they look the other way. Here, as there, is a fundamental adhesion which gathers all the powers of the soul around it, and draws them into its own movement. Here also are tendencies, tastes, joys, which lay hold on the soul, and excite a hunger and a blessed plenitude—"to hunger and thirst for justice is to be filled." [179] Here also, sin—as righteousness in the other case—becomes more and more difficult, and demands an abandonment, a turning back, a refusal which cannot spring spontaneously from a soul surrendered to the Holy Spirit. Herein lies the power, the beauty and the joy of Christian liberty. And we may note in passing that this is what St. Augustine meant by his famous and so much misunderstood doctrine of heavenly delectation. "With the Holy Spirit, by whose gift we are justified, we take delight in this, that we sin not,—and that is liberty; without the Spirit we take delight in sin, and that is slavery." [180] Sweetness, tenderness, pleasure—St. Augustine multiplies these terms in order to explain the rôle of grace in liberty. But he uses them first because he finds them in Scripture, especially in the Psalms; and quite apart from his personal experience, they have a doctrinal and theological weight in his eyes which rules their psychological and systematic significance. Further, these words denote spiritual realities, "these pure and intimate pleasures" [181] in which the body has no direct part, which live in the deep places of the soul, and of which the type, according to a celebrated formula, is "delectation in the truth." [182] And finally, this pleasure is identified with the love that governs liberty, with the choice in which it is expressed, with the impulsion that defines it.[183] In all these texts, in fact, St. Augustine is concerned with liberty only in its relation to its end, in its movement towards Beatitude and the *frui Deo*—the enjoyment of God; the thing that counts in his eyes is the central love, the essential adhesion, which appears in the successive choices made; and that is why, with the complex of this orientated liberty in view, he defines liberty by the love and joy that constitute its power, realize its orientation, and confer on it, if we may venture the word, its spontaneity. It must not be forgotten that St. Augustine regards true liberty as the health of the wounded soul,[184] and that the joy of which he speaks is something purified, strong, decided, springing from a spirit healed and a being rooted in the Holy Spirit—*Spiritus vivificans delectorem* [185]—and moving it to generosity and heroism. "The law is not to be fulfilled save by the exercise of the will; but by the law is the knowledge of sin; by faith comes grace to resist sin; by grace comes the soul's healing from the disease of sin; by the healing, liberty is given to the will; from this liberation springs love of justice, and from such love proceeds the fulfilment of the law." [186] And again, in connection with Peter's perseverance in the faith: "It is not in virtue of its liberty that the human will attains to grace, it is much rather by grace that it attains to liberty, and a delightly constancy and an insuperable fortitude, which enables it to persevere." [187] We see how far we are from every sentimental doctrine and every spiritual empiricism. We see also how dangerous it would be to transpose this concrete psychology, which deals with structures, states and complexes, into the terms and classifications of a psychology much more highly elaborated and systematized, and set upon distinguishing—because the abstract concepts demand it—what Augustine took good care not to dissociate— because the concrete data forbade him.

For the rest, this liberty is never fixed. It is itself but a dominant concrete complex, and always haunted by a real, tragic, and imminent possibility of sin. The Christian is always *en route,* never safely at home; he can always swerve from the path and betray himself and his Lord. A distinguished spiritual writer, Père Grou, notes in a beautiful chapter of his *Maximes Spirituelles* that: "We should always take the greatest care not to abuse our liberty, and to make it as like to God's as may be by love of the good and hatred of evil. The more we are morally necessitated to the good, the more we shall be free as God is free, who is necessitated to good by His very nature; the more we are morally necessitated to evil, the more our liberty will be in bonds. . . . Two servitudes, of which the first uplifts and perfects our liberty, and the second degrades it. . . . Now grace alone can set us free from servitude to sin, and assure us true liberty; whence it follows that the more the will submits itself to grace, the more it does all that in it lies to make itself absolutely, fully, and constantly dependent, so much the more will it be free. Complete deliverance will be attained nowhere save in heaven, where it will be for ever confirmed in good. But here below, however deep its submission to the rule of grace, it is always exposed to the danger of slipping the yoke, and should always go in fear of it." [188]

Thus the liberty of the Christian is never anything more than an effort at liberation; and it is the purity, force and spontaneity of this effort that measures the degree of the liberation. Bringing liberty and faith together into one conspectus, as we have done ourselves, Origen writes, in an admirable page: "Just as the knowledge now given to the saints is given them in a glass, darkly, and similarly with prophecy and all the other gifts of the Holy Spirit, so the liberty now offered to the saints is as yet no full liberty, but a liberty, so to speak, given in a glass and darkly, *in speculum et aenigmate;* wherefore the saints are still called slaves by comparison with the liberty which will be accorded them in face to face vision." [189] Only in the liberty of the glory of the children of God shall we be exempt from the possibility of further sin; only then will our freedom of choice be absorbed in perfect liberty, as the flower in its eternal fruit.

III

This would be the place to draw out the likeness of Christian liberty if we could undertake the task. A few traits, rapidly sketched, is all we can now offer.

Christian liberty is at once humble and glorious. It is humble because it knows itself to be the outcome of a gift. It is given, not simply as are all the rest, but infinitely more than all the rest, because it is a reality more spiritual, more divine, more directly involved in the creative benediction. It would be but a poor theology that would seek to withdraw this liberty from God in order to put it more firmly on its feet, seeing that only a pure divine mercy can make it exist at all. It is humble again because it knows itself to be a liberty healed. Of itself, as a result of sin, it tends to what God hates, desires what He forbids. Weak, tempted, divided against itself as it is, Christ alone nourishes, protects and unifies it, and makes of it at last a liberty victorious over sin. Conscious of being ceaselessly sustained and healed by Christ, it welcomes with wondering joy this grace which infuses it at once with health and holiness, it eagerly embraces this dependence which ever creates it anew, and it cries out with an infinity of adoration and thanksgiving: "Blessed be thou, O God, who dost daily deliver me."

Firmly based on the gift of Christ, it is also a glorious liberty, because it makes us capable of becoming wholly children of God. Divided, overcome, and filled with distaste for ourselves, grace quickens us with one sole love which unifies and tranquillizes and makes us strong. It unites us moreover with others; it excludes the domination that crushes, the concupiscence that abases, and brings us the liberty of generosity which respects our fellows and serves them, and bids them flourish in a fraternal air. And lastly this grace assimilates us to Christ, the free man *par excellence:* so wholly delivered from evil and sin, so wholly given up to the love of His Father, that, surmounting all the misery of choice, He could not sin at all. This is the liberty He would have us share, that we too many become obedient to the Father, serviceable to our brothers, sacrificed along with Him: that we should set out each morning in youth renewed to offer, to conquer, and sanctify the new day—*le vierge, le vivace, et le bel aujourd'hui.*

Christian liberty is at once deeply committed and very independent. More than any other, the Christian is called on to serve the human community, and therefore the Common Good in all its aspects, spiritual and material. He knows that without the elementary, essential and permanent values which society

alone can provide, a fully human life is not normally possible.
He must therefore be ready to take up all the tasks that aim at
making the social group a place where men can live and
breathe and grow; and in this context his liberty is simply a
power for service. Against all forms of liberalistic or anarchistic
freedom, which inevitably issue in tyranny and disaster, he will
try to achieve this evangelical liberty which consists in such a
seeking for the Kingdom of God and such a detachment from
all else, that without illusion, without calculation, without return on self, he can devote himself in simple love to the service
of all and to the good estate of the Community.

But precisely on that account his liberty is very independent.
For society is there to serve the human vocation; its mission is
to help the person to self-fulfilment in communion with his
brothers and his God; and God alone is its end, and bond, and
supreme power. The principle of Christian independence lies
in this: that Christians are free with respect to all that is not
God, or the will of God. On this plane, the only decisive one,
the social hierarchy and the constituted powers are things to
be judged and measured by the divine vocation to Christian
liberty. Social differences, for example—what do they signify?
Greek or barbarian, bond or free, all that is surmounted (I Cor.
VII, 21). A Christian may be a slave among men, but he is
the freeman of the Lord, and therein he finds the principle of
a liberty that lacks all common measure with social conditions,
and transcends them all even while it respects them. A Christian, though a freeman in society, is a bondman of the Lord,
and therein he finds the principle of an obedience so strict, a
service so total, that all juridical constraints are crude, loose
and strengthless in comparison. Is the Christian on that account a stranger in this world? Far from that, it is precisely
this very transcendence, this indifference by plenitude, that

makes of Christian liberty an ever active ferment in the bosom of human organisms. Moreover Christians know that temporal oppression has always borne heavily on human heads, that it pretends to bow them beneath a yoke that is sacred, and that Caesar has too often sought to have himself adored as a god. But he gives to Caesar the things that are Caesar's, and to God the things that are God's—to a God who Himself determines what belongs to each. To Caesar is the service of the citizen, the effort of the member in the body, voluntary collaboration, courageous, brotherly, with the Common Good,— money, toil, and sweat, even blood if need be. To God and to God alone is the inmost heart, the secret of conscience, service unreserved and love above all things.

The Lord Caesar and the Lord Jesus are not on the same plane. The former is insignificant beside the latter, provisional, passing, himself a servant, *for he is God's minister to thee for good* (Rom. XIII, 4) and a lord who must learn to obey before he commands. The latter is Lord indeed, the true Master, the true Head, the true Saviour, *King of Kings and Lord of Lords* (Apoc. XIX, 16). His is the Name that is above all names, the Power above all powers, absolute Primacy. He stands at the source of our being, at the centre of our liberty, at the term of our desire. We lie between His redemptive hands, and no one here below can take us out of His hands—none, unless it be our own unhappy liberty. When therefore these two lords are in opposition, and Caesar demands what Christ disallows, the answer made of old is always ready: *We must obey God rather than men.* It is our Christian vocation that makes us thus free, and it is our liberty that lends all its greatness to our obedience.

Finally let us add once more that Christian liberty remains, in all domains, a daily re-conquest. A conquest, that is, in the face of all the social obstacles, all the accepted routines, all the collective egoisms which ceaselessly close round the most liberating of initiatives, like the polar ice-floes round the explorer's ship. That is why the Christian forces are continually having to pull themselves together again, and risk everything afresh, to gain, defend or develop those social liberties which embody and protect our Christian liberty. It is one of the essential aims of Catholic Action to save, through the liberties of citizens, the imprescriptable liberty of consciences. The effort has to be ceaselessly renewed because the weight of social matter is always tending to stifle the spirit, and because the will of the group is always more repressive than liberating. Each new generation has to start the same work over again, to liberate its soul from the body its elders have left it; each begets its own obstacles, entangles itself in trammels of its own making even while seeking enfranchisement, and always runs the risk of a new slavery at the end of each new effort. The Church, the divinised body of Humanity on the march, plunged in the incessant movement of growth, of efforts and failures, of liberation and imprisonment—the City come down from above (Gal. IV, 26) to foster generations of free men in the human city—the Church cannot maintain her liberty save at the price of a never-ending liberation; nor can any generation, any more than any individual, "absolve itself from the duty of faithfully examining its conscience, of unsparingly purifying and energetically renewing itself, in its spirit and in its acts."

But the task will not be accomplished unless each of us sets out to achieve his own proper liberty. A daily achievement, since it is in time, in the sorrow of continual lapses and recoveries, that liberty is established, and the spiritual child becomes a man in judgment and generosity. A difficult achievement since the Christian is not exempt from temptation and is always having to quell his carnal reason and will which lust against his nascent liberty. An achievement which increasingly consists in making way for Another to work in the heart of our effort. Only on condition of allowing the Holy Spirit to work in the soul, of allowing ourselves to be led by the Spirit, can our souls find entrance into their divine liberty. The achievement therefore demands a radical renunciation of self, and a progressive self-abandonment to the leading of the Spirit. That is the paradox of Christian liberty: its full possession coincides with a full abandonment, because therein alone is realized a full communion. But we shall easily understand that when our liberty arrives on these heights it enters on dramas of which the simple warfare of flesh and spirit affords no idea. The great Saints are faced with choices and decisions which amount to agonies and crucifixions—*Father, not my will but thine be done*—because these heroes are charged with the task of prolonging, through their own hidden passion, the redemptive liberation of mankind and of bringing it to their brothers who sit captive in the shadow of sin and death. Through the joys of the liberty of grace fully recovered, they are penetrated and consumed with a burning desire for *the liberty of the glory of the children of God,* and they cry out with St. Teresa: "O life, enemy of my happiness, wherefore is it forbidden me to escape thee? I suffer thee because God suffers thee; I embrace thee because thou art His. But betray me not, and be not thankless. And in spite of all, O Lord, alas, how long is my exile! Time, it is true, is always short compared with thine eternity, but a single day, a single hour seems long when we know not whether we are about to offend thee, or when we fear to do so. O free-will of ours, so miserably the slave of thine own liberty when thou are not held by love and fear of Him who created thee! O when shall come that blessed day when thou shalt be drowned in the shoreless Ocean of the Sovereign Truth, where thou shalt have no more liberty to sin, and wouldst not have it, because then thou shalt be beyond reach of every misery and connaturalized with the very life of thy God." [190]

CHAPTER NINE

LOVE

LIBERTY HAS BROUGHT us to the centre of the person; but liberty too has its centre—which is love. And so, with love, we are at the very centre of man's being, and we can say that the man will be worth what his love is worth. But if love is generally recognized as the supreme value, the idea of love has been so distorted and falsified that we shall need a very special effort to recover it in all its purity. We shall try in what follows to set human love in its proper perspective, to indicate its essential structure, and to study it in its most typical expression—namely nuptial love.

I

The universe is the fruit of creative love. It was set in existence and recalled to God by one sole movement in which appears the gift of the First Cause, and the call of the Last End. It is borne along on the wave of a measureless desire, written in the secret depths of every being, and drawing all towards God. This great cosmic force which gathers all creatures together and sweeps them along, this movement of return to God, this appetite for unity striving towards the Infinite Good —this is the natural love of God. A love which is "the very inclination of nature implanted there by its Author." [191] A love that is necessitated and ineradicable because involved in the very structure of the created being as such, and constituting its radical dynamism. Love which is not an act, but the principle of all acts [192] because it is the relation which defines every created appetite in the face of its Creator: a relation of need and a relation of desire, both equally absolute. Thus God is present to His creature not simply in virtue of the being He bestows on it, but also by the love He excites in the very heart of its existence; whence it is that the whole world is tense with one immense aspiration, quickening and unifying, towards the First Beloved.

This movement, it need not be said, is verified in man: the spirit is nature before it is liberty, and it is defined by this natural love which is its original harmony with God, its incoercible impulsion towards Him, its constitutive relation to Him. If we look for the basis of this love we shall find it in the ontological link by which man is united to God. A union rooted in a participation—"every created being participates, so to speak, in the nature of Being"; a union involving a proper likeness to God, the spirit being an image of God in virtue of its capacity for knowing Him and loving Him, and in virtue of its "natural conformity" with God; a union which carries with it an appetite for unity because it is only a starting-point for this will which God "inclines to will what He Himself wills: the Sovereign Good." [193] We can now see the concrete implications of St. Thomas' words: "Natural love is the connaturality of the subject that desires, with the object of its desire"; [194] and we can say that the natural love of the human will is the radical dynamism which links it with and draws it to God as to its Principle, its Exemplar, and its End.

Hence when a man begins to will anything the secret and necessary spring of all his acts is his natural love of God. Because this is involved in the very structure of the will—to be, for the will, is to be drawn to God—there is neither liberty nor moral quality in it, but only a happy and constitutive necessity. For the will's object itself is desirable only as a participation of the Divine Good and as a reflection of its Beauty; and if it attracts, it is only because Another does so through it.[195] On the other hand, when the will seeks its own fulfilment it is still seeking a divine likeness, since the perfection of everything in the universe, like the perfection of the universe itself, is nothing other than a likeness to God. To love any object whatsoever is therefore to love a participation—though deficient—and a possession—though partial—of God; and thus: "in the love of every good it is the Sovereign Good that is loved." [196]

We must go further still, and doubly so. Every created good is at the same time both a likeness of God and a definite fulfilment for our desire; to desire it is to desire simultaneously the perfection it possesses and the divine likeness; to possess it is simultaneously to fulfil our own being and our likeness to God. Simultaneously; but an ontological priority has to be observed. Every perfection acquired supposes a principle of perfection, namely the good; every good attracts only in virtue of, and in the measure of, its likeness to God.[197] We must therefore say: it is because we love God that we love all else. Naturally to love a good is to be fraternal with that good; but the soul's fraternity with things is that of a spiritual being and so of a being attuned in advance, not to this or that particular good, but to the Good as such, the Good in all its amplitude; and this saturating object can only be God. In loving anything whatever therefore the soul loves God, and the natural and perfected form of its love is the love of God. None of its acts has any meaning or content save as a provisional step towards the last end, and as a partial possession of the divine Plenitude.

It is indeed the love of God that stirs up men to action, and if they love and seek their ends it is because *first* they love and desire, with a natural movement of desire, the God who created them and recalls them to Himself.

But if it is in love of God that all other loves are rooted, then it follows inevitably that man's first movement should be primarily love. The ultimate condition of love is that the lovers should be linked by a profound fraternity in their very beings, so that already in a way "they are one thing"; and love is so much the more sovereign, total and intense as the union in question is the more radical.[198] Now the person is, by nature, in life-giving contact with three objects: first with himself—and this substantial union, or rather unity, is the basis of the natural love of self; then with other human persons, since they all partake of the same nature, and can fulfil themselves only together within the whole body of humanity—and this unity of likeness and intimacy is the basis of the natural love of others; and finally with God—and this union of total dependence is the basis of the natural love of God. All three loves are implicated in the same movement; but here again a principle of order is needed, and therefore a First Loved who is loved absolutely—and evidently this can only be God. The will then is basically an inclination to love God above all things. St. Thomas repeats it again and again in texts that presuppose only this:[199] that to posit a nature which is to be a part in a hierarchised universe and a finite participation of the Infinite Being, is to posit it as ordered to God, the last End of the Whole; it is to give it an appetite and a love which, through its own proper good, tend directly to God, the Common Good of the universe, and subordinate all other loves to that. To love God above all things is therefore to hierarchise all ends, to set them all, whatever they be, on the way to a sole End, God

Himself, who rules them all by bringing them all into unity and calling them to Himself. Thus man's natural love is essentially open, disinterested, generous. It does not shut him up within himself, it opens him on the infinite, and attaches him thereto by way of a necessary, incoercible and indestructible inclination; it throws him back on the God from whom he came; it takes him out of himself, but only that he may find himself again in his Source and his End. The whole human drama arises from the fact that the free act of love blossoms on this natural tendency, and can either ratify or reject it; but all human hope will be founded on this other fact, that this natural tendency is one with the will itself, and no less indestructible; and that however disastrous may be the options we make, they will yet leave the natural inclination to love God above all things intact, and always ready for new initiatives.

For the rest, we must put this natural love of God in its proper place in the dynamism of the human being. It is not, as we have said, an act, but a movement written into the structure of the will, a natural inclination at the root of its acts, a necessary tendency whose energy is drawn upon even when its orientation is rejected. It lies beyond consciousness and direct knowledge, active without being known and present without being conscious. It is enveloped and concealed in the will's conscious tendency to its own Good even while tending naturally to the Infinite Good; and it is implicit in the love of any object that possesses a lovable character, but does so only by derivation and participation. Thus "just as it is God who is loved implicitly in every object, so it is God who is loved implicitly in every end." [200]

But this "implicitly" raises the formidable problem of the passage to the explicit, and it involves the possibility of an error and a deviation which will be love's misery and sin. Finally, this natural tendency, being necessary and prior to all voluntary choice, is devoid of freedom or moral quality; but is nevertheless the foundation of all freedom and of all morality: indeed these would be unintelligible unless grafted on a necessitating call and inclination; and it is the point at which will be received, as by a marvellous grace that comes not to destroy but to fulfil, the influx of divine charity.

However it be, it is on the basis of this natural love that all other loves will flourish. The corn that thrusts up from the earth, the bird that sings, the ocean that heaves and swells, the stars that pursue their courses, all love God in their own way; and when man seeks and toils, desires and wills, it is always God that he seeks in his. If the lower creatures remain unaware of the love that moves them, God knows it for them since He gave it; it is but the call within them of the love that created them. Man too is a creature like the rest; the summit of the world and therefore rooted in the world; destined to make its effort succeed and therefore partaking in that effort; placed in being by the creative will and therefore sustained and stirred throughout by that will. He is nature before he is liberty; willed before he wills; imposed on himself before choosing himself, or rather, since it is a Love that is here in action, he is *given to himself* before he *gives himself*. But because he is spirit he takes this given impulsion, this necessitating call, this natural love, into his own hands, not to suppress it, for that would be impossible, but to ratify it or refuse it. Here then arises the problem of love considered as a personal act.

II

Love, in the proper sense of the term, exists only between persons. Not to confine ourselves within the limits of a definition or lose ourselves in psychological description, let us rather try to seize love's inner reality through a series of its typical paradoxes. Thus perhaps we may catch some glimpse of its mystery.

Love is *passivity* and *activity*. It is in virtue of his deepest aspiration that man lies open to love, but the act of love is an impossibility unless he falls in with something capable of attracting it. Hence the essential passivity of love; if it is to exist at all another must first find entrance to the soul and awaken it to itself. The loved one acts always as the nourishment that comes to satisfy a hunger, as the beauty that comes to set a longing at rest, as the Plenitude that comes to fill a void; and love is always the offspring of riches and poverty. It supposes therefore a hold established by the other on the will, a transforming presence in the will of the lover; and since the beloved can neither enrich nor transform save only by communicating himself, he brings the will into tune with his own, he makes it vibrate to his own rhythm, and thus sets up a harmony and fraternity between these two which are love's first trait. They were two, and now are one, in this divine connaturality that henceforth links them together, in this gladdening presence which is now about to awaken the lover to action.

For we must be careful not to misconceive this passivity. If the beloved fulfils the radical desire of the will, if he makes himself the realization of this potency in quest of fulfilment, then, by that very fact, he sets it in full activity and makes it react in its turn. The will is tendency and inclination; for it, to act is to tend; to be brought to full realization is to be put into a state of tension, and that is why love is necessarily the spontaneous movement of the lover towards the beloved; [201] but a movement not initiated by oneself, a movement communicated by another, and this denotes the infirmity proper

to the creature. It cannot satisfy its own longing, it is desirous
and poor; its love implies at its source a trembling uncertainty,
an anxious expectation, and, if it comes to fruition, an encounter with the loved one which aways seems a gratuitous
marvel and a miraculous gift. There we have the first paradox
of love: it is an impulse, but an impulse that has to be aroused
by a gift; and to strip it of its character of imperfection would
demand that gift and impulse should be necessarily implied in
each other as equally absolute and eternal.

Love is next a *union* and a *movement*. It exists only by the
presence of the beloved, not simply *to* but *in* the lover: a profound internal presence of one being in the heart of another.
And nevertheless, since the will is inclination and movement,
the beloved is in it as something appealing to it and drawing
it on. He enters the lover's mind as a haunting image and
thought, a joyous spoil that the soul bears away in and with
itself; but that is only the condition of love. He enters the
lover's will as a force "inwardly impelling the lover to the beloved"; and that is love itself.[202] He who loves possesses thus
the object of his love not simply as a treasure he can hug to
himself, but as a principle of movement and a source of desire
—*amor ecstasim facit*. Because this hold and this call are
realized in a spiritual being they are taken up into his consciousness; because they introduce him to another person
who comes to enrich his being, fulfil his aspiration, and set his
inner impulse free, they are seized on as a source of joy, as a
principle of happiness. This conscious apprehension of an
aspiration at once fulfilled and inflamed is the affective phenomenon essential to love, the "affective union" in which
lover and beloved are henceforth one. But this union is essentially dynamic, it is brought about in and by the very movement that carries along those who love, and posits them as ir-

reducibly distinct and distant at the very moment that it
draws them together and unites.[203] Love is thus indeed an
appetite for a real and physical ontological unity; but one
which realizes its essence in this unitive inclination—*amor, vis
unitiva*—which is at once its misery and its greatness. Evidently therefore, if we wished to define love, we should have
to respect this mysterious conjunction of movement and repose,
of possession and desire, of presence and absence.

Love is *affectivity* and *liberty*. For there is a spiritual affectivity, too long ignored by the moderns and not always accorded its due place even by theology.[204] If the flesh can be
moved and made to quiver "like a great lyre," so too can the
spirit and even more readily. For the spirit is subtler, more
"sensitive," more open, more desirous, more capable of joy
and of sorrow. Accordingly, there are spiritual affections, radically irreducible to those of the sensibility—admiration, re-
pentance, fear, all kinds of sorrows and joys, and lastly the
sovereign affection, love. The ultimate seat and source of this
spiritual affectivity is therefore the will, and love is its most
essential and efficacious power.[205] It sets the whole will quivering; it is joy, it is "emotion" in the Bergsonian sense of the
term, it is the triumphant outpouring of a plenitude, a presenti-
ment of the infinite. Under this aspect it escapes all definition,
and all the philosophers, poets and saints together have only
been able to murmur a few vain words which wholly fail to
give it expression. But what it concerns us to note here is that
this affective movement is a call to our liberty. Love, as affective, is in us without us; it is a presence that offers itself and a
joy that calls; a movement of the spirit that solicits the spirit,
for the will that feels the affection has to will it freely. Love
does not truly come to birth until it is accepted and welcomed;
it calls out to be chosen, and to allow it to take root and grow

once it has been consciously felt is to have chosen it already. But then, once chosen, it is no longer simply *in* us, it is *ourselves;* and our freedom completes what the affectivity only began. There is therefore a necessary element of liberty in love, and it is precisely this that gives it its personal and personalizing character. For to accept a love is to accept a state of being which touches and transforms the entire person; it is deliberately to give one's life a certain direction; and that is why, if we take into account the choice and election that lies at the heart of love, we shall have to say, as we said above with St. Augustine, that love is liberty itself; and we shall have to add, with the moderns, that it is the act in which persons are spiritually brought to birth. Love is thus a complex of affectivity and liberty, in which the whole will is involved, and in which are found, in unbelievable depth and purity, both the activity and passivity, the weakness and power of the spirit.

Love, in us, is *spirit* and *flesh.* That it is spiritual, in spite of all prejudices to the contrary, is altogether evident. It exists only between persons, it is freedom, it is joy—all characteristic traits of the spirit. Against all the miserable sophistries which would place love in the sensibility or the senses this truth must be firmly maintained. Human love, which can carry so strong a charge of animal instinct, would never have the power, the infinity, one might almost say the divinity that it has, were it not rooted in a spirit capable of the infinite and an express image of God. But this love is necessarily embodied, since it is the act of a spirit that informs a body and can realize itself only by means of its body. Because it is the spirit's deepest activity it makes the whole body vibrate with these rich emotions, at once so new and so fulfilling for the entire person. All the body's resources are drawn upon. As means of action it does love's service; as means of expression it bears it witness;

as means of communion it nourishes or consummates. Love
must have a body, and it finds its body in all the highest functions of this body of ours: to serve, to reveal, to give life. And
just as the body can hide and oppress the spirit, so the body
that love takes on can mask, imprison or pervert its soul. And
yet it is still this imprisoned soul that gives love its life, its power,
and its terrible infinity. The body's revolt cannot alter the
natural order of things, which makes of love an embodied
power of the spirit.

There remains a last characteristic of love and the most important of all since it decides its whole significance. This appetite for unity, this onrush of liberty—do they return on themselves, or are they truly open to others? Are they egoistic and interested, or disinterested, generous and pure? We must answer,
as it seems to us, that love is at once desire and gift, and that the
real problem rather concerns the relation to be established
between the gift and the desire. Love implies a movement of
desire because man is a creature, therefore radically indigent,
a being definable in terms of this substantial indigence itself.
The will is the appetite, unsleeping, always seeking, of this
indigence; wherefore the love that attracts it must also be
desire, a movement tending to what it lacks and would have,
to the thing that has power to bring it to fulfilment, and which,
in virtue of its natural tendency, it seeks to embrace and incorporate into itself. *Desire and possession* are correlative terms,
and as long as the human creature is still in quest of its end and
its Beatitude, it cannot but seek the good which shall bring
its being to full expansion and stature.

But, on the other hand, love involves a movement of giving
that is more essential still because man holds from Another all
that he is. Our analyses of the person and of natural love will
help to make this clear. The person is subsistent and open. As

subsistent and closed, he loves by drawing things into himself, and that is the movement of desire. As open, as participating in human nature, and in God Himself, he loves by referring himself to his Whole: that is to say to his partial Whole which is humanity, in which he finds his place, his meaning, and his power to expansion; and to the Infinite Whole which is God, in whom he finds the source and the final consummation of his existence. And thus he is never *himself* save when he is surpassed, forgotten, and *given;* and love here terminates in communion linking me up with another human person as with another self, or with the Divine Being as with the One within me who is more myself than myself.[206]

Moreover our analysis of natural love has shown that it is the first, fundamental, and necessary movement of the person; and that as such it is a love of God above all things, essentially open, disinterested, generous. Now it is from this natural love that the free act of love proceeds; and if the will follows its law, if it expresses itself in a rightful appetition, then its love will be an act of gift. Desire expresses one essential aspect of the creature: it is indigent; gift expresses the other: this indigent creature *is;* and exists that all its riches may be given, spent, if need be sacrificed. That is the only way to fulfil and exalt them.

And further: what this creature is, is destined to make the loved one *be* the more. Love brings growth in being. It reveals men to themselves. It seeks them out in their intimate depths to set their energies free, to answer their deepest call, to find their still veiled and ambiguous meaning and bring it to light. In this sense only, but in this sense very truly, love is creative: because it creates that community in fact to which humanity tends by nature, and therein all who still seek themselves may find. But this it does only because it is a gift that calls forth a gift, and which, in this mutual giving, finds its own perfection by realizing that of the person and the community. And when there is question of God, whom none can make greater than He is in Himself, love at least can make His Kingdom grow, is able to fulfil the creative will by giving itself to that will, and realize the fraternal and divine community which the Father would establish among us and by us.[207]

The relations of desire and gift in the act of love can now be formulated thus. Just as the person finds his full subsistence only in the act which links him with his fellows and with God, so love realizes its veritable essence only in the act in which desire (i.e. desire to possess) is penetrated and borne on by the gift (i.e. desire to give oneself). Desire is measured by the human person, which is why it is so strongly apparent in love; the gift is measured by Him who created the person, which is why it is more radical and profound. In love as desire man loves himself in loving another; he makes himself a *centre,* and rightly so, for such he is. In love as self-giving he purely loves the other in whom he places his centre; he makes himself an *excentric point,* and rightly so again, for such he is.[208] His mystery consists in being both at once; and in attaining to his consummation only when this centre which he is, is voluntarily attached to the mysterious and infinite centre which is the universe of persons in the Infinite Personal Being. True love is therefore the impulsion in which desire is enveloped and carried away by self-giving; so that nothing egoistic remains in the desire, and nothing mutilating in the gift; so that persons are fulfilled in their true communion at the very moment when they are wholly surrendered to each other; so that to God from whom all proceeds, love makes everything return in a desire and a gift for ever reconciled, equally peaceful and ardent, equally substantial, equally eternal.

This rapid analysis would remain in part ineffective if we did not go on to indicate briefly the concrete condition of love in man. All we need do here is to resume and apply what we have already said of the concrete condition of the person. The love to which man is called is supernatural, springing from the personal mystery of a God who is Love, who would have sons animated by the love wherewith He loves Himself, and who brings this Kingdom of love to realization by giving them the Christ, *the Son of His love* (Col. I, 13). It is this strictly personal love (personal in its source and term) that at one and the same stroke has chosen, predestinated, called and justified us—and already glorified us. But, like the person, love is wounded; or rather the person himself is wounded because this supernatural love no longer exists in him. He has ceased to love as he should the God who loves him, and from this primal wound flow all the others. He loves neither himself, nor his fellows, nor the world, with a rightful love, pure, efficacious and divine; because his love is tainted it is halting and impotent and blind, and all has turned to confusion in the world of persons. At last, and once more like the person, love is healed in Christ; or rather restored to us in Christ. Sinners and enemies as we are, God has nevertheless loved us anew in giving us His Christ; and Christ reconciles His Father and His brothers by loving both with one same love, by offering Himself to God and delivering Himself up for us; the Holy Spirit, whom His sacrifice has merited for us, pours out mysteriously into the depths of our hearts the Love which is the very life of the Trinity. Then begins the drama of the slow, difficult and magnificent growth of the children of God. The "miracle of miracles" is thus the visible apparition of the eternal Love among men; and the redemptive Incarnation is the unique event which transforms our human condition, and inaugurates the new Man, the new Heavens, and the new Earth in the midst of this world of sin, where human hopes so often founder in a welter of mud and blood. But since this subject is inexhaustible let us content ourselves with a few reflections on two capital points: the love of man and woman, and man's love for God.

III

The love in which man and woman are made one engages the human being in all his corporeal and spiritual unity; and that is why we shall have to distinguish three components in this act of love. The first of them is the *call of instinct,* the movement that comes from the depths of the ages and assures the survival of the species, the quiver that comes from the depths of the flesh and makes it vibrate through and through to the rhythm of another; the power that seizes on a man and in one way or another, discreetly veiled or brusquely open, makes him the servant of its own ends. That is the carnal aspect of love—opaque, hungry, violent. The second component is the *act of the spirit,* the definitive choice that excludes all others, the absolute gift that is given for ever, the absolute generosity stronger than death. That is the spiritual aspect of love—radiant, infinite, creative. The third component is the *intoxication of the affectivity,* a whole world of specific feelings, sensible and spiritual together. The former, as efflorescence of instinct, stand for the carnal hunger and thirst, and awaken a desire at once precise and imperious. The latter, an overflow of the spirit, bring with them an infinitude of purity and joy, like "music awakened" in the soul. Indissolubly united, the two reinforce and colour each other and issue together in a radically new and potent joy. The three components—instinctive, spiritual, and affective—integrate a sole reality which is that of nuptial love; a sole act, the act of loving; and a sole state which is a kind of experience of the infinite.

Normally it is in the affective region that love first stirs, and this fact goes to explain the essential double ambiguity that surrounds it: there is the ambiguity with which it is invested by its *felt passivity*, for it appears in us without us, and the freedom of the act which accepts it is masked by the strength of a desire fully "experienced" and triumphant: and there is the ambiguity which comes of its *spiritual plenitude,* for it moves our appetite for the infinite, our desire for an absolute beauty, our eager impulse to generosity; and the call of instinct is enveloped and masked by this spiritual flowering. But love, being the act of the person, is always instinct, liberty and affectivity at once; these three awaken and develop together unequally, in accordance with a rhythm that is highly complex and a permanent source of gratification and of danger. Love is made up of the interior tension between these three inter-linked and opposed forces—a tension always variable because living, always imperilled because maintained with difficulty, always harmonic because voluntarily maintained, and one which alone enables the person to give himself, body and soul, to another.

If now we look for the outcome and end of this nuptial love, we shall find it, first, in the fulfilment of the two spiritual persons concerned. They cannot fulfil themselves save in communion; and now, here, is a union of persons in all the fullness of their power to complete each other. For a soul that informs and is one with a body is "affected" to its depths by the sexual difference. After what we have said already on the part played by the body we need not further insist on it. Let us say simply that man and woman are here doubly fulfilled: first as *human persons,* representing two irreducible vocations, two images of

God for ever distinct, albeit convergent and fraternal; and then as *masculine and feminine persons,* representing two essential possibilities of one and the same nature, each essentially incomplete, and essentially orientated to the other (whatever may be the detail of their complementary divergencies, a matter on which precision is difficult and one on which our science has little to say as yet). Moreover, linked as they are already by the way in which they complement each other, man and woman are united *in their personal mystery.* For each individual human being is a profound secret, living and inviolable, sealed in the very union of the soul with its body. In nuptial love, availing itself of all its quality as embodied spirit, and therefore of its carnal possibilities, the soul is given by means of the body. Not clearly, not in a light that absorbs every shadow, for that is impossible as long as the soul remains in the body, a sign that reveals only by always concealing and achieves a presence only by hiding it under a veil. And yet these two will very really give themselves to each other in the mystery of their embodied souls. "These twain are one flesh," each regards the other as an extension and a prolongation of self, as his body or hers, as the case may be—a body augmented in which the soul can live, desire and act; and each is surrendered to be inhabited and possessed by the other, as a flesh to be informed, and animated, and made to bloom and grow. Thus attached, each to the other, they leave father and mother, they quit the community that gave them being, to live and affirm themselves in a new community in which an absolute intimacy shall be the source of a mutual fulfilment. Then in the union of these two a new and mysterious being is realized, a real and living "We" arises from this "Thou" and "I"; a "We" posterior to either since they are the persons who realize it, and yet prior, since they come together within it and are given for it. Possessing each other, given to each other, in a relationship in which the possession is enveloped and caught up in the gift, in an outpouring in which the growth and greatness and joy of the other are the first thought, the first desire, and the supreme joy, husband and wife commune together through the flesh and in time, but above time and the flesh. They unite in a total offering and consecration in which are embraced a generosity and a pure faith, a humble loyalty, chastity, and an exquisite modesty—in short in an absolute religious reverence not far removed from adoration, since it contains a note of divine greatness which already lifts their love to the realm of the holy and makes it fructify in unity and indissolubility.

But the persons are fulfilled in nuptial love in another mystery that surpasses themselves and their "We." A two-fold call—from beneath and above—penetrates their union. The vital call in the first place, that of the cosmic progression and movement of life, which carries their partial "whole" into the specific "whole" of humanity. The persons, being members, fulfil themselves in fulfilling the species. Their community is normally fruitful since it is orientated by nature towards the child in whom their own life is to be continued and the future assured. Man and woman come together not simply to bring forth themselves but to bring forth another being who shall still be themselves and realize nevertheless another step in the progressive development of humanity. Their love is thus creative not simply because it reveals themselves to themselves and opens them out to their full dimensions, but because it issues in this other human person, the child, in this substantial gift henceforth subsistent and open to a destiny that is infinite. And that is why the woman who gives birth rejoices, *because a man is born into the world* (John XVI, 21).

And yet this too must be surpassed. For the family and

humanity were not made for themselves but for God, and
nuptial love cannot be fulfilled save in making of the human
community God's own world. For love, in the spouses, is the
call of the Creator who would accomplish in them the communal aspect of their vocation, would develop, through them,
the divine image borne by humanity; and who associates them
for that end with His own dignity as Cause, and with His own
creative fecundity. So that nuptial love is henceforth in itself
a cry of their nature and their very being for the personal and
immediate intervention of God: the creation of a human soul.
Here the vital and the spiritual alike are caught up into the
divine. In virtue of this unexampled relation to the divine
causality human love once more finds entrance to the realm
of the Holy, and the movement that runs through it, if it
begins in the flesh, reaches its consummation only in the kiss
of God.

* * *

So far we have studied nuptial love in its structure only.
Now we have to consider its concrete condition in fallen man,
and look at the wounded and unhappy reality. A thing so
complex is naturally exposed to danger, and can hardly fail to
carry the seeds of conflict. When man fell the dangers became
open wounds, and the conflict was envenomed by defeat. Here
are the essential facts.

Fallen man comes into the world to-day in a state of separation from Christ, in whom he would otherwise have found the
God who is Love; and human love, accordingly, comes to birth
in separation from its Source and from its End. Its purpose
remains: it is still there to help men and women to enter into
union with God and to extend His Kingdom. Its power however has gone. It can no longer really attain to God because

it no longer springs from the merciful Heart of the Lord; it
cannot achieve the holy community in which the Father stands
at the centre as at the source, and in which the children are
equally sons of men and sons of God; it cannot build the
Kingdom because it is no longer really itself, because it has
lost its supernatural substance, because from this standpoint
it is but flesh and blood, which cannot, as such, inherit the
Kingdom of God. This lack of being, this unreality, this hidden
disorientation towards the animal man which is only perceptible to the eyes of faith—this is love's deepest wound; and
we shall have to return to it when we take up the study of the
love of God. Let us dwell for a moment here on its consequences.

Since love is a complex, its first danger lies in the *separability*
of its elements. After sin, this became a *separation*. The internal unity of an act—like that of a being—lies in the efficacious attraction of its end. Now love is dissociated from its real
end,—God and man loved in Christ; it has lost at once its
internal proportion to this end and its efficacious movement
towards it; and its elements, instead of being bound up together and integrated in a single impulsion, have fallen apart.
Urges of instinct, movements of affectivity, calls of the spirit,
each go their own way, and dominate the unhappy human
creature in turn. At the limit, we have the man of instinct, the
man of feeling, and the man of calculation. The first is
abandoned to his reflexes, and love, for him, is a physical need
and a merely animal reality. For the second, absorbed in
emotion, love is a dream-life full of alluring mirage. The third
regards it as a kind of social necessity designed to secure the
continuance of the species—consider for instance what becomes
of love in the hands of the Plato of the *Republic* and the
Laws,[209] and what becomes of marriage in the corruption of a

bourgeois and puritan society.[210] In this triple division love perishes. Perhaps the most remarkable case is that of the emancipation of the emotional life (that of instinct being natural). Poets and novelists speak of the "thunderclap" of love at first sight to which their heroes so readily succumb, and it is easy to smile at this facile conventionalism. But we must also note those cases, by no means so rare, in which a love lays hold on the sensibility with irresistible force and infixes a sting which the most prolonged efforts cannot eradicate. A disordered passivity has here taken control of the spirit, and rules it henceforth on its own account in the bosom of the dissociated personality.

But, further, love is flesh and spirit, and exposed to the risk of tending unduly to one side or the other. Now in fallen man the spirit is weakened and the flesh emancipated, so that for all practical purposes it governs. So it is with love. The bodily component has become the strongest and its pull the heaviest. If the flesh can do nothing without the spirit, it attracts it nevertheless, seduces it, turns it to its own ends; and the spirit brings its own infinity into a love which is now no more than an appetite. Subjected to sense, emancipated from its spiritual law—the movement to God—love becomes passion, the passion that utters its song through all our Western literature to be laboriously deciphered by callow youth on the school benches. At one degree lower it becomes the sexual attraction discussed by learned psychologists in studies of animal behaviour, exploited by a host of commercial interests in novels, plays and movie-shows, and finally drained to the dregs by the unhappy crowds that people our cities. The flesh-spirit tension, essential to love, is no longer supportable; it breaks down, and makes way for the progressive degradation of mankind, for this "aphrodisiac civilization" [211] which the philoso-

pher himself can only regard with horror. If, finally, love is
desire caught up in a gift, in fallen man the relation is only too
easily reversed. Man is naturally generous, and sin makes him
naturally egoist. When the two tendencies come to grips it is
commonly egoism that gains the day; and, in love, the desire
is quick to engulf and govern and corrupt the gift. There is a
force of egoism henceforth, at once spiritual and sensual, which
exploits the dissociation and disequilibrium of love, sets it on
the downward track, reorganises it to its own profit, and makes
of it at last the hard, blind, tormenting and pitiless power
whose inhuman face we know too well.

Weighed down under such a load of miseries, nuptial love is
like a great wounded bird. When it looks up to the summits
for which it was destined, at the chastity in which the soul
would envelop its body, the fidelity that pledges one man to
one woman for ever, the generosity that gives life and growth
to those it holds embraced, the sanctity which offers to God for
their transfiguration the pair who have already surrendered
themselves to each other to the point of sacrifice—when it
looks up to these heights it can only despair of itself, and turning its back on the everlasting hills it sinks either into an
insipid and pitiable commonplace or a frenzied sensual abandonment—"when the furious winds of concupiscence make
your flesh flap like an old flag"—or even perhaps into denial,
incredulity and blasphemy. In any case, the real tragedy of
love lies less in its fall than in the struggle between its fall and
its true vocation, for it is always at once a prisoner to the flesh
and called to freedom in God.

The influence of sex on human behaviour is enormous and
the Freudians are certainly not wrong to make this animal
component the subject of a systematic study. But at the same
time we can never sufficiently emphasize the immeasurable

aspiration that traverses this foundered love; for it remains destined to receive the benediction of the God who is Love and to collaborate with Him in the work of His Kingdom; it is always sustained by this natural love of God, however sunken it may be in the night of unconscious powers, impotent to lift itself up alone; there is always at the root of the act of love a wounded power crying out to be healed, an indestructible hope that awaits its fulfilment. Love's tragedy lies in the conjoint fact of an aspiration crushed, at the heart of lust triumphant. Because the aspiration is infinite, the lust will never satisfy it; because the aspiration is spiritual and the lust carnal, it is commonly in tears and disgust that sexual adventures end; because the aspiration is less easily destroyed than the lust, which is organic and exhausted in its own exercise, a longing for purity lives on in the midst of the worst befoulments of the flesh, and a possibility of redemption is present in the deepest fall. God alone, in Christ, can actualise that possibility; and wounded love has but one resource to fall back upon: to kneel and pray for a new purity like Magdalen at the feet of the Lord Jesus.

IV

Christ came to save human love. He brought it first the radical cure effected at baptism. Christian grace reunites the person to God by filling up his spiritual emptiness and restoring him to his supernatural being. Then the spirit recovers its power and efficacy, it becomes capable of really loving God and really overcoming the flesh. Equilibrium is re-established in principle, love is freed from the tyranny of the senses, and chastity—the rightful ordering of the several elements in love—becomes possible and attainable. Before ever nuptial

love is born, it is healed in its deepest sources. If liberty collaborates with grace the human being is spiritualized and he
brings into his love an instinct already subdued (though always a danger), an affectivity already "ordered" and edu-
cated, and a will strengthened and rectified. The climate has
changed, the man become chaste, and a truly generous love
can therefore come to birth and grow.

Love however is too potent a force, instinct is too violent,
the affectivity too perfidious, for the birth and growth of love
to be left to themselves without the help of any special grace
from Christ. And so, for the Christian, there is a grace "destined to perfect the natural love" and the fruit of the sacrament of matrimony.[212] The peculiarity of this grace is that
it flows from the love that unites Christ with His Church (Eph.
V, 22–23). For there is a First Bridegroom and a First Bride,
by whom the others are to be judged, and a first nuptial love
which is their law. The nuptials of Christ and His Church
began at the Incarnation when the Word of God entered into
union with a human nature, and, through this unique nature,
embraced the whole human race in order to save it. They were
consummated on the Cross, whereon Christ *loved his Church
and delivered himself up for it, that he might present it to
himself a glorious Church, not having spot or wrinkle or any
such thing; but that it should be holy and without blemish;*
and they produce their full fruit whenever sons and daughters
are born and grow up to people the heavenly Jerusalem. And
while Christ *nourishes and cherishes the Church as his own
body,* in a submission which is love's absolute sacrifice, the
Church in her turn gives herself to Christ. Such is the first
love on which the others are founded. It is the source of Christian love, for it penetrates the soul with a grace that transfigures and divinises human affection. It is its model, for it

calls and draws us to imitation of Christ, to generosity, to
service and to sacrifice even as His. It is its end, for the riches
and power and joy it bestows on the heart are there to bring
to full bloom these images of Christ, the spouses and their
children, to spread abroad the Church, and to make way for
the Sole Love to achieve its plenitude in all. Christian love is
thus a fruit, an image, and an instrument of Christ and of the
Church.

Love however is too potent a force, instinct is too violent,
sistency, purity and fruitfulness when it is rooted in the Christ-
Church relationship; and the mystery of the nuptial union
derives its decisive significance and nobility from its participation—as effect, symbol, and means—in the mystery of the
union of Christ with His Church, the mystery of Christ as
Head of the Body. Here once more the mystery of the Head is
the principle of the healing of the members. Henceforth it is *by*
Christ that the spouses love, since it is He who has merited for
them and given them the power to seek and find themselves
in God. It is *in* Christ that they love, because it is in Him that
human persons receive their supernatural being and love; and
in the measure in which this gift is a grace that informs in
order to divinise their love, it is Christ Himself helping them
to love. And likewise it is *for* Christ that they love, because
He is the centre, the focus, and the absolute end of their love,
and all the delicacy of Christian chastity has no other aim than
to make the image of Christ shine out in His members, and so
invest them, as St. Thomas says, with a "heavenly likeness."
Consequently, it must needs be *as* Christ that the spouses love.
If persons are living relations to Christ, it is easy to see how
such a love will deepen and personalise them.

Love moreover knits up the spouses in a community involving certain profound relations of which it is difficult to speak

precisely. As persons, man and woman are equals. They have the same vocation; both are spiritual and free; both are *of God* (I Cor. XI, 12), and husbands should *give honour to the female as to the weaker vessel, and as to the co-heirs of the grace of life* (I Peter III, 7). Each, in God, is freely given to the other, and the man has true possession of his wife and the wife of her husband; each is in the other's power (I Cor. VII, 1–5). Because love issues in a gift of the soul through the body, and because both the man and the woman are members of Christ, temples of the Holy Spirit, consecrated to the glory of God in their very bodies, there is no room for inequality on this point: they must be *subject to one another in the fear of Christ* (Eph. V, 21), like all Christians; and so completely are they given that *the wife hath not the power of her own body, but the husband: and in like manner the husband also hath not power of his own body, but the wife* (I Cor. VII, 4). Two persons of equal standing, equally their own masters, equally called, and surrendering themselves to each other in all the fullness of their rights and their liberty—such is the first Christian affirmation.

Yet husband and wife are nevertheless unequal in so far as their union involves a human community *qua* community. Community implies order, that is to say differentiation and hierarchy of function, authority, a head and subordinate members, all at the service of the Common Good of the community. When St. Paul considers the relation of man and woman from this angle, he sees the Christian couple as situated at once with respect to the original couple—Adam and Eve—and with respect to the mystery they prefigured, the Divine Bridegroom and the redeemed Bride. He sees the spouses as two beings both involved in a creation, a fall, and a redemption which mark them at once in a common fashion (they *are* created, fallen, redeemed), and in a special fashion (each is so *in his or her own way*). If we bring together the texts in which St. Paul's thought is expressed, we might perhaps put it thus. The conjugal community needs a head, and this head is the man, because in him is continued the first Adam, and because he thus shares the prerogatives of him who was *formed first* (I Tim. II, 13), who is the direct *image* and *glory* of God (I Cor. XI, 7), and *a figure of him who was to come* (Rom. V. 14), in other words the image of the Head. As to the woman, her part here is to obey because she was *formed afterwards* (I Tim. II, 13), because she was *created for the man* (I Cor. XI, 9), and is therefore *the glory of the man,* just as the man is the glory of God (*Ibid.* 7),—an image that completes and glorifies him in his turn.

Nothing would be simpler, in the purity of an order willed by God, than this insertion of an authority and an obedience into a love which would animate, harmonise, and transfigure them with its ardour,—the order of love! But sin did its work, and henceforth all was thrown out of joint, and made difficult and painful; everything would need to be redeemed in Christ to recover its power and splendour. The Adam-Eve relationship must itself be inserted into and renewed in the Christ-Church relationship; and here are St. Paul's formulas: *Let women be subject to their husbands, as to the Lord . . . as the Church is subject to Christ;* and: *Husbands, love your wives as Christ also loved the Church and delivered himself up for it* (Eph. V, 22–25).

These formulas touch the sensitive point in a love that is fallen and redeemed. For the woman, who has to love and obey at the same time, the difficulty lies not so much in the first as in the second. There was doubtless a special need to recall this due submission to the woman of ancient times, for

Christianity had freed her from her social inferiority—*in Christ
there is neither male nor female* (Gal. III, 28)— and she
might easily find a pretext there for emancipating herself from
her duties. But such submission is also a permanent difficulty.
Every woman has a touch about her of this Eve who ought to
obey but in fact, *being seduced was in the transgression* (I Tim.
II, 14–15). This unsubmissiveness, that is to say a certain
egoistic independence—half-concealed, caressing, but none the
less obstinate, stubborn and dangerous—is the subtle temptation of the weaker and less heavily carnal vessel, and quite
capable of destroying the purity of her love. And St. Paul
wants to forewarn her against her formidable power as much
as against her weakness; for the woman is loved and knows
it, and is tempted to presume on this love to get herself
pampered, served, and adored even to the point of betrayal of
God. She has become a temptation to the man and he is weak
in her presence. Well then, let her be subject to her husband as
the Church is subject to Christ, in purity, in faith, and in
honour; and, for her, let submission be the abandonment
which is so quietly magnanimous a form of love, and the holy
reverence—*subject to her husband as to the Lord* (Eph. V,
22)—which is a form of faith and adoration towards the
Christ present in the heart of her love.[213]

For the man, on the other hand, for the head, the chief difficulty is to learn to command as one who serves: that is to say at
once to conquer his weakness in the face of too carnal a love, a
weakness readily leading to abdication of his task of ruling and
"saving"; and to overcome the egoism, the "hardness of
heart" as the Gospel calls it (Matt. XIX, 8), which tempts him
to use the woman for the satisfaction of his appetite either for
pleasure or for domination. Well then, let the husband love
his wife *as Christ also loved the Church* (Eph. V, 25), with a

love that keeps the instincts in check and knows when to set
them aside, a love that is generous and pledged till death, a
delicate, respectful and tender love which *nourishes and
cherishes* (Eph. V, 29) like the breasts of a mother. To such a
love, since it is a will to service and to sanctity, it is possible
to be *subject in all things* (*Ibid.* 24). But so great a mystery is
not to be understood or lived save by one who has entered
into personal, even heroic bonds, with Christ and with the
Church (*Ibid.* 32).

A last step has to be taken. For *the head of every man is
Christ: and the head of the woman is the man: and the head
of Christ is God* (I Cor. XI, 3). There, in a phrase, is traced
the unique movement which ought to lift everything from
carnal depths to God. Man and woman are to enter into union
in virtue at once of their spiritual liberty as equal persons, and
of their functional differences as head and body. When this
organic relation is established God's purpose is achieved, the
community is knit up by the mutual completion of the spouses,
because in the substantial equality of one same love the woman
submits to the man as to her head, and the man gives himself
to the woman as to his own body. But this unity is at once
taken up into another, for it cannot either come to birth or
grow unless founded on Christ, animated by Christ, and directed to Christ. He is the Head in the plenary sense of the
term, since it is He who saves the persons and gives them to
themselves, who establishes the conjugal community and integrates it into the unity of His Body. Here again, He assures
the solidity and intimacy of the union only by drawing it into
a movement which perfects it by surpassing it. But Christ
Himself is the Head in virtue of being *the Mediator,* of receiving from God, in His humanity, all that He bestows on His
brothers; and this Man, who is our Head, is altogether pos-

sessed by God as by the unique Principle of His being and of
all His redemptive riches; and He is wholly given to God as
to the sole beatifying End of His life and His action. In this
absolute sense God is the Head of Christ. And so, in Christ,
the conjugal community is drawn into God Himself, in whom
it finds its mysterious cohesion, its invisible momentum, and
its unspeakable consummation. Now perhaps we can begin
to divine the dimensions of the "great mystery," as St. Paul
calls marriage, and see by how much it surpasses our human
calculations. For the love of man and woman is really consecrated and divinised by being taken up into Christ; and if
the woman is ordered to the man, she is so as an equal ordered
to one who, for her, is not a term but a starting-point, who
embraces her to carry her higher, to give her, along with
himself, to Christ; that so united to the Head they may find
each other in their Principle: the Eternal Love who created
each for the other, purified each as the other, and gave them
each to the other that they might be sanctified by each other.

For they are to grow greater and to give themselves to
Christ by rooting up all that remains to them of concupiscence.
There is nothing authentically human they will have to renounce for that. The grace of Christ is human and brotherly,
and the Christian knows of no essential opposition between
the man and the child of God, between the love that springs
from the depths of nature and that which descends from the
God of Benediction, between Eros and Agape. Eros is wounded
and soiled by man's sin. Christ comes to bring it healing, to
purify and sanctify it by Agape. By this divine contact He re-
generates it from within; He makes it a new love—a love that
has recovered in principle its dissociated unity, since grace envelops it and blesses in it instinct and affectivity and liberty,
and helps the spirit to hierachise, consolidate, and spiritualize

all three powers. But we know that if the spirit is fully redeemed, the flesh as yet is redeemed only in hope. Because the
healing is not total, the flesh escapes the spirit in the very heart
of love: the children of Christians are not born Christians.
Because it is not instantaneous the effort at generosity has to
be daily renewed, and there is always a *tribulatio carnis,* a
trial of the flesh inherent in nuptial love. Trials of endurance
and fidelity, of purity and fruitfulness, of mutual understanding and forgiveness; trials of souls so slow to sustain each other,
so dull and awkward; trials that come with children, and want
of bread, the day's burden and thought for the morrow—that
is why the grace of matrimony is also a grace of sacrifice. It
sprang from the foot of the Cross. It was there that man and
woman found once more their power to love and the law of
their love; and there, in the shadow of the Cross, blood-
stained but reconciling, serene, overflowing with triumphant
charity, their love must live and grow. Thus, under this aspect
too, the mystery of Christ and the Church is prolonged in
nuptial love. For Christ and the Church together are built up
in the spouses, in their community, in their love; and the
Passion continues in them no less than the Resurrection. The
true remedy, the true strength, the true joy are to be found
here as always, in attachment to Christ; it is from above that
love is redeemed, and it has to be protected and made fruitful
in a perpetual *sursum corda.* Tempted, threatened and trembling as it is in its carnal elements, Christian love will find its
strength, its purity and its youth in the joyous embrace of
Christ.

All this the Christian accomplishes by a magnificent act of
faith, a scandal and folly no doubt for the animal man, but for
the Christian the power of God in his life. In pledged fidelity,
in resolute chastity, in consecrated fruitfulness, he confronts

time and the flesh and existence itself, and envelops them all
in the power of Christ and in the promises of God. Thus he
relies on no strength of his own, but only on the gift that he
daily receives of a generous and truly divine love—a life-giving
love, stronger than the flesh, more durable than time. And so
his purest dream is linked up once more with its deepest
sources; his free action coincides with the tendency of this
natural love whereby God calls him and by which humanity
is fulfilled; by way of this faith in Christ he assures and realizes
an essential aspect of his vocation to love. We must not be
afraid to say it: without this deliberate and enthusiastic act
of faith, Christian love is a dream and an impossibility; by
this act of faith alone can it take on consistency and reality.
And the reason is the same in both cases: Christian love is
the presence of the new world, of the Kingdom of God, of the
mystery of Christ and the Church, in the very heart of this
magnificent and miserable human love. We speak of the solemn
engagements that are entered into in Christian marriage, but
all of them rest on a prior engagement, fundamental and absolute, by which the person is pledged to God in faith. How
should the priest not tremble when he blesses the pair whose
faith he knows to be vacillating, or sleeping, or absent; when
he sees them standing before him in love, forgetful of its source,
its greatness, its exigencies, to build on sands the house which
winds and waves will soon demolish? But how can he fail to
turn in gratitude to God when, thanks to the love of the
Father, the blood of Christ, and the fire of the Holy Spirit,
they come before him in faith unfeigned, and hope in things
invisible? For them, at least, the future is safe, for they know
that the true love comes from God, that its bonds are knit by
God, that in God it is nourished and for God it bears its fruit.
They in their turn can say, closing up love's circle, what Pierre

Dupouey wrote one day to Mireille: "Apart from duty and things divine, I have need of none but you; or rather I need you because you too are part of the divine things of my life, because it was the good God who brought you into it, and because you, under my roof, are His living and effectual benediction."

CHAPTER TEN

CHARITY

"MAN IS THE PERFECTION of the universe; the spirit is the perfection of man; love, that of the spirit; and charity, that of love. Wherefore the love of God is the end, the perfection, and the excellence of the universe." [214] We may be forgiven perhaps for citing these well-known words once more at the outset of a chapter on charity. They suggest the difficulty of the task, and may help to excuse the inadequacy of the pages that follow. For charity is the mystery that *surpasseth all knowledge* (Eph. III, 19); "it is not a thing that can be taught from without"; [215] it is purely divine, and "he who would speak of the charity of God, takes it upon him to speak of God Himself —a thing that is full of pitfalls for one who fails to give it all his attention." [216] Not underestimating the task therefore, let us set out to catch a glimpse of the mystery of charity by disengaging some of its essential traits as they are revealed to us in the word of the God who is Charity Itself.

I

The first mark of the love that comes to us from on high is this—it is an absolute and magnificent *gift*. Fallen man cannot love God supernaturally. He is an exile from that paradise. He no longer has the divine substance and strength that would enable him to know God as He knows Himself, and to love God as He loves Himself. Because he has ceased to be a child of God in the strict sense of the term, he is no longer in touch with God by the essential activity of the child, which is filial love. Because intimacy with God is God's prerogative, he cannot now, of his own power, recapture the mystery of divine love, the marvellous marriage-portion that the race has lost. Because he is still called to this supernatural communion, he suffers here the deepest of all his wounds. In short, because he does not love, he is as one dead in the sight of God; and that is the innermost quick of all our human miseries.

Let us go further. Fallen man, with the powers that remain to him, cannot any longer love God above all things. He retains the natural inclination, but has lost the efficacious power to love God freely more than all things. He can imagine the act, dream of it, desire it, and please himself by toying with these ineffectual shadows of it; but he cannot produce it in deed and in truth. Now this act is the very perfection of the human being. Suppose a man who should really love God with his whole self, even were this by his own sole powers. Then that man would be wholly given to God, rectified and unified in principle, able to fulfil his human vocation. He would not be truly a son of God but, among other things, he would have restored, pacified and healed himself; he would no longer be *wounded* but simply *unfulfilled*. But is this a possibility? The Christian will find it difficult to admit it. Fallen man remains wounded in so far as Christ has not yet touched him, and Christian grace always comes to heal as well as to elevate. Without it, therefore, the spontaneous and natural movement to God is deprived of its outlet; it cannot succeed, it falls back powerless on itself, it ends by absorption in the human; and the love

of self—which springs from the same root as the love of God—
tends to usurp the first place, to mask the higher love and rule
it on its own account. Not loving God as he ought, man does
not love himself as he ought, he becomes "egoist" in the strict
sense of the term, and henceforth he stands before God as a
sinner and an *enemy* (Rom. V, 8, 10). To love God now,
stripped as he is of his supernatural resources and wounded
in his natural powers, he will need to be created anew. There
precisely is the marvel of divine charity: God loves us first in
Jesus Christ, and enables us to love Him in return in Jesus
Christ; so that charity is God's gift calling forth man's. This
statement can be considered either on the eternal plane or the
historical. Let us begin with the latter.

*In this is charity: not as though we had loved God, but be-
cause he hath first loved us, and sent his Son to be a propitiation for our sins* (I John IV, 10). *But God commendeth his
charity towards us; because when as yet we were sinners according to the time, Christ died for us* (Rom. V, 8–9). The
love of God manifested in His gift of Christ to mankind—that
is the central event of history and the principle of the new
life. If we are to characterize it by its aim we must say that
this love is an act of *salvation* which transforms our human condition, bestows supernatural existence on man, and re-creates
him in justice and holiness. Because this love has no other
raison d'être than its own joyous outpouring and plenitude, we
must take it as an absolute beginning behind which we cannot
go; it is the mystery that illuminates and vivifies everything
else. Because it stoops to a fallen being who is nought but
misery and sin, that is to say offence, refusal and impotence,
this love is, in the proper sense, a *mercy,* and this is indicated
in the Gospel when it speaks of the Father as Merciful. Because it suppresses misery and sin and makes the fallen creature

alive from the dead (Rom. VI, 13), this love is the Omnipotence that creates and divinises: the love of God, from its earliest dawning in the soul, is a love that transforms.

Nevertheless the marvel is that this saving act should be, in itself, an *act of gift*. God does not give this or that; He gives Himself. To give, for the Father, is to give His Son, in whom His joy is exhausted, and by whom is so overwhelmingly revealed His love for men. As for the Son, He gives Himself even to death, like a poor human being who bears witness; and, having passed through death, like a God who lays down His life to take it up again and diffuse it sovereignly through the world. He communicates it by giving this other self of His, the Holy Spirit, who comes to seal the union and complete the work because He is the mysterious completion of the Trinity Itself. Thus all the fullness of joy and power and life comprised in God's love is hid in Christ, who is at once the fruit, the sign, and the reality of love. The God who is Charity concentrates this charity in Christ, and through Christ He holds embraced the entire human race (II Cor. V, 14). Moreover, what is in question here is by no means an envelopment only but a penetration: the love of God is poured forth in our hearts by the Spirit; it flows unceasingly from God's heart into ours; and this divine act is at once a communication and a drawing upward. A communication, because in Christ God stoops to us, enters the soul, transforms the heart and reconciles us to Himself; and thus *the fullness of which we have all received* overruns the soul like a flood, and where sin abounded grace abounds the more. But God gives Himself thus only to bring us back to Himself, to draw from the soul another gift to answer His, to awaken a love that freely goes to meet His own. In this sense, God draws us to Himself, and since He was lifted up—on the Cross and into glory—the Son *draws all men to Himself.* More than any other divine favour, love—in which all others are resumed and concentrated—verifies this law of the divine action, which posits creatures in being only to bring them back to itself: by the gift of charity God stirs up a filial love in the heart of His child and thereby brings about *the fellowship of man with the Father and with His Son, Jesus Christ* (I John, 1, 3).

But this love governs human history only because its roots are planted in eternity. Before the creation of the world, before the beginning of time, God enveloped us in His love. This means, in the first place, that He destines us to Life by an act of creative knowledge—merciful, because it awakes nothingness to existence; beatifying, because it would communicate the divine beatitude; efficacious because it posits man in being at the moment fixed in the eternal counsels. And moreover this love is a *choice,* there is nothing merely general or abstract about it; it is both universal because it embraces mankind as a whole, and particular because it looks to each one of the persons. It chooses each in the act of fixing his proper differences; it predestines each to be a unique image of the *Son of his love,* and to play a unique part among his brothers. Each is therefore elected according to all his proper "dimensions," individual, communal or divine; and by that very fact the love of God, the love of self, and the love of the neighbour are all implicated in this choice, and written into the radical dynamism of the being. This love is lastly a *vocation;* it is love in the last resort that calls us to being, to life and to charity, and this essential and active exigence within us is precisely our vocation: we come from love and our vocation is to love. Knowledge, election, vocation—three acts all integrated into the unique mystery of love. For to be loved is to be known, chosen, and called in view of a divine filiation and communion. And conversely, when grace has awakened love in a man's heart, then *he who loves God, the same is known by him* (I Cor. VIII, 3) ; and *those who love God are those that according to his purpose are called to be saints* (Rom. VIII, 28) ; and finally, since this knowledge and this call in the bosom of love engender to life, *he who loves is born of God* (I John IV, 7). This love is therefore wonderfully personal, and its proper character is to raise up persons who can enter into communion through Christ with the Three ever-blessed Persons. From every standpoint we ought to regard love as something that comes from on high: love is *of God* (I John IV, 7) because *God is Love.*

If this love is a gift—*the unspeakable gift of God* (II Cor. IX, 15)—it should call the deepest passivity of the human will into play. Man can neither create it nor make it spring up in his own soul, he can only open himself and receive it. That is a metaphysical necessity, since love always presupposes at its source the transforming action of the being loved; it is also a necessity of the concrete case, since here we have to do with a love that introduces us to the intimacy of God, and wholly surpasses the powers of nature. If then we are thus to love, God Himself must love us first, make good in man the power of loving, bestow the active capacity and efficacious power to love Him in return. Thus, by a purely gratuitous grace, He makes Himself the Act of this potency, and makes it divine by participation. And so there is a radical and substantial *pati divina*—a being acted upon by God—at the source of all supernatural love: [217] in other words, to love is first of all *to be* loved, *to be* known, chosen and called, *to be* created anew by God. A transforming donation and presence, in themselves not apprehensible, unconscious, unknown, but lying at the source of this other *pati divina,* that of the mystics, in which the soul becomes aware of the divine action within it. But even this gift has to be accepted. For God's own sovereignly free love is addressed to a full liberty: God who knocks will enter only if we open to Him, God who chooses would be chosen, God who offers Himself would have us give ourselves, God who transforms, demands—and produces—man's consent to his own transformation. And thus supernatural love, more than any other, is a passivity and a liberty equally radical; always forestalled, always called, always stirred up, it is always a love that responds.

Consequently, it knits up the holy fellowship of man with God. These two, who love each other, become interior each to the other by the very energy of their love. God is in man in virtue of His creative and redemptive love; man is in God in virtue of his resolute, humble and adoring love, which is but a gift in return. This immanence is, of itself, so deep, so durable, so "constitutive" for man; it is—in man—such an envelopment of time by eternity, such an assumption of the fleeting life by the life eternal, that by love *God abides in man and man in God* (I John IV, 13). Because it consolidates, enriches, and truly realizes the human being, this immanence is a source of life; it blossoms in an efficacious and generous outpouring; it fructifies in "grapes of righteousness": *He that abideth in me and I in him the same beareth much fruit* (John XV, 5). And these fruits are essentially the activities of faith and of love, along with all that these imply; they are the very life of the child of God, overflowing with divine vigour, perfumed as the ripening fields and rich with the harvests of eternity.

The admirable thing is moreover that this communion of God and man is normally in continual process of growth. Man is free in his love; and in the measure in which he loves with

the love that God gives, in that measure also God loves
him the more. For man very truly gives himself to his God; and
God, looking at this activity that He Himself has called forth,
sees not so much what He Himself contributes as what man
does with it in return: He looks at the free generosity, He welcomes its joyous outpouring, He rewards it as if it were a true
beginning on man's part; He embraces the proffered love in
order to make it purer, more solid, more fruitful. And thus begins the infinite circling of these two loves, calling and answering each other, and every answer bringing a new call, and
every joy a new desire. *And he that loveth me shall be loved*
(in return) *by my Father: and I will love him and will manifest myself to him.* . . . . *If anyone love me, he will keep my word
and my Father will love him* (in return) *and we will come
to him, and will make our abode with him* (John XIV, 21, 23).
And so it always continues until the human being shall have
reached the fullness of his growth in love, and shall have become, according to his measure, a full image of Him who is the
Only Beloved; thus definitively fulfilling his eternal election
and predestination in this fellowship with God which is at
once a unity and a union. Because one sole and same life
fructifies in one sole love circulating from God to man, and
from man to God, these two are One; because they remain
for ever distinct as creature and Creator, as Father and child,
these two are united. This is the marvel of divine charity,
which is the image of the Trinitarian Beatitude, that it re-
duplicates unity by Union, that it makes united those that it
makes one, that it consummates the human person by so
making of him a voluntary Relation to God that he becomes
thereby more fully subsistent than ever. By way of love man
definitively stabilizes his own being and enters into the eternal
world. Fixed in God and possessed by God, he is snatched

away from time,[218] and from *this world which passeth away
with the lusts thereof.* That part of his soul which naturally
breathes an air beyond time is supernaturally plunged in
eternal life. And henceforth, even in the midst of this world
which ceaselessly flows away and crumbles and disintegrates,
the man who is born into a life that does not pass, *abideth for
ever* (I John II, 17).

In this mysterious immanence however God and man always
keep the relation and distance due to their respective natures.
Man is as dust and ashes before his God; however much he
abounds he is always a poverty-stricken thing hanging on the
divine mercy, and however much he may be purified he is still
the sinner face to face with Holiness. And that is why his love
is always penetrated with a great wave of adoration that comes
from the depths of his being, and is clothed in a pure and holy
fear before the Majesty of Him who loves him, before the
inaccessibility of Him who is nevertheless his Father, before
the formidable transcendence of Him who dwells within his
heart—*O best-beloved Lord and Master, what am I compared
with thee?* [219] But then at the same time he cannot but be uplifted in thankfulness for the "unspeakable gift" of the mighty
God, for the charity which passes the thought, desire and
capacity of the created spirit, for the love that was before all
ages, that embraces the universe, and sovereignly chooses its
loved ones—which has no dimensions save those that are infinite and divine—and he cannot but overflow with praise and
benediction: *Blessed be the God and Father of our Lord Jesus
Christ who has blessed us with spiritual blessings in heavenly
places, in Christ* (Eph. I, 3). Finally therefore this love is more
generous, more active, and more fully embodied than any
other; it tends of its own abounding energy to pour itself out
in manifold gifts and fruitfulness which are altogether inex-

haustible, triumphant and divine. Eager as fire, joyous as living water—*Fons vivus, Ignis, Caritas*—capable of facing sorrow, sacrifice and death itself, since all is overcome in advance and already consumed in the charity of Christ.

Love is therefore absolute generosity; but in giving itself thus it simply prolongs the gift by which it is constituted—it gives what it receives. It can flourish and bloom because it is welcomed, it can act because it is activated, and all the infinitude of its power comes from the adoring passivity in which it lies open to God. *Love is of God* (I John IV, 7), and *by him we live* (*Ibid.* 9), and only in ever closer attachment to God, in ever more direct return on its Source, can love reach its consummation and put forth all its vitalising energy to quicken the new and eternal world from on High in the midst of the world of sin. Whenever a little Christian child says to God: "My God, I love thee with all my heart," then the mystery of divine charity is renewed among men, and the Kingdom of Love expands in the midst of the Kingdom of Shadows, because a soul has renewed its embrace, its union, and its unity with the God of Benediction who would build up in us and by us here below the Kingdom of Heaven, the Kingdom of the Son of God, the Kingdom of Love.

II

But love, from God's side, is not only a gift, it is a *commandment*. An unheard-of demand without doubt, but at bottom inevitable, and big with consequences.

The love of God is commanded because God is the source and end of the human creature, the Saviour of the creature wounded and the Beatitude of the creature redeemed. Man's dependence is therefore total and absolute. It appears in the necessary and indestructible tendency of the created being which we know as the natural love of God, and in the gratuitously given tendency of the supernaturalized being which we know as charity; and these two tendencies are signs, the first of the creative Sovereignty, and the second of the redemptive Omnipotence. Here God appears as *Master and Lord,* as He who has all rights because He gives being itself, as He whom we cannot love without total submission. The gift, essential to love, takes on therefore the form of obedience and service: to give oneself to Him who is Master and Lord is to give Him one's liberty by the interior act of obedience, and all one's living powers by actions directed to His service. That is a necessary exigence of love, and one in which some of its essential traits will appear.

Such a love is, and more than ever, an act of the spirit. The world of emotion and feeling and sentiment is here entirely left behind. Only the fine point of the spiritual being is engaged directly, but this, when it submits itself to God, has to draw after it all the rest in a great outpouring of liberty, abandonment and energy. *Not everyone that saith to me, Lord, Lord, shall enter into the kingdom of heaven, but he that doth the will of my Father who is in heaven* (Matt. VII, 21). Thus is clearly marked, and within the very bosom of love, the essential opposition between Christianity and all religions centered on the sensibility, on the "pathetic," on a *pati divina* experienced, savoured, at need provoked, and always more and more submerging the spirit beneath the waves of the sensibility. Christian love, on the contrary, is a spiritual generosity; it is rooted in faith, which is an energy purely born of God, and not *of blood, nor of the will of the flesh, nor of the will of man* (John I, 13); it lives and grows on this mysterious plane, it apprehends God through signs that have to be transcended, it seeks

Him as one absent and *loves Him without seeing* (I Peter I, 8).
It is a love that grows purer and deeper in a triple and unique
effort: the effort to overcome the exigence, the ascendency,
the resistance of an emancipated and insatiable sensibility; the
effort to commune by faith with the God who is both given
and inaccessible, who is Life because He is spirit; and the
effort to cleave to the will of the Father in order to give it out-
ward expression, and realize it by thought and will and action.

Adoration therefore becomes more than ever essential to
this love. None can enter into union here without total submission, without conforming his will to the divine will, without
acknowledging himself a servant and conducting himself as
such. This consideration adds further force to the point already noted: it is not simply God our Father whom we love,
but God our Master who commands us to love Him. All
love is a "submission" to the being loved in the measure in
which it is a passivity accepted,[220] in the measure in which it
follows the call of the Beloved. But here the passivity is that
of a creature laid bare and touched in the very foundations of
his being by the Creator Himself; and the call is that of a God
who gives the very acts of existing and willing and loving to
the will itself. Hence the submission has to be absolute, and
to envelop a renunciation of self, a consent to God, an abandonment to His mastery, and a joy in our trembling nothingness in the face of Being, which are the authentic notes of
adoration. The gift that stops short of that is not a total gift;
and this should help us to understand that love *par excellence,*
the love that fully realizes its definition, is not the love of equals,
not the love of man and woman, but the love which so marvel-
lously unites the creature and the Creator.[221]

To love, in effect, is to refer oneself to another as to one's
end; to love God is to refer oneself to Him as to the Last End;

and it is therefore to submit oneself to Him without reserve, and to give oneself living into His hands. That is the profoundly religious meaning of this *fruition* which characterizes love according to St. Augustine. "To enjoy God" is in no wise, in his eyes, to feel God and to take delight in the feeling, it is rather *to cleave to God for His own sake,*[222] and to refer to Him all our love of self and love of others by bowing before the infinite majesty of Him we love, by submitting to all the demands of the absolute Master—*Totum exigit te qui fecit te*—by transcending self, forgetting self, and submitting self along with all its loves to the immutable and beatifying Good. This attitude of obedience, adhesion and joyful submission is altogether essential to love, and St. Thomas merely echoes St. Augustine when he writes that: "Charity, by its very nature, consists in man's loving God above all things, and subjecting himself to Him entirely by referring all that is his to God. It is therefore essential to charity that man should so love God as to wish to submit to him in all things, and always to follow the rule of His commandments." [223] So essential is this attitude that it defines the whole order of the relations between man and God, that it still subsists in Paradise, and that the beatitude of the Saints consists "in their perfect submission to God." [224] Thus, this submission is interior to love, and indeed, in a sense, they coincide, since both utter the same "yes" to the creative and redemptive will. There we have the *obsequium divini amoris.*[225]

Lastly, this love is of necessity a service. We are called to an exacting and magnificent task: *to become holy and unspotted in his sight in charity* (Eph. I, 4), to become thus sons in Jesus Christ, to help others to become sons likewise on their own account as members of His Body the Church. Our love is therefore to bear fruit in keeping the Commandments; and by "commandments" is not here meant a multiplicity of observances, but more especially the "love and faith" whence all the rest should flow:[226] if we are truly to love Christ, we shall have—in an act of faith quickened by charity—to embrace the Commandments interiorly and make them bring forth fruit in generous actions: *He that hath my commandments and keepeth them, he it is that loveth me* (John XIV, 21). All legalism is here ruled out; the accent falls on the interior adhesion, the voluntary engagement, the obedience of a loving faith, which are to animate all the powers of the soul and produce a humble and literal fidelity. If on the other hand we took this love to be something affective beside which acts would hardly seem to count, Our Lord's insistence on the practical observance of the commandments would soon show us our error and how completely we should have missed the genuine Christian outlook.

Love and obedience are therefore indissolubly bound up with each other, but the mode of connection still calls for attention. We cannot simply reduce love to obedience and service and so sink the divine and marvellous *agape* in a mere moralism without force, horizon or life, for that would contradict the very essence of the Christian revelation which makes of love the First Reality, creative of the new world because it is none other than God Himself. We must therefore integrate obedience in love by conceiving the former, not as the bare act of a will that yields because it must, but as the generous act of a will that submits itself because it loves. Then love floods over into everything! It blossoms out into obedience and service; it transfigures both; under its touch the very commandments cease to be *heavy* (I John V, 3), and that precisely because it has become a love *in deed and in truth* (I John III, 18).

In throwing itself thus into the work commanded love does not cease to be itself. There, on the contrary, it finds its purity, its depth and its fruitfulness—after the likeness of Him who never wished to do anything but the will of His Father, who made of obedience the offspring of love, of service the fruit and the sign of charity, and who has thus definitively integrated the keeping of the commandments in love: *If you keep my commandments you shall abide in my love; as I also have kept my Father's commandments and do abide in his love* (John XV, 10). The reciprocal immanence of God and man is therefore not simply the fruit of a mutual affection, it is even more the fruit of fidelity and of courage, it is generous obedience that knits the embrace, draws down the presence of God, and enables love to bear its fruits of light and of joy: *He that hath my commandments and keepeth them, he it is that loveth me. And he that loveth me shall be loved of my Father; and I will love him, and will manifest myself to him* (John XIV, 21). Thus once more the circle is closed, obedience deepens the impulse, service multiplies the gift, work for God draws closer the bond of union with God; and it is in possession and communion ever more deep and joyous that the movement of love is fulfilled until it shall spring up in us with a new impulsion to receive a new increase.

III

God's love is lastly Redemption, since it falls on one who is fallen, wounded and sinful. It has had to be said already since the gift is bestowed on an "enemy" and the commandment bears on a rebel liberty. Now we have to insist on it.

Love is God who *gave his Son to be a propitiation for our sins* (I John IV, 10), and *we have known the charity of God because he* (i.e. Christ) *hath laid down his life for us* (I John III, 16). The Father's love is a charity that gives His Son and delivers Him to death, not in the least by abandoning Him to human cruelty, but by filling his soul with such love for His God and for His brothers that of Himself He offers Himself in sacrifice for them. Christ's love is a love that expiates—*He loved us and delivered himself for us*—a love that redeems by unrecognized and costly service, by a fervent obedience but sorrowful even to agony—*non quod ego volo, sed quod Tu*—by cries and tears, by the Passion and the Cross. It is the whole humiliated, tragic, and bloody aspect of adoration, of obedience, of service, that Christ integrates with love, and it is this that makes the redemptive offering a sacrifice in the strict sense of the term. Now this precisely is the love that Christ has merited for us and bestows on us by the Holy Spirit.[227] And hence our love for God will also be sacrifice, and that by the very characters which it stamps upon our gift and our service.

The service of God demands the sacrifice of all that makes for egoism and refusal, whether it be a question of the flesh—*if thy right hand scandalize thee, cut it off* (Matt. V, 30), or of the spirit—*he that loveth father or mother more than me, is not worthy of me* (Matt. X, 37)—or of daily life with all its burdens—*If any man will come after me, let him deny himself, and take up his cross daily, and follow me* (Luke IX, 23). This service also demands that we spend and hazard and wear out our strength and our life for our brothers, as also did Christ: *In this we have known the charity of God, because he hath laid down his life for us; and we ought to lay down our lives for the brethren* (I John III, 16). Because love is desire for unity, the essential thing here is imitation of Christ and communion with His life; now sacrifice effects both, and it is in an intimate conscience of this likeness and this union which purifies and inflames our love, and consequently envelops sacrifice in a joy more profound, more substantial, and more irresistible than all its suffering: *For as the sufferings of Christ abound in us, so also by Christ doth our comfort abound* (II Cor. I, 5). Henceforth we shall understand the song that rises to the lips of Christian heroes, and the joy that they have in communion with Christ—Paul in his tribulations, Ignatius of Antioch on the road to martyrdom, Francis of Assisi in perfect nakedness. . . .

There is another sacrifice and a deeper, not the sacrifice made in the service love asks of us, but the sacrifice of the gift itself which is love. Love is joyous by essence since love is communion, and joy is the fruit of realized communion. This joy is, in itself, both spiritual and sensible, since love gives all and inflames all. If a man were not fallen this joy would be *given* in and with the love, and the words of the Psalm would express love's normal and natural state: *My heart and my flesh have rejoiced in the living God* (Psalm LXXXIII, 3) ; and then the Christian would be able to verify the truth of St. Augustine's words about our first parents: "They were pleasing to God, and God pleased them." [228] But sin entailed a disjunction between spirit and sense, and since the unity is not restored by God it has to be regained by a bitter struggle. The result is that grace and faith and love are purely spiritual, living in the spirit as such, and able indeed to move the spiritual affectivity but not the sensible. For man as he is, so deeply immersed in the senses, these realities have been banished into the mystery of the spirit. The love of God is therefore not, in itself, a thing that can be sensibly felt ; it stirs no chords in the sensibility, and will have to subdue and purify it before it can fill it ; and in this respect it once more shows itself as redemptive and brings the cross with it. It is so much the easier to see why love is the subject of a commandment: since it is not sensible, not a centre of contagious emotion, it will be essentially the act in which the spirit surrenders itself, submits, obeys, even in the absence of any felt attraction or any experienced sweetness. Its stability and power are due precisely to this nudity, this limpidity, this holy preference for God.

Man however is too deeply immersed in the world of feeling for God to leave his love thus always reduced to its bare essence. And that is why, first of all, we have the consolation that God gives to wean the soul from sin and from itself. How indeed could man abandon all things if the sovereign delights—illuminations, calls, yearnings, tendernesses, embraces, foretastes of surpassing joy—did not sometimes enter his miserable heart? But this sensible joy is given only for a time; it does not knit up the unity of spirit and flesh; the sensibility awakes for a moment and under the swift fingers of the Spirit the hidden chords are swept, and then the song falls back, the vibrations are damped, sleep overtakes the mysterious musician, and the spirit finds itself alone once more as emerging from a dream, in the face of a sensibility unpurified, dead, unresponsive or hostile to its calls: no longer in the fresh oasis but the desert. Then the struggle begins again, the toil is renewed until the day comes when now subdued, purified, and transfigured by the fire of love the sensibility shall respond to the call from the heights and fill up the joy of the spirit with her own gladness. Then "that soul is perfected whose sensitive part is wholly turned towards God," and "happy is he who loves God as the amorous swain his best-beloved." [229]

Up to these moments of beatitude, and through all these passing consolations, both of which depend wholly on God and have no other law than that of a charity that surpasses us at all points, imperfect man has to live in pure faith and a love above all feeling, a love which is preference, obedience and fidelity. That is why, when commenting on St. Paul's phrase, *I desire to be dissolved and to be with Christ,* St. Thomas explains that man naturally desires union with God without being separated from his body; but, since this is impossible, a struggle ensues between the two desires, and "the desire of charity triumphs over the desire of nature in a fashion so much the more sensible *(sensibilius)* as the charity is the more perfect; while amongst those whose love is yet imperfect, if the desire of charity should achieve its triumph the victory is rendered insensible on account of the resistance of the natural desire." And therefore "to say with the Apostle in so direct, assured and bold a manner: 'I desire to be dissolved and be with Christ,' is perfect charity; but to prefer, in no matter what way, even insensibly *(qualitercumque, licet insensibiliter),* the fruition of God to union with the body, this is necessary charity." [230] And this insensibility is, for the "wayfarer far from the Lord," one of the inevitable renunciations of love.

There remains however a last sacrifice, and the most terrible of all. If the sensibility has to be purified, *the spirit* in its turn must be stripped bare to be fully divinised. The outpouring of love is normally accompanied by admirable spiritual sentiments—joy and peace in the Holy Spirit—which flow from it and nourish it in their turn. On this summit where the theological virtues reign, lifted high above the senses, clear of all their turbulence, the spirit breathes a divine air. There it lives in cloudless faith, in confident hope, in fervent charity which go together to make up the incomparable force of love; and when our hearts are uplifted by all this how easy, how generous becomes our gift! But too many clinging impurities are still present, a "natural sediment" [231] still too thick, and these too will have to pass to the crucible in obscurity, anxiety and dryness. Hours without light, without warmth, without support—

all true Christians know them and find them hard. Love is banished so far into the mystery of the spirit that its presence is neither felt nor known. It is pure obedience, pure fidelity, and pure preference for God; so simple, so despoiled, that it seems to have disappeared, and the Christian finds himself alone and confronted—as with some Alpine wall of inexorable rock—with all the array of the commandments of God. And yet in virtue of its very nudity this love attains a force and a limpidity hitherto unknown.

This sacrifice however is only a beginning. For truly great souls, at any rate, there comes an hour when they have to love God in the darkness of night, in anguish and in desolation. Because they remain as yet unpurified, imperfect, miserable, divine charity would burn away their last impurities and, as says St. John of the Cross, its flame for them is not friendly but hostile, not clear but obscure, not gentle but tormenting, not savorous but dry; not in the least comforting and pacifying but devouring and killing.[232] A terrible trial by which the soul is forged anew in the fires of God, united with the agony of Christ, conformed to His crucified love, made holy in God's sight and terrible to the devils, capable of making a sacrifice of all things for the Lord: "Nothing, nothing, nothing, leave skin and all for Christ." [233] Then love reaches its plenitude, it emerges from Passion into Resurrection, it becomes an extraordinary power for Redemption, and of such souls it is written: "A little of this pure love is of more use to the Church than all other works put together." [234]

IV

"Of more use to the Church": for in Christianity the love of God of necessity means love of the neighbour. That is a

point of obedience to start with. The second commandment,
like to the first, is this:*thou shalt love thy neighbour as thyself*.
A new commandment and proper to Christ, for He is its model,
its efficacious principle, and its last reason. A commandment
in which the law finds its fulfilment, and one which is accordingly emphasized in the New Testament on all occasions, in
all its forms, and in all its force. Love of the neighbour is therefore a matter of obedience, a strict and essential obligation;
and here again we have something to be integrated into our
love: *If any man say: I love God, and hateth his brother, he
is a liar* (I John IV, 20).

But this commandment is rooted in God's attitude towards
us, and obedience should therefore be rooted in desire for conformity. Now the Father is by definition the merciful God. He
is always stooping to fill us with His benedictions; He sends
His rain on the just and the unjust; He bestows life, health,
talents; He grants forgiveness, grants reward, gives "the good
spirit," gives His Son in whom all the gifts of grace and nature
are resumed, and through whom come all good things. The
law of love is here to imitate the Father, to conform ourselves
inwardly to His infinite mercy, to give of what we have and
of what we are to our brothers, to love both the good and the
bad, ingrates and enemies, and thus to be merciful *as our
Father also is merciful* (Luke VI, 36). Still more strictly
should our love be conformed to Christ, the perfect Image of
the Infinite Love, the first-born Brother in whose likeness we
have been modelled in advance. Now *He loved us and delivered Himself for us,* and has left us this law: love therefore
each other *as I have loved you;* and thereafter one who loves
discovers some reflection of the love of Christ in every human
countenance. When he stoops to one of his brothers, were he
the lowest of outcasts, he sees him as one *for whom Christ*

died (Rom. XIV, 15) ; and he must expend his life for others if he would know conformity with Christ, and would love Him in deed and in truth.

But love is not content with conformity in act and effort: it would have participation of life, it would have the communion that makes of man *one spirit* with God; and it is precisely the love of the neighbour that brings us into intimacy with God. From all eternity God carried all men in the bosom of His love, He saw them in Christ, willed and blessed them in Christ. The filial love that springs in the heart of Christ gives Him so great joy that He would fain diffuse it among all peoples and multiply even to infinity the voices that shall cry out, Abba, Father! If He continues to stoop to the sinful and miserable race it is to transform them in Christ into a divine race, and *to bring many children into glory* (Heb. II, 10). Since men are thus gathered up in the embrace of one sole love, of one sole call, of one sole Saviour, to love God *as He is* is to love Him as a Father, and so to love all those whom He chooses, calls, and redeems; and, on the other hand, to love men *as they are* is to love their deepest and most personal reality, that is to say their divine vocation, and through that vocation the eternal will and the eternal love that are God Himself. Henceforth, to spend oneself for one's brothers is to rejoin and serve one's God; and to hide oneself in God is to discover and embrace one's brothers more than ever before.[235] This, moreover, is still further strengthened in Christ in whom both God and humanity are wholly embraced. Christ is at once the Word, inseparable from the Father, and the Son, in whom dwells the fullness of the Godhead; and the Head of redeemed humanity, carried in His mind, sustained by His love, mysteriously identified with Himself. And so to love a man as a Christian should is not simply to love a divine vocation, it is to love a member of Christ and therefore Christ in person, and God Himself in Christ. And not only the just, the generous and the holy, but also the hungry, the poor, the sick and the prisoner, all are so many facets of Christ, and all that is done to the least of these is done unto Christ Himself (Matt. XXV, 35–45). Because there is a mystical identity between Christ and His members, because the faith affirms this identity, because charity springs from the heart of faith and sees only with the eyes of faith, there is but one love which never separates men from Him in whom they are called, nor Christ from those He bears within Himself; a sole love which loves together that which God has joined together for ever: the total Christ, the Head and members in one.

If the love of God is bound up with the love of His sons and the love of Christ with the love of His members, then our charity towards our brothers will have all the same characteristics as our charity towards God. It will be a gift whereby man offers himself to those whom God has willed to be His sons, it will be service done to these needy, weak and miserable human beings, it will be sacrifice, it will be life worn out in daily toil or relinquished at a single blow, in deprivation, humility, weariness, tears and blood, to the likeness of Christ. That is why the Christian forbears and forgives, binds up wounds, consoles souls, joyfully performs the meanest services—*you ought also to wash one another's feet* (John XIII, 14)—refrains from judging his brothers, renounces the exercise of his natural rights if that would scandalize one of these little ones, renounces —as near as may be—the joy of seeing God, should he still be called upon to serve his fellows: *For whereas I was free as to all, I made myself the servant of all* (I Cor. IX, 19),—like Christ, and for the love of Christ! The whole array of the Saints bears similar witness. From St. Paul, whose words have just been quoted, down to St. Peter Claver who signed the formula of his profession after ten terrible years spent in the service of the negroes: "Peter, slave of the black slaves for always"—down to Father Damien, who wrote during his first months at Molokai: "For me, I make myself a leper among the lepers to gain them all for Christ; and so, when I preach, I make it my custom to speak of 'we lepers' . . ."

The way in which this fraternal charity bears on the love of God is easy to see. For the Christian, it is the great safeguard against illusion. We can readily deceive ourselves as regards our standing with God, but hardly on our treatment of our neighbours. They are there in flesh and blood, and that obliges us to love them "in the sweat of our brows," to lend our hands to the work, to give our bodies as well as our souls to a service that is quite concrete and definite and ever demanded anew. Wherefore *he that loveth not his brother whom he seeth, how can he love God whom he seeth not?* (I John IV, 20). Moreover, for unbelievers, fraternal charity is the supreme sign of the presence of God among Christians. So deeply rooted in mankind are the forces of concupiscence and egoism and pride, that such as are seen to overcome them, to consider others, to give and forgive and do service, to live in communion stronger than all distances, all discords—such as these are evident signs that a new world is born, the world of Light, of Truth, of Life, the world of the God who is Love, in the midst of men. Nor does this charity only testify to the presence of the new world, it literally *constructs* it. It is the charity of God who created all things, and gave His Christ, and redeemed mankind; it is the charity of men whose task it is, in Christ and in the Spirit, to build up the Church, to set up the Temple, and to fill up the Body of the Lord. Time is given us for nothing else but this: that thanks to charity redeemed humanity may reach its full stature in Christ. The task is hard. To the end of his days the mutable human creature is the prey of sin, of misery and of death. Even redeemed he is still vulnerable, he falls, he betrays his vocation. He must always be looking anxiously into himself, washing off his stains, binding up his wounds, comforting his own miserable heart. Charity accomplishes all.[236] Charity is the redeeming power, incessantly at work to heal, redress and save; it is the *power from above*, that envelops and lifts up this ravaged humanity and transforms it; it is the *eternal power*, that nothing can destroy because it is purely divine, and therefore surpasses time, possesses the future, and already brings it into this present world *whose fashion passeth away* (I Cor. VII, 31); whereas itself, and only itself, *never falleth away* (I Cor. XIII, 8).

V

A last problem remains, embroiled by multitudinous solutions, exasperated by endless dispute, and one which only a theologian, an historian, and a psychologist rolled into one could hope to unravel from top to bottom—the problem namely of *the disinterestedness of charity*.[237] It comes home to us French especially through the Bossuet-Fénelon controversy; and if we made this our starting-point we should probably never emerge from it. We shall not stir up old quarrels. We propose to go higher, and following the Gospel and St. Thomas, we shall endeavour to bring out the relation between the love of desire and the love of gift in charity; the relation, in other words, between the love of self and the love of God.

If we envisage charity as a virtue, as a force that enters and draws the soul, then it is very evident that it tends to God, embraces Him, rejoices in Him.[238] Desire, union, joy—here we

find once more all the magnificent efflorescence of love. But if
we strictly envisage the act itself of loving, then the question
remains: is charity desire of God or simply gift to God?—Does
it love man's beatitude or simply God's "honour"?—Does it
seek to enjoy God, or simply to glorify Him? [239] Here again, it
is in the paradox of love that the sole coherent solution lies,
and the terms we are tempted to disjoin must be affirmed together: charity is at once desire of God and gift to God.

* * *

Charity is desire of God, and it is impossible that it should
not be so. In charity God is loved as the Last End, therefore as
He who shall wholly supply my lack, who is at once *the* Absolute Good and *my* total good. As *the* Good, He is absolute
happiness; as *my* good, He opens this source of happiness to
me. And with every fibre of my being, with flesh and spirit
together, I cannot but desire this beatifying Presence, this
Abiding of God within me, this consummation of love in
closest society with the Father, through the Son, and in the
Holy Spirit. If in such embrace my soul finds its fullest expansion, its definitive density, its radiant plenitude, how should
I not desire God with all my heart and all my strength? And
if moreover I love God thus, is it not because He calls me to
this intimate possession, and because the natural movement of
my love is founded on the explicit will of my Lord? God
loves me with the gratuitous and all-embracing love we have
tried to depict; and because love wills the good of the beloved,
"by this (supernatural) love God simply wishes the eternal
Good, which is Himself, for the creature." [240] He *wishes* it;
and when I *desire* it I simply conform myself to this intention
of His love, and ratify moreover the spontaneous tendency of

my own created being, dependent, needy, and necessarily in quest of its end. Even in this desire there is obedience and consent, together with a liberty that gives itself freely since it accepts the conditions of its existence, of its action, and of its love.

The proper aim of this desire is the possession of God. Because I am a subsistent, solid and inviolable being I would have God for myself; I would have this eternal life which is God possessed as the principle and object of my thought, of my will, of my joy. As realized already here below by living faith, eternal life is *to know the Father, the only true God, and Jesus Christ whom he has sent* (John XVII, 3); but this with a knowledge which is "a total possession of God by the soul, and at the same time a total penetration of the soul by God." [241] The Fourth Gospel insists on this possession which is brought about by faith animated by love: *he that believeth in the Son hath life everlasting* (John III, 36. Cf. III, 15, 16—V, 24—VI, 40, 47). And since this everlasting life is union with Christ, and, through Christ, with the Divine Persons, the Christian possesses the Persons in himself, so as to live by Them and partake of Their happiness. St. John explicitly affirms this consequence: *God hath given us eternal life; and this life is in his Son. He that hath the Son hath life* (I John V, 11–12)—*He that confesseth the Son hath the Father also* (*Ibid.*, 11, 23)—*He that continueth in the doctrine, the same hath both the Father and the Son* (II John 9). God therefore gives Himself, and does so that He may be possessed by man. Because here below this possession is enveloped in faith, the desire of God grows along with love, and continually opens out the soul's capacity for plenary possession of God. When this is attained, and when the charity of the blessed is wholly inflamed, then "possessing Him, they enjoy Him as the last end satiating all their desire" [242]—and satiating it moreover only while making it eternally spring up anew.[243] But even here below the Christian possesses the Divine Persons, that is to say he has the power to enjoy Them freely,[244] to love Them, to contemplate Them, to taste Them, to embrace Them and to fill himself with a joy that embraces the universe and all things created because it embraces God: "Mine are the heavens, and mine the earth, mine are mankind and the just and the sinners; the angels are mine and the Mother of God, and all things are mine; and God Himself is mine and for me, for Christ is mine and wholly for me." [245]

This love of desire which aims at possession is a love of God identical with love of self. For to love God thus is to love oneself in accordance with the highest exigencies of the natural impulsion; it is to love one's own consummation and full participation in God; it is to love oneself as one whom God Himself would make happy in the joy of this possession. Then we perceive that the act by which "man loves himself in God and for God" and thus wills "to enjoy God and His glory," is an act comprehended in charity.[246] We perceive that this "movement of the human spirit towards the fruition of the divine Good is the proper act of charity whereby all the acts of the other virtues are ordered to their end." [247] We perceive finally that this act, when it achieves the vehemence that burns away all impurities, belongs of right to the "perfect who desire to be dissolved and to be with Christ." [248] Nothing but a fundamental misunderstanding could induce us to consider such a love as interested and egoistic. If there is such a thing as an egoistic love it represents a deviation from the natural tendency resulting from sin. But charity is there precisely to restore, purify and divinise the natural tendency. Consequently the act of desire that springs from charity itself cannot be egoistic, it is necessarily as right and true as the impulse whence it proceeds, and which is planted by the creative and redeeming God in the very heart of the spirit. For the rest, a love that would not desire to possess its God is a mere chimaera. For this human love, coming from a created person, is subject to strict metaphysical conditions; it is the love of one who is not his own end, who cannot but tend to his end, and who cannot reach it save in possession and fruition of the Sovereign Good. Such a love, far from being egoistic, is the sign of our condition as creatures and as adopted sons, and is necessarily pure and true.

But it is not the highest of loves. For love is more gift than desire. Now the love of charity does not go to a limited being, an imperfect person, a partial beauty, but to the infinite God, the adorable Being, the beatifying Beauty. It is therefore with absolute fullness, without limit and without reserve, that this love will be gift, service and sacrifice. It will be so much the more so since charity, far from destroying, comes to consummate and fulfil everything. It lays hold therefore of this spring of love which is the will and which leaps up towards God but falls back powerless without grace; it strengthens it inwardly, fills it with Christ, opens it out divinely and makes it bear fruit.[249] Now this movement of the will is a love of God above all things, and divine grace does but dilate the power of gift, purify the movement of abandonment to the Lord, support and strengthen the tendency of the soul to refer itself wholly to God, to submit itself wholly to God, to fasten wholly on this life, beauty, holiness, joy which God possesses in Himself and gives to none but Himself—and far more than on what itself can seize and drink of it, for all the burning thirst of its desire.[250] Love of adoration and of praise, of exultation and of thanksgiving, of obedience and conformity, of consent and abandonment, of abnegation and sacrifice—the very love we have tried to depict in these pages.

Now this love terminates no longer in possession but in communion. Its centre is no longer the human being who possesses, but the God with whom he enters into union. Here love no longer seeks to possess itself of God, but to give itself to God and to be possessed by Him. It enters into God, it lives in Him, abides in Him. It forgets itself in order to plunge itself joyfully into its Source, into its Model, into its End. If love seeks its own good, "God is a greater good than any other, and more the proper good of man than any other, because He is more intimately present to the soul than is the soul to itself." [251] That is why the soul abandons itself to give itself over to God.

Possession of God and communion with God are terms that designate one and the same reality, but looked at from two different angles. In the first case, man draws God to himself, and in the second, he gives himself over to God, and exists only as relation to God; and thus inaugurates his own spiritual unity and his living communion with the Father, through the Son, in the Holy Spirit—so that he gives himself wholly and with no reserve to the trinitarian love, and is thus achieved in being at the very moment when he ceases to seek himself. And this doubtless explains why St. Thomas, when defining this essential act of charity, normally avails himself, not of the vocabulary of possession, but of that of union: "Charity is formally union with the Infinite Good." "Charity realizes the society of the rational soul with God, by a kind of spiritual union." It brings about "this spiritual union by which we are, so to speak, transformed into the end itself." Hope tends to God as to a good yet to be attained, but "charity makes us tend to God by so cleaving to God in love that we no longer live for ourselves but for God." [252] To live for God is charity's last word: to will the good and the honour of God, to spend ourselves for His Kingdom and the glory of His name, to rejoice in His Beauty, His Holiness and His Joy. And not as a stranger but as one redeemed, "become by grace God and son of God," [253] given to God as the Divine Persons are given to Each Other, admitted through Christ to the movement of the Infinite Love, assimilated to the Son who is joyous Return to His Father and purest Ecstasy in Him; and thus altogether given to God, established in God, passed into God—because He is God, because He is Lord, because He is Glory and Beatitude.

* * *

Charity therefore is both love as desire and love as gift, and we have to determine the interrelations—ontological, not psychological—between these two. There can be no question of *suppressing* either. It would contradict the very condition of the creature to eliminate either the radical misery that gives rise to desire, or the substantial greatness which makes possible the gift; and moreover we should be unfaithful to the exigencies of the supernatural vocation which calls us to possess God as well as to give ourselves to God. Nor can we *reduce* one of these loves to the other so as ultimately to make them coalesce, since they represent two movements of different and strictly irreducible tendency. To resolve desire into gift would be to attempt an impossible purification and to force oneself into an attitude pregnant with every kind of illusion and dissimulated egoism. To resolve gift into desire would be an interior corruption of the gift itself and a simple suppression of charity. One way only is open: to include the two loves in each other and set them in hierarchical order.

The outcome is not in doubt: in the nature of things it is

the gift that comes first and takes the lead. First, in virtue of the general law we have already noted in its place: all love as desire is enveloped in a love as gift which is radical and primary.[254] Thus, to love oneself as a real being and as a subsistent person is something simply necessary, and this is the love of desire which seeks to incorporate all that it loves; but to love oneself as a created being and as a person called, is something that goes deeper, something more radical and absolutely first, and this is the love of gift which goes to God while nevertheless enveloping the desire. To love others as a source of happiness for ourselves is love of desire; but to love them as ends in themselves, as living images of the invisible God, as magnificent vocations to be fulfilled, this is the love of gift, more radical because it reaches to the deepest essence of the person loved, and also first because it springs thus more directly from the creative call. Consequently, to love God as the infinite and overflowing Source of benediction, of beatitude, of eternal life, is love of desire both legitimate and necessary; but to love Him as absolute Plenitude, Beatitude, and Holiness, as the Love both One and triply outpoured, this is the love of gift, more radical than the other because, by bringing the creature back to his Source, it rejoins the movement that gave him his being, and because it thus coincides with the substantial call that constitutes the creature. Accordingly the love of desire is wholly enveloped and borne away by the love of gift, and from these two integrated movements there arises one sole complex and organic movement. For I love God as my good, but this good is also the absolute Good, and it leads me on to overpass desire and throw myself into the gift. On the other hand, I will God for myself, but in virtue of a power that essentially leads me to will myself for God, and thus obliges me to overpass the possession to give myself to communion. The movement that carries me towards God is therefore a desire for full possession, but enveloped, orientated and surpassed by the striving for full communion; and it is the flux and reflux of these two movements in the interior of one and the same effort, that constitute the riches, the torment, and the joy of the love of God.

Let us now add that charity, far from destroying the radical tendency of the human being, comes to heal it (since it is wounded) and, by divinising, to make it fully itself. God calls up from the depths of the soul by grace a spring of that same love which enternally springs by nature in the Bosom of the Three Persons. Now in this love is no desire, but only gift, and generosity and infinite communion; and when God decides to create new beings who are to be His sons, that is still nothing but pure liberality and an outpouring of the eternal generosity. When this love finds entrance to the soul it cannot but carry the love of gift to an unprecedented pitch of force and purity; but because it perfects and does not destroy, it cannot but strengthen also the springs of desire in the divinised soul and augment its thirst for God. Thus the man is altogether transformed; and more than ever are found together in his soul, enveloped, hierarchised, purified and carried to the infinite, both desire for the God of Beatitude and gift to the God of Holiness. The final consummation of man! Because the person is subsistent and open, he finds his full dimensions in this love which exalts within him both desire and gift at once; because he is above all a living vocation, he is normally fulfilled by a gift that more and more envelops desire, and makes him ever more and more respond to this eternal predestination; because he is subsistent and called in Christ, it is in Christ that he finds his true perfection,—which is to be so much the more subsistent as he is the more open, so much the richer as he is the more given, so much the more himself as he is more an image of God in Christ, so much the more satiated in his desire as he is the more irrevocably given to his God.

* * *

We may easily now perceive the essential thing that assures the purity of divine love: it lies in the hierarchy of the loves that are integrated within it. The ontological purity of a love is nothing other in fact than the conformity of its effort with its essence and with its radical orientation. The love of God which is destined to "accomplish" everything comes to put all our loves in their proper place, to develop each on its own plane, and to make them all flourish in its own light and warmth. Charity according to its essence, writes St. Thomas, "consists in man's loving God above all things and submitting himself to Him entirely, by referring all that is his to God." [255] And elsewhere and still more explicitly: "In the state of perfect nature man referred the love of himself and of all other things to the love of God as to its end; and thus he loved God more than himself and above all things." [256] The purity of love here fully appears as a hierarchy of ends and a preference for God. There is nothing to be excluded, nothing suppressed, nothing destroyed, but everything has to be orientated, subordinated, and consecrated. To desire God with all our strength, and to envelop this desire in a radical offering to God of the whole being—that is pure and perfect love. Such was the love of St. Paul when he spoke of himself as *straitened between two: having a desire to be dissolved and to be with Christ, a thing by far the better; but to abide still in the flesh is needful for you. And having this confidence I know that I shall abide and continue with you all for your furtherance and joy of faith* (Phil. I, 23–25). Desire enveloped by gift! For St. Paul, for

whom death is the way to Christ, and entrance into His joy
and highest gain,—St. Paul subordinates this desire to the call
of the apostolate, and *defers his joy for the glory of his God*.
He does not renounce his desire. He hierarchises his loves; he
prefers the good and the glory of his God—and therein his love
finds its purity.[257]

For the rest, no one arrives at this purity save after a severe
purification. Fallen man, egoistic and carnal, puts up a stiff
resistance to the exigencies of charity. If a pure desire for God
is really to dominate the soul we shall have to overcome a whole
host of concupiscences, decisively subdue the flesh, and rise
well above the level on which fear of punishment and hope of
reward predominate—a zone in which our own "proper good"
is still too much in evidence. We shall have to eradicate the
essential vices, plant solid virtues in their place, and thus be
freed and transformed if we are to put the necessary effort
into our desire for God. Now this work covers the stages of
renunciation and purification which lead to perfect charity, to
a love that is truly purified, to a love that implies a purity
of desire which goes beyond that demanded of "beginners" and
is the prerogative of the "perfect." [258]

Moreover even in this love there may well remain elements
that are too human, too mixed, too impermeable as yet by
pure divine charity. Then God Himself takes up the work. He
calls the soul to absolute self-renunciation and tempers it in
unsparing flames. When the log that is soaked in hissing sap
becomes one glowing mass of fire, when the soul becomes one
spirit with God and its love one love with God's, then love
attains to perfect purity, and the spirit compasses an absolute
gift to God, a perfect coincidence of its willing with the divine
Will, an acceptance unreserved, joyous and triumphant, by
which the whole immense force of desire will be made clean,

rectified, integrated and consecrated. In the end we shall find ourselves neither with Bossuet nor with Fénelon, but with St. John of the Cross.

Finally, this lived dialectic of desire and gift may help us to understand the pure and magnificent cry which runs through Christian literature from one end to the other, from Moses and St. Paul down to St. Margaret Mary and St. Theresa of the Child Jesus. *I have great sadness and continual sorrow in my heart. For I wished myself to be an anathema from Christ, for my brethren, who are my kinsmen according to the flesh.*[259] So spoke St. Paul, and all such cries spring from the same source: the obscure and tragic condition of love in this life here below. They suppose, in effect, a conceptual separation and a thought opposition between the elements of desire and gift. Now the separation is made possible by the conditions of human knowledge. As long as the soul is in the body it apprehends spiritual things only through signs. It apprehends God, not by any direct vision face to face, but through a whole complex of truths, of religious attitudes and of spiritual affections. It tends to God as to a Being it would possess—by desire, and would serve—by gift. But desire and gift are presented in two concepts, which are distinct in themselves and are oriented moreover in opposed directions, so that their mutual exclusion is much more readily seized than their inclusion. As for the opposition of desire and gift, it is made possible by the conditions of the supernatural action. On the one hand, the soul in a state of trial knows itself to be imperfect, entangled in spiritual impurities that are subtle and not easily discerned, still tainted by an egoism that persists in the very bosom of love. On the other hand, it feels itself increasingly apt to work with Christ, to continue His sacrifice, to redeem souls, and to co-operate in building up His Kingdom. To exclude so much as a shadow of egoism and to give itself fully to the redemptive work, love can never be too much purified.

Suppose now a soul fully conscious that its love is desire as well as gift, that it seeks its own happiness as well as the glory of God; suppose it exalted and set on fire by the consuming ardour of its love, by the passion for service, by the anguish of the Redemption; and then the very onrush of its generosity will make it long for new sacrifice and look into itself for something more to offer up as a holocaust. Now in the secret heart of its longing it finds these two elements of desire and gift, *experienced* as linked together, *known* as distinct, *conceived* as opposable. Henceforth if a choice is to be made between desire and gift, between possession and communion, between the soul's own good and the divine good, it does not hesitate for a moment. It chooses the divine good and sacrifices its personal joy to the honour of its God and the salvation of its brothers. This is the sacrifice of a love so ardent that the mere thought of offence to God, of the loss of souls, of the blood of Christ spilt in vain, is an inexpressible anguish and calls for the most despoiling, consuming and reckless of offerings by way of the most absolute self-immolation. The positive and admirable element in this is the will to give without reserve, the will that is wholly forgetful of self on the plane of explicit thoughts, of particular choices and free sacrifices. And yet the separation of desire and gift, of possession and communion, is an impossibility; the very idea of it is conceptual, not real; and the soul knows it as soon as it begins to reflect. But then, precisely, at the moment when it formulates this "hypothesis of an impossible thing," there is no question of reflection on its part, but only of love and service and sacrifice. And within this soul, obscure to itself, imperfectly conscious of its love and of its God, partly a prisoner to and betrayed by its own "ideas," but vowed to Christ for the salvation of its brothers and the glory of its God, "wounded thus with a blessed folly," [260] the cry of renunciation does no more than express, by this very choice of the impossible, the consuming fire of the purest, the most absolute, and the most realist of loves.

RES SACRA, HOMO

CHRISTIAN REFLECTION on man cannot but terminate in a feeling of religious admiration and of infinite respect. The more indeed we explore his being the more does man appear paradoxical, mysterious, in one word sacred. For each of these successive paradoxes and mysteries we have been considering rests on some new relation to God, plunging him ever deeper into the mystery of the Holy. Now the sense of the Holy would seem to have disappeared from the modern mind and sensibility,[261] leaving a void which is one of our cruellest wounds. Having made God a stranger to man, it ends by making men strangers to each other.

The Sacred is the proper character of God considered precisely as God, that is to say in the infinity of His power, of His sanctity, and of His love. But it is also the character of all that manifests God, so that to call a thing sacred (as our contemporaries still do), is to adopt a religious attitude towards it, to see it as so surpassingly great and worthy that it becomes an object of fear and desire at once, a thing that claims an absolute respect, whose violation is as heinous as its service is ennobling. What is at stake in our civilization is whether man shall remain—or re-become—a sacred thing. Let us do what we can for our part to restore man to his dignity by showing how

267

Christianity makes of man in all his entirety a mystery rooted in the Holy; and how this mystery is entirely enveloped in the tragedy of his wayfaring condition.

* * *

Man is a mystery first because he is a kind of limit or horizon between two worlds.[262] He is immersed in the flesh, but constituted by the spirit; occupied with matter, but drawn towards God; growing in time, but already breathing the air of eternity; a being of nature and of the world, but also transcending the universe in virtue of his liberty and capacity for union with God. It is doubtless because they had some sense of this mystery, which can be so much of an irritant at times, that certain philosophers (Scheler for instance) have yielded to the temptation to make of man—this medium between nothingness and all—a limit pure and simple, and to deny him all consistence and definition. But if man is two-fold he is also one; and this mystery, far from destroying, is the very basis of his individual existence—that of a being who has to integrate (spiritually) what is already one (ontologically); who is susceptible of a full unity and, on the other hand, of a full disaggregation; who has to acquire a significance of his own, and is tossed about meanwhile in all the whirlpools of the flesh and the world. We live out this drama, we suffer from it and bleed, but remain for the most part inwardly withdrawn from it because without acute sense of it. On the day when, by some flash of intellectual enlightenment, or some effort at spiritual progress, we come to realize what we really are, we are seized with a kind of shiver. Pascal was indulging in no rhetorical exaggeration when he wrote: "Whoever considers himself in this light will be terrified at himself . . ."

Man then is radically a "mystery" that refuses to be "de-

graded into a problem"; and this profound resistance comes
of his sacred character. For man is a spirit and, as such, a
proper image of God. He is made for a mysterious life with
God, to seek Him by thought and by love, to serve Him and to
spend himself for His glory; and thus to achieve the perfection
of that image of God in himself which is likewise the perfection
of his own being. This capacity and this orientation are bound
up with his structure and define his substantial mystery. To say
that God is Spirit is not to define God, but rather to place Him
beyond all definition; and to say that we are spirits, linked to
Him by an indestructible likeness, is to plunge also ourselves
into the mystery of God. Regarded as a living relation to God,
and as signed upon for ever by the light of His Countenance,
man surpasses man, he slips beyond his own grasp, he is not to
be understood or judged or violated in his personal secret. He
belongs to God alone. No human power can claim him. He
cannot be destroyed, for the very act of killing him simply
gives him entrance to the mystery of God and the society of
immortal spirits. In the midst of the world he is a being from
beyond the world. In one word, he is sacred.

* * *

This first mystery leads to a second. The essential thing
about the human being is his relation to God, and therefore
his vocation. Now here the paradox goes still deeper because
man is fallen and redeemed. He is fallen, and therefore affected
by all sorts of evil forces which penetrate and attract him,
which awaken the strangest complicities within him, and which
appear to be so much incorporated in his nature—although
in truth they have other and remoter sources—that they seem
to spring from the very depths of his heart. And yet this fallen
creature is redeemed, and therefore taken up again into the

grace of Christ. Other forces are at work in him, other calls
sustain his interior energies, another love comes to snatch him
from evil hands and to give him to God. Even from the very
midst of concupiscence we may see rising to the light, humble,
pure and potent, the aspiration to God who is Truth and
Love, and Holiness. At this stage, the mystery of man lies in
the dynamic coexistence, so to call it, of these two forces
which dispute the human being between them by disputing
his love and his liberty. And while sin does its best to seduce
him and browbeat him into submission, grace sets out to
convert him and deliver. The entire person, soul and body,
instincts and passions, love and intelligence: and, around the
person as well as within him, the world of things, the world of
men, the world of invisible spirits—all that is one immense field
of battle, the seat and subject of an inexpiable war waged
between the powers of sin, grouped around the Prince of this
world, and the powers of grace which radiate from the heart of
the King of Kings. Man's mystery is here deepened in both
directions. It is more opaque, more carnal, more terrible—and
at the same time more luminous, more spiritual, and more
joyous than we could ever have dared to think. Man's paradox
is more and more accentuated in interior tension, for here
he appears as capable of falling into the abyss of sin and of
becoming a prisoner to the Evil One—*he that committeth sin
is of the devil* (I John III, 8) ; but none the less capable of
being uplifted above his earthly condition and exalted even to
deification—*he that doth justice is born of God* (I John
II, 29).

But these two traits—fallen and redeemed—make man a
sacred being again in another way. Paradoxical as it may seem,
to be fallen is a sign of his sacred character. For the fall was
essentially a separation from God. But only a being capable of

divine communion is capable of being excluded from it, capable moreover of finding his own worst misery, his own eternal death, in that very exclusion. For man's fall was not primarily concerned with the cosmic element of his being, with what he has in common with the world around him; he fell primarily from his heavenly estate, he lost his divine substance and the bonds of grace that united him with his God. That is why he can indeed be fallen from God's world and yet remain a magnificent denizen of ours. The fall means nothing if not a fall from divine grace; and an age that has lost all sense of the Holy has lost all normal means of appreciating its fallen state; it misses man's misery because it misses his greatness. But now man is taken up again into the divine hands and redeemed in Christ. He is no longer sacred only in virtue of the radical capacity which makes it possible for him to be called to life in God, he is so also in virtue of the efficacious call to life in God in Christ, which introduces him into the inviolable world of divine charity. Called by the Three Persons, redeemed by the Incarnate God, he is once more linked up with God by this eternal election and love that silently penetrate his being; and even the most polluted of souls retains this touch of the redemptive love in its hidden depths and this call to transformation in Christ.

* * *

Finally, when man has become Christian, he finds entrance to a new mystery. He is born a second time and of God Himself, he has become a member of Christ, possessed of eternal life, he is the temple of the Holy Spirit, "signed upon" and consecrated even as to his body, he participates the life of the Society which links the Father, the Son, and the Spirit in the bonds of Infinite Love. Thereby he is rapt away into the holiness of God, and by this contact with the divine fire he becomes even more of a holy thing than before because God Himself now dwells within him; because in the eyes of the Father and in reality he is indeed another Christ; because he is thus taken out of the whole order of things profane, and is destined to glorify God in his soul and in his body till the Glory Itself shall consume him and divinise him for ever. *Agnosce, O Christiane, dignitatem tuam!*

And nevertheless we have not yet formulated the mystery of the new man with precision. For the Christian is redeemed, and not yet redeemed; he is son of God, and not yet wholly son; supernaturally he is and he is not. All that he has is but a pledge, all that he is is but a germ; all that he has and is are only first-fruits. He knows God by faith, and compared with the night of sin this faith is light indeed, it is nothing less than a divine epiphany; but compared with final vision it is no more than a partial, indirect, and obscure knowledge, in which God by no means truly "appears." We love God, and we know that we love Him *when we keep his commandments and do the things that are pleasing in his sight, and our hearts do not reprehend us* (I John III, 21–22). But then, how frail an assurance! All the obscurities of faith reappear in it and envelop it in their moving shadows. And then, too, the consciousness of our sins, of our miseries, of our readiness to betray; and the growing revelation of God's holiness which makes us daily seem the greater sinners in our own eyes; and the revelation of His infinite love which shows up so vividly the weakness of our own and wrings from us a cry like Madame Acarie's: "To die, and never to have loved!" So that it is in security always hedged about with uneasiness, in confidence always chastened by fear, in joy always shot through with sorrow, that we go to God. We are always plucked back from our miseries, always re-comforted by His mercy, always mysteriously flooded with peace, because we really possess *Him who is eternal life,* but yet with a peace that goes deeper than our experience because it comes from *Him whom we love without seeing* (I Peter I, 8).

If, furthermore, we all live through the same griefs and the same joys, it is because we all play our parts in the same drama. Growth of a man and growth of humanity, salvation of a man and salvation of humanity, are all one. We are called to our God together and we have to win our way to Him side by side; and this fraternal collaboration, sustained and quickened by the Spirit, is precisely the task of the Church. We accomplish it in a world and in a society which are at once an obstacle and a support, a means to try our strength as well as an aid to progress, an allurement spread before our cupidities as well as a call to sacrifice. There is an essential and tragic ambiguity in all our world. That is why the Christian is called upon to purify it and to transform it into an instrument of redemption. Thus we may see that he is truly attached to the world, committed to the work of its reconstruction, thrown into the thick of the fight against all its miseries and injustices, so that the human community may become gradually more habitable by the sons of God and may reach its consummation at last in a community divinised. But we see also that he is detached, most thoroughly detached, from the perishable forms in which human effort embodies itself, from these "miserable inns" it has to put up with while awaiting the day of entry into the Father's house. However intent he may be on the temporal task, the Christian knows too well that here he has no abiding city, that he is still an exile from his native land, and that he will never be truly at home until he rests fully and definitively in God.

The tragedy of this wayfaring condition affects the whole of the triple relation—of likeness, vocation, and filiation—which defines the sacred character of the Christian, and throws its enveloping folds around them all. Each is involved in the movement of becoming and growth, for they are but the first faint outlines of a picture traced by the moving fingers of the Spirit and of human free-will, and apprehensible only through the veil of faith. Each is involved in the fall, since in man now alienated from his God the light of the Divine Countenance has faded; and his understanding, too strongly attracted to the sensible and the carnal, is unapt to perceive the divine traces in an image so grievously deformed. Each is enveloped in sin, for even the Christian does not escape it; and when he freely rejects his God he destroys his divine life, smothers his vocation, effaces his likeness to God, divests himself of every trace of his sacredness, and becomes, by his own act, a creature profaned. Put all this together and we may realize the triple darkness in which a world that has ceased to be Christian is plunged: supernatural existence absent, the call unheard and in vain, the likeness effaced and forgotten. How should we expect man to retain the stamp of the holy and not rather founder in some vague paganism which shall exalt him for a moment only the more effectively to remove the last traces of God from his poor countenance? We see then how closely the human and the sacred go hand in hand—the sacred being simply the noblest name and the deepest truth of the human. We see too that man's essential tragedy lies precisely in being thus profaned, that the first task—the sole Christian task—is to help him to recover his lost likeness, to renew his vocation, and regain his life in God; we see to what an extent he stands in need of this new and ceaseless "sacring" which comes to him by the Spirit; how much he needs to be restored to the truth

of his holiness by Him who is the "Holy One of God," that he
may never fall away and betray himself again.

* * *

Here, however, Catholicism shows an astonishing boldness.
Not content with tracing this shifting, mixed and miserable
image of man, it sets before us a human creature who even
here below was fully conformed to the divine idea, and, in
consequence, fully holy. We do not speak of Christ, of the
Word made flesh, whose human nature terminates in the
Person of the Son of God, but of His Mother, the Virgin Mary.
She was *a woman among women*. She was born and grew up
like others. She became a very perfect mother. She wrapped her
Son in swaddling clothes, she fed Him at her breast, she folded
Him in her arms. She brought Him up and formed Him. She
saw Him go forth in due time, and she knew all the anguish
of the mothers whose children grow up and go out into the
world. She followed Him lovingly, but in the background. She
went by His side to Calvary and shared His martyrdom, and
her heart was pierced like His. A true woman indeed, a true
mother, and yet unique; for had she not been called *blessed
among women?* She stands apart, a whole world in herself,
the world of intact humanity. In such wise had she been redeemed that sin had never touched her at all. She had been
conceived as a daughter of man, but conceived without sin.
She is the Immaculate, the creature that evil has never soiled,
the Panagia. If Christ, who redeemed her, is the perfect
Image of the invisible God, she is the perfect image of divinised
humanity. All that we could ever imagine or desire for a
creature, all the beauty, all the purity, all the holiness for
which we long, all was realized in the Virgin in a plenitude that
had no other measure than Infinite Love. *Inviolata, integra et*

casta: here, in the bosom of fallen humanity, we behold at last the creature fresh and unstained, joyous as Paradise, and so redeemed as to be in her own sole self the promise and pledge of our Redemption. The problem of man at which we have been toiling is resolved in her *who cometh forth as the dawn;* and we understand the saying of Péguy: "Everything turns for me on the Immaculate Conception."

And nevertheless the human problem is resolved in hope alone by the existence of the Virgin Mary. When a soul is so totally possessed by God that it totally possesses its own body, when the radiance of its love is of infinite purity, then that is something so beautiful that we hardly dare to look it in the face. When a creature is full of grace, when the Lord is with her, when she is blessed among women, then she escapes us by her very greatness, by her likeness to God, by her communion with Him, by this silence in which she rejoins the silent love of the Three. When she is an image unstained, a vocation fully accepted, a perfect Daughter of God, and when all this culminates in a divine Maternity, then she is so bathed in the consuming Fire of the Holy that she becomes altogether lost to our eyes. Thereafter her presence is all around us, but not unveiled; she acts in us and among us, but we cannot clasp her in our hands; she is our Mother, but the Mother of a child of God as yet not fully formed, and not yet able to know or to love in perfection. Thus the Virgin is not by us to be apprehended save in faith, and the perfect human creature remains for us a hope. *Exules filii Hevae. . . .*

* * *

We must therefore always come back to this fundamental position: here below we are still pilgrims far from the Lord, we are still less than we should be and have to press on to the future when we shall be like to Him because we shall see Him as he is. The Christian therefore, if he understands himself, is always as one who stretches forward towards the Parousia. He is plunged into a world in travail, groaning in expectation of final deliverance, and in this expectation he shares. He is a member of the Church of God, at once militant, suffering and triumphant; but here below the Church presents only her beginnings, she is always, in her members, in the act of passing from the militant state to the suffering and the glorious; by a formidable movement of growth she passes out beyond this world, beyond death and time, and in the movement towards this Beyond lies the life of the Christian. For the rest, he plays out his personal part in the cosmic drama and in the ecclesiastical drama, participating in a definite moment of the growth, of the trial, of the call to eternity. His life is already a life in God, but it is *hid with Christ in God* (Col. III, 3), and of its own energies it still presses forward to the day when it can expand in the light because Christ, appearing in His glory, shall come to gather up all His elect.

Pressing thus with all his powers towards the Coming of the Lord the Christian is, quite literally, a man who seeks his country; and, like his fathers in the faith, he *beholds the promises from afar off, and salutes them, and confesses that he is a pilgrim and a stranger on the earth* (Heb. XI, 13). And so he uses the world as though he used it not; so strongly is he drawn towards the Invisible and the Hoped-for that all the rest is caught up into this immeasurable aspiration. He is no escapist, he does not run away and hide himself; he finds his place in the world and strikes roots; but all his temporal effort is sustained, surpassed and uplifted by the thought of his abiding City. "He holds to the things of this world so as not to be held in the world by them, so possesses them that he is not possessed by them, so keeps them under the vigilant rule of his mind that he is not overcome by the love of worldly things, nor held in the grip of his own havings." [263] To revert to Pauline terms, if he has a wife he is as if he had none, for he would try to please her without displeasing God. He weeps as if he wept not, for all the troubles of this world are swallowed up in expectation of eternal joy. He rejoices as if he rejoiced not, for all joys here below throw him back of themselves on the risk and the fear of eternal death. In short, for him the *fashion of this world passeth away* (I Cor. VII, 29–31) and he looks for the light of the Countenance that does not pass; the kingdoms of this world daily crumble and he would have the Kingdom that time can never touch.

But he knows too that it is in this instant that passes and in the midst of things that change that the Lord comes and His Kingdom appears. Henceforth, far from consuming his heart in useless longing, he works and wears himself out and spends himself to hasten His Coming. Because Christ is always He who is to come and because He is impatient to fulfil Himself in His members and to recapitulate all things in Himself, because the insistent call that draws all men to the Father is but one of the names for the Redemption, the Christian dedicates himself to his sacred function *par excellence* which is *to testify to the Gospel of the grace of God* (Acts XX, 24). He adds his own voice to the call, he unites himself with the work of redemption, he accepts the sufferings asked of him that the Body which is the Church may be daily built up like a holy Temple and that the day of its consummation may draw near—the day of the final Coming of its Head. How well he understands that all the world's sorrow is no more than the sorrow of a childbirth! How eagerly he accepts it in his soul, how deeply he shares it in tears and in hope, because it brings all things to birth and to growth!

And how much also he rejoices at every human joy and fosters and protects and loves it because it helps the wayfaring creature to breathe, and because it is a faraway shadow of Joy Ever-lasting!

By such communion in joy and in sorrow he becomes not only more fully man, but also more Christian than ever. He enters so much the more deeply into the great well-spring of the invincible hope of the whole Church. For *the Spirit and the Bride say: Come. And he that heareth let him say: Come—Come, Lord Jesus!* (Apoc. XXII, 17–20). A trembling supplication, that goes up so many thousands of times in a Christain's life—every time that he says the Our Father: "Hallowed be thy name. Thy kingdom come. Thy will be done!" A cry to which he awaits the response that shall end the day of growth and of hope by inaugurating the Kingdom which lives above time and sorrow and death: *Behold, I make all things new!* (Apoc. XXI, 5). And when he has served God well and done good work for His glory, when by his humble and steadfast faith he has enabled Christ to re-build the divine image in his soul, when his last hour has come and he is about to pass from this world to his Father, then the pilgrim far from the Lord understands that he is at last realized in the truth of his eternal vocation; that the new man—and the holy!—is formed in him for ever; that redeemed humanity has once more achieved success in himself. And he who was made to know, to love, and to live, and has longed for nought else, can now do no more than exclaim with Elizabeth of the Trinity as she lay dying, in a cry which is at once the fulfilment of human hope and the dawn of the eternal certitudes: *I go to the Light, to Love, and to Life.*

NOTES

1. We shall not make use of the opposition "Temporal-Spiritual," and that for two reasons. First, because these words at once evoke certain definite historical problems: those concerning the relations of the ecclesiastical and the civil power, the Sacerdotium and the Empire, as they presented themselves in the Middle Ages. These historical questions are outside the scope of our study, and we shall leave them aside. But furthermore, the terms "temporal-spiritual" are taken in the end by some to mean the material and the immaterial, the world of bodies and the world of spirits. But a temporal reduced to the material is mutilated, emptied of substance, and ruined. In the modern meaning of the word the spiritual is included in the temporal.

2. Thus, as Pius XI writes, the finalities of the State are not simply "corporeal and material, but are, in themselves, necessarily contained within the limits of the natural, the earthly and the temporal." The Church's mandate "extends to the eternal, to the celestial, and the supernatural. . . ." *Doc. Cath.* XXVI (1931) 83. And the formula of Leo XIII is well known: "God has divided the care of the human race between the two powers, ecclesiastical and civil, the one charged with the care of divine things and the other with that of human things." Encyclical, *Immortale Dei* (Denzinger, 1866).

3. St. Thomas, *Sum. Theol.* I, q. 65, art. 3: "Creatures, as far as in them lies, do not turn us away from God but lead us to God. . . . If they turn us away from God, that is due to those who by their own fault, use them in ways that are contrary to reason."

4. St. Thomas, *Sermo V, in Dom 2 de Adventu* (Vivès XXIX, 194).

5. "In the great body of the world the divine murmur finds

281

as many veins whereby it may come at us as there are creatures over which the very divinity rules. Thus when we look on all that is created we are uplifted to admiration of the Creator." St. Gregory the Great, *Moral.* V, 29 (P. L. LXXV, 707).

6. Cf. *Contra Gentes,* III, 24.

7. St. Gregory of Nyssa, *In verba "Faciamus . . ."* (P. G. XLIV, 264 d). Cf. *Sap.* IX, 1–4: "God of my fathers . . . who by thy wisdom hast appointed man that he should have dominion over the creature that was made by thee, that he should order the world according to equity and justice, and execute justice with an upright heart . . ."

8. *In homine quodammodo sunt omnia; et ideo secundum modum quo dominatur in his quae in seipso sunt, secundum hunc modum competit ei dominare aliis. Sum. Theol.* I, q. 96, art. 2.

9. Cf. Huby, *Epître aux Romains* (Paris, 1940), pp. 296–301, and the citation of Goguel, 301, n. 2.

10. "*Creaturae quantum est de se, non retrahunt a Deo, sed in ipsum ducunt . . . Sed quod avertant a Deo, hoc est ex culpa eorum qui insipienter eis utuntur . . . Non enim abducunt a Deo, nisi alliciendo secundum aliquid boni in eis existens, quod habent a Deo.*" *Sum. Theol.* I, 65, 1 ad 3.

11. *In Rom.* XIV, 5 (P. G. LX, 530). Cf. St. Augustine: "The man (Adam) lived in friendship with God in a double paradise, corporeal and spiritual. There was no corporeal paradise for the goods of the body without a spiritual, for those of the soul; any more than there was a spiritual paradise for interior joys, without a corporeal for exterior joys. Thus there was a two-fold paradise for a two-fold happiness." (*Civ. Dei.* XIV, 11).

12. St. Ambrose, cited by De la Taille, *Myst. Fidei,* 567.

13. St. Gregory of Nazianzen, *Orat.* 39, 16 (P. G. XXXVI, 352).

14. Cited by R. d'Harcourt, in *l'Esprit de la Liturgie,* p. 70.

15. This is one of the themes that penetrate all Claudel's work. We may find its direct expression, full of humour and force, in the *Conversations dans le Loir-et-Cher,* pp. 253–270.

16. Joergensen, *Saint Francis of Assisi* (trs. Sloane), pp. 308–315.

17. *Ibid.* p. 312, note 1.

18. When he is really himself, be it understood, as in this portrait of hunting dogs:

"Ils [les chasseurs] ont choisi ceux-là dont le mufle est camus,
Les yeux ardents et noirs, le sourcil par-dessus
S'avalent refrogné, une tête petite,
Une oreille pendante, une gueule dépite,
Les dents comme une scie, un col petit, le dos
Long, large, bien fourni de peau, de chair et d'os,
L'estomac rond et fort, et la jambe derrière
Plus longuette un petit que la jambe première,
La queue déliée, et bref quand tout le corps
Etait ferme planté sur membres beaux et forts.
Puis ils les ont nommés dès leur jeunesse tendre
De noms aigus et courts, pour soudain les entendre . . ."

The hunters have chosen flat-nosed dogs, with burning black eyes beneath beetling brows, louring and knitted, a small head, a drooping ear, a defiant jaw, teeth like a saw, a short neck and a long broad back well covered with skin, flesh and bone, a strong round body, hind legs a little longer than the fore, a slender tail yet a shortish body firmly planted on fine strong limbs. And even as puppies they gave them names that are short and sharp, to be instantly understood.

19. Rom. I, 20; cf. Huby, *Comment.*, 82, sq., who writes: "Creatures are signs of the divine perfections and man has power to decipher the great book of the universe."

20. On this point note the very just remarks of M. Gilson, *Christianisme et Philosophie*, 103 et sq.

21. We indulge in no mythology. What we call "spiritual instincts" are, to put it shortly, those spontaneous, universal, and irreducible functions of reason which lead to the perception of values.

22. *De Baptismo*, 2 (P. L. I, 1202).

23. *Catech.* XVI, 12 (P. G. XXXIII, 933).

24. *Interior Castle*, IV, 2.

25. Claudel, *Cinq grandes Odes*, 64.

26. *Spiritual Canticle*, Stanza V (Trs. D. Lewis).

27. *Adversus haereses* IV, 17, n. 4, and 18, n. 4–6 (P. G. VII, 1023 and 1026–29).

28. Dupré, *Pathologie de l'imagination et de l'émotivité*, p. 487. Dide et Guiraud, *Psychiatrie du médecin practicien*, p. 7.

29. *De Anima*, Art. VIII, 15.

30. See on this point Lhermitte, *L'Image de notre corps* (Paris, 1939). And, by the same author, *Les méchanismes du cerveau* (Paris, 1938).

31. Wallon, in *Nouveau Traité de Psychologie*, I, 324.

32. Lhermitte, *Les méchanismes du cerveau*, 118.

33. *Positions et Propositions*, I, 95–96. There is an identical but still more curious case in Valery in connection with the *Cimetière Marin*, which at first was "only an empty rhythmic figure" (*Variété*, III, 68–69). And we know that Berlioz, who had chanced one day at Rome to fall into the Tiber, came up triumphantly singing a refrain he had vainly sought for two years. (Delacroix, *Psychologie de l'Art*, 192).

34. Cited in Lhermitte, 122.

35. *L'homme, cet inconnu*, 169.

36. St. Thomas, *Sum. Theol.* II–II, 156, I, ad 1: "The human soul is the form of the body, it possesses certain powers which make use of bodily organs. The operations of these organs conduce somewhat to those actions of the soul which are accomplished without corporeal instruments, namely to the acts of the intellect and the will."

37. "We have the feeling to-day that every rhythm perceived, perhaps every rhythm imagined, is accompanied by a rhythm really produced in the body of the subject, that it cannot be perceived or imagined save as produced or reproduced, and that it cannot be exactly perceived unless one is in the way to reproduce it." Landry, cited in Madinier, *Conscience et Mouvement*, 412.

38. Lhermitte, *L'Image de notre corps*, 156–157. Cf. 15.

39. Madinier, *ibid.*, 449–450.

40. St. Augustine, *Confessions*, I, 8.

41. R. P. Aupiais, *Vie intellectuelle*, 10th. April, 1939, pp. 92–93.

42. On the body as radiating the beauty it receives from the soul, cf. St. Bernard, *In Cantic. Serm.* 85 (P. L. CLXXXIII, 1193).

43. Valery, *Eupalinos ou l'Architecte*, pp. 117–118.

44. M. Louis Arnould's fine book, *Ames en prison*, is well

known; M. BLONDEL has given an admirable philosophical commentary on these facts in *La Pensée*, I, p. 86 et seq.

45. ST. ATHANASIUS, *De Incarnato Verbi* (P. G. XXV, 9, d). Cf. ST. PAUL, I Tim. 2, 8.

46. Cf. LACOMBE, *Sur la Yoga indien*, in *Etudes Carméli-taines*, Oct. 1937. 163.

47. Cf. MARITAIN, in *Ransoming the Time*, Chap. X (Trs. Binsse).

48. *De Anima*, 8, ad 7. Cf. *De Malo*, V, 1 and 5; *De Veritate*, XIII, 4; II–II, 29, 1.

49. So much is this so that for St. Thomas, as for the whole Catholic tradition, nothing less than a supernatural grace is needed to compose the conflict. The reply to the objection just cited goes on as follows: "To overcome this repugnance there was given to man in the state of innocence a remedy by means of grace, such that the lower powers no longer set themselves in opposition to the reason. But this remedy was lost to man by sin."

50. Some of these syntheses are demonstrated in Pierre JANET's book: *L'évolution psychologique de la personnalité* (Paris, 1929).

51. Affective tonicity is "the confused affective disposition which makes our activity more or less easy, and which reveals itself in a vague state of satisfaction or, conversely, in a dull and indefinable dissatisfaction." DWELSHAUVERS, *Traité de Psychologie*, p. 219.

52. Cf. Rémy COLLIN, *Les Hormones* (Paris, 1938).

53. DE GREEFF, *Notes sur la psychologie des foules. Vie intellectuelle*, 25th February, 1939, 66.

54. *Ibid.* p. 75.

55. I Cor. VI, 9–10; Rom. XIII, 13; Eph. V, 3 sq.; Col. III, 5.

56. For example, Inquiry of the J.O.C.F. *La Santé des jeunes travailleuses;* CARREL, *L'Homme, cet inconnu,* 72, 180–181, 323; BERGSON, *Les deux Sources,* 326.

57. *Illustration,* 1934, p. 306.

58. ST. THOMAS, *De Ver.* XXVII, 6, ad 2: "Original sin is in the soul, according to its essence, by which it is united as form to the flesh, from which it contracted the original stain; and although nothing essential was taken away from the soul,

nevertheless the relation of the essence of the soul (to the body) was hampered, and so to speak loosened (*per modum cujusdam elongationis*), just as contrary dispositions loosen the potency of matter from the act of the form."

59. *In Cant. Cant. Sermo* XXIV, 6 (P. L., CLXXXIII, 897).

60. Cited by P. DE GRANDMAISON, *Jésus-Christ*, II, 168.

61. On this text, cf. LAGRANGE, *Rev. Biblique*, 1936, 26–27; and HUBY, *Epîtres de la captivité*, 66–67.

62. ST. SOPHRONIUS OF JERUSALEM, cited by GALTIER, in *L'Unité du Christ*, 15.

63. ST. JOHN DAMASCENE, *Ibid.* 157.

64. See KITTEL, *Theologisches Wörterbuch zum N. Test.*, at the word eikón, 386 sq.

65. ST. THOMAS, *In Ephes.* I, lect. 8, n. 3.

66. Cf. Vatican Council, Constitution de Fide, c. 3 (Den., 1794).

67. This view must be completed by the inverse relation, which we can merely indicate: Christ, for God, *is the divine face of humanity.* He presents to God the Father—He and His mystical body—the unique and perfect man, conformed to his eternal type, and God's glory here below.

68. And that is why the priest, when placing the sacred body between the lips of the faithful, says: *Corpus Domini Nostri Jesu Christi custodiat animam tuam in vitam aeternam.*

69. On this point see P. DE LA TAILLE, *Mysterium Fidei*, Eluc. 45 and 49. We make no attempt here to explain the whole unifying rôle of the Eucharist, and therefore do not insist on the rôle of the abiding and unifying oblation of Christ.

70. Cited by P. PARIS, *Retraite sur le Baptême*, p. 3. The text, very slightly modified, occurs in the Roman Ritual for the baptism of adults. Cf. another fine text in MARTENE, *De antiquis Ecclesiae ritibus*, L. I. art. 18, ordo XIII.

71. And thus, tearing away his body from God he tears it away from himself and alienates it. The expression may be found in ST. CYRIL OF JERUSALEM, *Catech.* 18 (P. G. XXXIII, 1017b and 1041a).

72. A contact which in certain cases becomes really perceptible: Cf. R. SCHWOB, *Moi Juif.*

73. This comes from the classical theology. Cf. for example,

SUAREZ, *de Euch.,* disp. 64, sect. 1: or better still, FRANZELIN, *De sacramento Euch.* Th. 19. Let us detach this beautiful text: "Although our bodies, inasmuch as by the state of grace they are temples of the Holy Spirit, are, by that very fact, members of Christ, bone of His bone and flesh of His flesh. . . . yet this mystical unity of our flesh with His flesh receives its full consummation, and, so to speak, its *sacramental consecration* by the union of the glorified body and blood with our own bodies, a union in which are celebrated the nuptials of the Lamb with the Church, His Bride, still in the state of a wayfarer in each of its individual members. . . ." (p. 304).

74. Secret for Dom. III Quadr. and Postcomm. of Mass for the grace of continence.

75. Various prayers: *A cunctis, Concede,* Postcomm. of the Feast of the Holy Trinity, Secret, Feria 4 post Dom. IV, Quadrag.

76. Cf. M. DE LA TAILLE, *Mysterium Fidei,* el. 38 (Text of IRENAEUS cited on p. 492), and cf. ST. THOMAS, *In Joan.* VI, lect. 7, n. 3–4: "The virtue of this nourishment is great because it gives everlasting life to the soul; but also because it gives everlasting life to the body. . . . As Augustine said, and we too said above, the Word raises up souls, *but the Word made flesh gives life to the body.* Now this sacrament contains not only the Word according to his divinity but also the Word in the reality of his flesh; and that is why it is the cause not only of the resurrection of souls, but also of bodies . . ." On this resurrection in hope, cf. ST. AUGUSTINE, *Contra Faust. manich.,* II, 7 (P. L. XLII, 251).

77. ST. THOMAS, *in I Cor.* VI, lect. 3, n. 4. Cf. *in Phil.* I, lect. 3, n. 2.

78. Secret, *Contra persecutores Ecclesiae.*

79. *Ad Polyc.,* 2.

80. ST. JOHN CHRYSOSTOM, *in I Cor., Hom.* XVII, 1, and XVIII, 2.

81. Cf. LOT-BORODINE, *La doctrine de la déification dans l'Eglise Grecque,* Rev. de l'Hist. des Religions, 1933 (t. 107), 528–540; more severe, *Apatheia,* in Dic. de Spiritualité, 727–746; Vg. on the Fathers of the Fourth century in the East: ". . . The greater part give *apatheia* a profoundly Christian significance. It is in fact a gift of God, a grace merited for men by

the incarnation of the Word. . . . and it does not prevent men being tempted by the demons . . ." (738). The return to the state of original liberty is a theme known also to the West. Limiting ourselves to two belated examples, we may note that St. Bonaventure interprets the case of St. Francis in this sense (Cf. Longpre, Dict. Spirit., *Bonaventure*, col. 1775); and cf. St. John of the Cross, *Cantico*, str. 37.

82. *In I Cor. Hom.* XVIII, 2.

83. St. Thomas, *Sum Theol.* II–II, 17, 3: "Hope involves a movement or a stretching forth (*protensionem*) of the appetite towards an arduous good."

84. St. Bernard, *De diligendo Deo*, XI, 31 (P. L. CLXXXII, 993).

85. St. Bernard, *Lib. de precepto et dispensat.* XX, 59 (P. L. CLXXXII, 892).

86. St. Thomas, *De Anima*, 2, 14: The soul is united to the body for the perfection of its nature. But that the body becomes a prison, and sullies it, is due to the first sin.

87. Victor Hugo, *Pleurs dans le nuit*, IX (*Contemplations*, VI, 6).

88. St. Irenaeus, *Adv. Haereses*, V, 2 (P. G. VII, 1127).

89. St. Bernard, *De diligendo Deo*, XI, 30–31 (P. L. CLXXXII, 993). These beautiful texts of St. Bernard's, which we cite of set purpose, will show, if need be, the lucid appreciation and deep love of the body which animated the great Christian ascetics. There is no need, after that, to make excuses for a contempt they never professed.

90. II Cor. V, 4; and after him, St. Hilary, in this untranslatable text: *cum incorruptio corruptionem, et aeternitas infirmitatem, et forma Dei formam terrenae carnis absorpserit.* Tract. in Ps. I, 13 (P. L. IX, 258).

91. St. Augustine, *Sermo* 242, II (P. L. XXXVIII, 1142).

92. St. Thomas, In I Cor. XV, I, 6: *Primo (anima) dat esse; unde quando erit in summo perfectionis dabit esse spirituale.*

93. St. Irenaeus, *Adv. Haer.* V, 8 (P. G. VII, 1142).

94. Note here that we set aside the technical problem of the "formal constituent" of personality, and study only the real structure of the person. This by definition is "a being that subsists *per se* in a spiritual nature"; and calls for exploration, not only of its mode of existence, but also of the nature in which

it subsists, and which is "included in its signification" (St. Thomas, *De Pot.* IX, 3).

95. *Etiam nos, secundum quod aliquid aeternum mente sapimus, non in hoc mundo sumus.* St. Augustine, cited in *Sum. Theol.* I, 112, I ad 1.

96. It is the constant—and too often forgotten—teaching of St. Thomas, that: *anima mensurata tempore, secundum esse quo unitur corpori; quamvis prout consideratur ut substantia quaedam spiritualis mensuratur aevo* (*De Pot.* III, 10 ad 8); *pars intellectiva animae secundum se est supra tempus, sed pars sensitiva subjacet tempori . . .* (I–II, 53, 3 ad 3); . . . *Intelligit (intellectus) quod quid est, abstrahendo intelligibilia a sensibilium conditionibus: unde, secundum illam operationem neque sub tempore, neque sub aliqua conditione sensibilium rerum intelligibile comprehendit . . .* (II *Con. Gen.* 96). Cf. I, 10, 5 ad 1; I, 85, 4, ad 1; and 5 ad; *Spir. creat.* 5, ad 4.

97. *Omne sensibile est quasi quoddam particulare; intellectualia autem sunt quasi totalia quaedam.* St. Thomas, *In Joan.* c. 8, lect. 2, n. 1.

98. I–II, 53, 3, ad 3.

99. *Cum enim anima rationalis excedat proportionem materiae corporalis, pars animae quae est ab organo corporeo absoluta quamdam habet infinitatem respectu ipsius corporis et partium animae corpori concreatarum* (I–II, 2, 6). On the soul as "exceeding" see *Spir. Creat.* 2, corp. and ad 3, 4, 18, 19: *anima secundum suam essentiam est forma corporalis, et non secundum aliquid additum. Tamen in quantum attingitur a corpore, est forma: in quantum vero superexcedit proportionem corporis, dicitur spiritus, vel spiritualis substantia* (ad 4), *Ibid.* 4, corp. and ad 3; 5, corp; 9 ad 15; 11, ad 12, 14. *De Pot.* 3, 11 c and ad 15: *anima rationalis, ut dictum est, excedit totum ordinem corporalium principiorum.*

100. *Contra Gentes,* II, 81.

101. *De Anima,* 7, c. and ad 16: *Licet sola species definiatur proprie, non tamen oportet quod omnis species sit definibilis. Species enim immaterialium rerum non cognoscuntur per definitionem vel demonstrationem . . . Unde nec angelus proprie potest definiri . . . Anima etiam definitur ut est corporis forma.*

102. Cf. *De Pot.* 9, 3, c.; 6, c, and ad 3, 4.

103. *Redire ad essentiam suam* (Proclus' expression) *nihil*

aliud est quam rem subsistere in seipsa. Forma enim, in quantum perficit materiam dando ei esse, quodammodo supra ipsam effunditur; in quantum vero in seipsa habet esse, in seipsam redit. I, 14, 2, ad 1. Cf. *I Sent.* 17, 5, 3, and *Ver.* 2, 2 ad 2. On these texts see R. P. WEBERT, *Reflexio,* in *Mel. Mandonnet,* I, 322–323.

104. *Pot.* 9, 9, ad 18.

105. In his very formal language St. Thomas does not say that the created being is a relation. The relation of creation (*Pot.* 3, 3, c. and ad 3) is inherent in the creature, and created along with the creature; it is an accident. But an accident of a unique kind. For if, according to its *being,* it is posterior to the created thing, yet according to its *essence* as relation, it is *quodammodo prior subjecto.* On the one side this relation is an *esse ad* which has an *esse in;* on the other, *it must needs exist that the being itself may be* (Cf. *Pot.* 10, 1, ad 3). All this is naturally still more true of the person than of any other creature, because the person participates more in God. Borrowing the formula by which M. Forest characterizes matter (*La structure métaphysique du concret d'après S. Thomas* 215, n. 3), we could say: the being of the person is "to be relative, but not to be a relation"; in other words, it is a *relativum,* not a *relatio.* But just on that account we can say without inconvenience (as we have done in the text) that this essentially relative being is a living relation.

106. *De Anima,* 6, c. and *ad* 8; *Spir. Creat.* 3, c.

107. *De anima,* 6, *ad* 13.

108. On all this, see *Spir. creat.* 2, c. and *ad* 4; *De An.* 7, c.

109 *De Malo,* 4, 6, *ad* 9.

110. *Sum. Theol.* III, 2, 5, *ad* 2. So true is this that if Christ had assumed human nature thus He would have assumed all men into His personal unity. *Ibid.,* and 4, 4, c.; 4, 5, c.

111. This is the standpoint St. Thomas adopts when he writes: *Peccatum originale non pertinet ad naturam hominis absolute, sed secundum quod derivatur ab Adam per viam seminalem. De Malo,* 4, 7, ad 3; or again: *Omnes homines sunt unus homo, in quantum conveniunt in natura, quam accipiunt a promo parente. Sicut etiam Porphyrius dicit quod participatione speciei, plures homines sunt unus homo* I–II, 81, 1, c. For the reference to Porphyry, cf. III *Sent.* d. 18, q. I a, 6, sol. I and *Comp. Theol.,* 201.

112. *De Pot.* 2, 1, ad 14.

113. *Natura reflectitur in seipsam, non solum quantum ad id quod est ei singulare, sed multo magis quantum ad commune. Inclinatur enim unumquodque ad conservandum, non solum individuum sed etiam suam speciem. Sum. Theol.* I, 60, 5, ad 3.

114. *Sicut in una persona multa sunt membra, ita in una natura humana multae sunt personae, ut participatione speciei multi homines intelligantur quasi unus homo, ut Porphyrius dicit. Comp. Theol.,* 201.

115. R. P. Teilhard de Chardin, *Etudes,* 20 Oct. 1937. Cf. also the chapter by R. P. de Lubac, *Personne et Société* (in *Catholicisme,* 253–275).

116. Here we follow (and cite) the R. P. Malevez, whose remarkable work may be found in *Rech. de Science Rel.* 1935, 418 et seq. Cf. also the convergent reflections of R. P. Congar, in *Rev. des Sc. Phil. et Théol.* 1936, 489 et seq. That this position should be criticized by R. P. Bouesse (*Théologie et Sacerdoce,* 161) for its "platonic idealism" appears to us surprising.

117. . . . *Cum anima rationalis sit forma penitus spiritualis, non dependens a corpore, nec communicans corpori in operatione* . . . *De Pot.* 3, 9, c.

118. *Anima intellectiva excedit totum genus corporeum, quum habeat operationem supra omnia corpora elevatam, quae est intelligere. Con. Gent.* II, 86.

119. *Anima rationalis non solum secundum speciem est perpetuitatis capax, sicut aliae creaturae, sed etiam secundum individuum. Con. Gent.* III, 113.

120. *Con. Gent.* II, 49.

121. *Ibid.* II, 46.

122. *Ibid.* III, 111–113.

123. *Ibid.* III, 112.

124. "Each of us is born by his own choice . . . and we are in some sort our own fathers because we bring ourselves to birth as we will." St. Gregory of Nyssa, *Vita Moysis,* P. G. XLIV, 327 b.

125. We do not treat the *whole* problem of supernatural vocation. We envisage the man of to-day, as he stands in the actual economy of the redemptive incarnation.

126. *Gratia secundum se considerata perficit essentiam ani-*

mae, in quantum participat quamdam similitudinem divini esse.
Sum. Theol. III, 62, 2, c.

127. *Sum. Theol.* III, 23, 1 ad 2. Cf. *Filiatio adoptionis est participata similitudo filiationis naturalis. Ibid.* 23, 4, c.

128. Cf. Huby, *Les Epîtres de la captivité,* p. 40–42, 45.

129. It will be recalled that to *participate* a thing is precisely not to be that thing, and thus all danger of confusionism is avoided: to say that we are *by grace* what Christ is *by nature,* is to affirm within the bosom of the union the most irreducible distinction. Moreover—need we say it?—a relation to the Person of the Son of God, does not of itself include a relation to this Person in His character as pure relation to the Father, which as such is not participable. We know that the Incarnation itself was explained by St. Thomas as the union of two natures in the Person of the Word, considered not according to *id quod est proprium personae Filii scil. relatio qua refertur ad Patrem,* but *secundum communem rationem personae, prout significat quoddam subsistens. De Unione Verbi Inc.* I, ad 8.

130. In consequence of original sin, which touches the essence of the soul, human nature is, in each man, *extracta a naturali dispositione quam ex Deo accepit, proindeque non jam illud ipsum quod est, totum Dei est.* Salmanticenses, *de Gratia,* Disp. 2, dub. 3, n. 103.

131. *Sicut informis.* St. Thomas, *in Rom.* 8, 19, lect. 4. Cf. *in II Cor.* V, 17 (lect. 4, 3): "Renewal in grace is called a creation. For creation is a movement from nothingness to being. Now being is two-fold: of nature and of grace. The first creation took place when creatures were produced *ex nihilo* by God, in their *esse naturae.* The creature was then new, but became 'aged' by sin. . . . He therefore needed a new creation, that by which creatures were produced in their *esse gratiae*: and this is a creation *ex nihilo,* because those who lack grace are nothing (I Cor. XIII, 2)." Cf. *De Ver.* 27, 6, c.: "grace is in the essence of the soul, and it perfects it inasmuch as it gives it a kind of spiritual being, and makes it participate, by way of a certain assimilation, in the divine nature." And compare *De Ver.* 27, 2, ad 7: grace is ordered "not to an act, but to this *esse spirituale* that it realizes in the soul." A unique and mysterious because supernatural case: "Nothing comparable to grace is to be found in those accidents of the soul that are known to philosophers;

because philosophers know only those accidents that are ordered
to acts proportioned to human nature."

132. St. Gregory of Nyssa, *de perf. christiani forma.* P. G.
XLVI, 280a.

133. The person (*De Pot.* 9, 3, c.) is a certain nature (=in-
tellectual) with a certain mode of being (=subsistence). The
human person, as he actually is, carries a nature originating
from Adam as its principle; and this nature, on account of its
relation with Adam, is de-supernaturalised; it is characterised
by its lack of participation in the divine nature. Consequently,
its mode of being is also impaired: it carries with it no *esse
supernaturale.* And thus the whole person is impaired: *natura
corrumpit personam.*

134. "In human nature called to supernatural beatitude there
must needs be a new subjective disposition, a new exigence,
anterior to all deliberate exercise of will, anterior even to faith
and sanctifying grace, finalising human nature to its supernatural destiny under the form of a necessary and undeliberated
need of the absolute last Good. . . . The calling of man by
God to his supernatural end is therefore not simply a call from
without. Before any call from without, the divine call has already sounded in the depths of human nature, there to excite
a new and undeliberated will, analogous to the primary natural
will, a need for this possession of the perfect Good according
to its essence which did not exist in the will left to its natural
conditions. Man's vocation to his supernatural perfection therefore physically modifies human nature to order it already in a
certain way before all free cooperation on his part to this new
destiny; a remote ordination without doubt, for there is no
question here of sanctifying grace, nor of an act of faith, nor
even of habitual faith, but only of this preliminary subjective
disposition which is to make these possible, and which consists
in the need, the exigence, of the absolute last good, expressed
by a first indeliberate act of willing." R. P. Brisbois, *Le désir
de voir Dieu, et la métaphysique de vouloir selon St. Thomas*
(*Nouv. Rev. Théol.* 1936, 1011). The systematic explanations
of the Rev. Father are open to discussion; but the need for this
physical modification of human nature, which he emphasises
so strongly seems to me to be incontestable.

135. Huby, *op. cit.* p. 89.

136. R. P. Bonsirven, *Epîtres de S. Jean*, p. 275, n. 1.

137. This is the formula of R. P. de Lubac, *op. cit.* p. 267.

138. Cf. *Sum. Theol.* III, 79, 1, ad 1: *ad hoc quod homo "in seipso perfectus existat per conjunctionem ad Deum."*

139. *De Malo*, 4, 6, ad 4: "By baptism original sin is taken away inasmuch as grace is given which unites the higher part of the soul to God, but the soul does not receive the strength which would enable it to preserve its body from corruption, or would enable the higher part of the soul to keep the lower powers in full submission; and that is why, after baptism, there still remains the need of dying to concupiscence which is the material element in original sin. And thus man, as to the higher part of his soul, participates the newness of Christ; but as to his lower powers, and also as to the body, there remains the 'decrepitude' that comes from Adam."

140. Cf. Gal. V, 16–17. On these texts see Lagrange, *Comment.*, 147 and 153.

141. St. Gregory of Nazianzen, *Orat.* 40: For the Christian there are three kinds of birth: carnal, baptismal, and glorious. "The first is a birth in the night, in slavery, in passion; the second is a birth in the day, in liberty, and in deliverance from passion, lifting all this veil (of sorrow) which covers us from our birth, and leading us to life above; the third is a sudden and formidable birth which, in an instant, in the flash of an eye, reunites the whole human race that it may stand in the presence of the Creator." P. G. XXXVI, 360, 2.

142. "Now we begin already to be *like to God* since we have the first-fruits of the Spirit; and yet we are *still unlike* because the old Adam is still with us. . . . Now we have the first-fruits of the Spirit, and so have already really become the sons of God. For the rest, it is in hope that we are saved, and renewed, and, in the same way become sons of God: because we are not yet saved in all reality, we are not yet fully renewed, not yet even sons of God, but sons of this world. . . . Let all that then be consumed that keeps us still sons of the flesh and of the world, and let all that be perfected that makes us sons of God and renewed in the Spirit." St. Augustine, *De peccat. meritis et remissione*, II, 7, 10. Cf. *de Perfectione justitiae*. XVIII, 39.

143. *De Veritate*, 24, 4, c.

144. *De Veritate*, 24, *passim*, and in particular, 4, c. and

ad 10; 6, c. ad 1 and 4. Note the precision of the ad 4: man is free inasmuch as he is rational, that is to say, as St. Thomas explains, inasmuch as he possesses a rational soul, and therefore intelligence and will.

145. "An act of the person as person" writes M. MARITAIN, *L'idée thomiste de la liberté*, Rev. Thomiste, 1939, 446.

146. This is the language of the Councils, from Orange to Trent. It is also that of theologians. For St. Thomas, for example, see *De Ver.* 28, 4, c. and 5, c; *Sum. Theol.* II–II 52, 1, ad 3: "the sons of God are moved by the Holy Spirit according to their mode (of being), that is to say, in a way that saves their free-will, which is the power of the will and the reason."

147. *Sum. Theol.* III, 34, 3, ad 1: "Free will has not the same relation to good and to evil. It has an essential and natural relation (*per se et naturaliter*) with the good; and a relation by defect and deviation from nature (*per modum defectus et praeter naturam*) with evil." Cf. II Sent. d. 26, q. 1, a. 1, 2.

148. This has been strongly emphasised in a remarkable study, to which we have been much indebted, by M. MARITAIN: *Une philosophie de la liberté*, in "Du Régime temporel et de la liberté," 37 et seq.

149. In *Les caves du Vatican*, the free act becomes the *gratuitous act*, whose whole meaning is contained in the power of refusal it expresses; that is, to say the truth, it is an act that has lost all meaning whatsoever.

150. "All the beauty and sublimity with which we have invested real and imagined things, I will show to be the property and product of man, and this should be his most beautiful apology. Man as a poet, as a thinker, as a god, as love, as power . . ." NIETZSCHE, *The Will to Power*, Book II (translated by A. M. Ludovici, Vol. I, p. 113. London and Edinburgh, 1909).

151. *Thus Spake Zarathustra*, Prol. 3, and II, 12.

152. Taken from 3rd. note book (unpublished) and cited by Y. SIMON, *Critique de la connaissance morale*, p. 49.

153. Here we might appropriately study the human reaction to the obstacle. In fact, men are always more or less given to two extreme reactions: benumbed apathy and violence. Both destroy the freshness and easy mastery that liberty demands.

154. "There are two contrary inclinations in the human spirit. The one goes to the good, following the lead of reason. . . . The

other comes from the lower powers, especially seeing that these are tainted by original sin; and thereby the spirit is inclined to choose whatever may be pleasing to the senses..." *De Ver.* 24, 12.

155. On all these points see *De Malo,* 4, 2, c; *Sum. Theol.* II–II, 164, 1, c; II *Sent.* d. 30, q. 1 (As such, "the force of desire tends naturally to sensible pleasure; as human, it does so according to the order of reason; and consequently, to do so in an unbridled manner is not natural to this force as human, rather it is against nature") : I–II, 82, 3, ad 1.

156. *Sum. Theol.* I–II, 82, 4 ad 1.

157. Cf. the studies of R. P. MOTTE, *"Vers une solution doctrinale du problème de la philosophie chrétienne"* (in *La Philosophie Chrétienne,* 1933, 76 seq.) and *"Théologie et Theo-dicée chez St. Thomas"* (in *Revue des Sc. Phil. et Theol.* 1937, 5 seq.).

158. *Sum. Theol.* I, 94, 1; II–II, 2, 4 c.

159. *Ibid.* II–II, 1, 8, ad 1, and 5, 1, ad 1.

160. Cf. the note by P. HUGUENY, Bulletin Thom., Jan. 1933, 819.

161. Cf. NEWMAN's suggestive sermon *"Religion a weariness to the natural man"* (Sermon CXXX, Plain Sermons).

162. Cf. J. DE FINANCE, *La Sophia chez S. Paul,* Rech. de Science Relig. 1935, 393 seq.

163. To the classic texts of St. Thomas add this one also, which links up knowledge of the moral law with knowledge of God: "As to the precepts of the moral law, the human reason is unable to go astray in the abstract, in respect of the universal principles of the law; but through habituation to sin it does in fact become obscured in respect of the detailed things to be done. But with regard to those other moral precepts which are like conclusions drawn from the universal principles of the natural law, the reason of men went astray to the extent of judging some things to be lawful which in fact are evil in themselves. Hence there was need for the authority of the divine law to rescue men from these defects. Just as in the articles of faith not only are there truths set forth to which our reason cannot reach—such as the Trinity of the Godhead—but also some that are attainable by right reason—such as the Unity of the Godhead: and this precisely for the purpose of excluding error

into which our human reason often falls." *Sum. Theol.* I–II, 99, 2 ad 2.

164. Pius IX, *Singulari quadam* (Denz. 1642–4); *Gravissimas inter* (D. 1670); *Qui pluribus* (D. 1635). The Council of the Vatican had to re-affirm this doctrine: Sess. III, c. 2 (D. 1786), c. 4 (D. 1799).

165. *De Ver.* 24, 12, ad 2.

166. *Sum. Theol.* I–II, 85, 3, ad 2.

167. A wonderful description of this complex may be found in St. Gregory of Nyssa, *De Beatitudinibus,* VIII (P. G. XLIV 1296–97). He compares all these agglutinated forces to "a carapace, as of a tortoise" which cripples the soul; and he exhibits this latter as "attached to the pleasures of life by the power of feeling as by a nail," and "indissociable with those powers with which it is entangled and which act along with it."

168. A sort of natural inclination, *quasi naturale: De Ver.* 24, 10, esp. 1 to 5.

169. A verification of St. Thomas' word (*De Ver.* 24, 10, ad 14) that sin takes away nothing from free-will, but adds a union with a perverse end.

170. *Sum. Theol.* I–II, 73, 1, c. and ad 3: "The love of God is unitive (*congregativus*) because it draws men's affections from the many to the one . . . but self-love disunites (*disgregat*) man's affections, because when a man loves himself he desires temporal goods for himself, and these are many and diverse."

171. *De Ver.* 24, 11, ad 3 and ad 6.

172. *De Ver.* 24, 12, ad 13.

173. *Conc. Trid.* VI, cap. 16 (cf. XIV, c. 8). When Baius affirms that man, once fallen, could only sin; but that he remains free because, although he is constrained interiorly, he is not so exteriorly, and that he loves what he does, the Church condemns this confusion between spontaneity and freedom. Sin demands a power of choice, and the Church rejects this necessity of sin which Baius pretends to find in the Catholic tradition: fallen man can perform other acts besides sins, and his power of choice can really pass to act.

174. St. Bernard, *Serm. in Cant.* 81, 7 and 9.

175. St. Irenaeus, *Adv. Haer.,* IV, 33 (P. G. VII, 1072 b).

176. *Contra Gentes,* IV, 22.

177. *Ibid.* III, 128 (Cf. IV, 22).

178. St. Gregory of Nyssa, *De Beatitudine* (P. G. XLIV, 1289c).

179. Origen, in *Joann.* XIII, 4 (P. G. XIV, 404).

180. *De Spiritu et litt.* XVI, 28.

181. Grou, *Maximes Spirituelles,* XV.

182. *In Joann.,* Tr. 26, 4–5.

183. On this delicate point see Gilson's excellent remarks, *Introduction a l'étude de S. Augustine,* 203, sq. (Cf. 205 . . . "delectation is simply love, which itself is but the interior 'weight' of the will, which in turn is but free-will itself.")

184. *De perfectione Justitiae,* IV, 9.

185. *De Spiritu et litt.,* 16, 29.

186. *Ibid.* 30, 52.

187. *De Corrupt. et Gratia,* VIII, 17.

188. *Maximes Spirituelles,* II, (cf. XXIII).

189. Origen, *In Rom.* I, 1 (P. G. XIV, 839–840).

190. Exclamation XVII.

191. *Sum. Theol.* I, 60, 1 ad 3, and I–II, 29, 1.

192. "We call that love in every inclination, which is the principle of the movement towards the end loved." I–II, 26, 1.

193. Participation: *Sum. Theol.* I, 45, 5, ad 1; image: I, 93, 8; conformity: *De Ver.* 23, 7; call: *De Malo,* I, 5, c.

194. *Sum. Theol.* I–II, 26, 1.

195. *De Ver.* 22, 2.

196. *De Car.* 12, ad 16. Cf. I, 44 ad 3.

197. *Con. Gen.* III, 24.

198. *Id unde amans est unum cum amato. C. G.* I, 91.

199. The appetite of a man in the universe is the appetite of a part, and is therefore directly ordered to the good of the Whole (I–II, 19, 10); all that holds its being from another is inclined more, and more radically, to its principle than to itself, for the principle is the total reason of its existence, its desire and its beatitude (I, 60, 5); every part naturally loves its own proper good for the sake of the Common Good of the universe, which is God, and "that is why, before sin, man referred to the love of God as to its end, both the love of self and the love of all things else, and thus he loved God above all things." I–II, 109, 3. Cf. II–II, 26, 3; *De Spe,* I, 9.

200. *De Car.* 12, ad 16.

201. *Sum. Theol.* II–II, 25, 2, c.

202. *C. G.* IV, 19. Cf. *ib.* "The beloved is in the will of the lover as the term of a movement is in its proportionate motive principle by reason of the proportion and aptitude of the principle to that term."

203. On this point see the analyses of M. MADINIER, in *Conscience et Amour.*

204. For an idealist philosophy a spiritual affectivity is not far short of a scandal, and it is not difficult to understand why it has been neglected or denied. Our language moreover lends itself to the worst confusions: sadness, emotion, love are all words that can bear both senses, but which have been appropriated to the benefit of the sensitive affectivity. The rediscovery of the spiritual affectivity is precisely one of our modern philosophy's titles to greatness. Bergson made it for one, and he calls "emotion" one of the highest forms of spiritual activity (cf. BORNE, *Rev. de Philo.*, 1935, p. 439). Lavelle does the same thing when he distinguishes in the spirit the three acts of understanding, willing and loving ("Love may therefore be defined as the very perfection of the will, precisely because it is the synthesis of will and intelligence, or an act of the rational will."—*De l'acte,* p. 515).

205. This was formerly apparent in the very words used: St. Thomas commonly calls the will *affectus;* he pointed to love as its first and most essential act; and he did not hesitate to write: *Affici ad aliquid in quantum hujusmodi, est amare ipsum (C. G.,* IV, 19). For all sorts of spiritual problems, both philosophical and theological, a thorough and systematic study of this affectivity is greatly to be desired,—even after Scheler's great book, so deep and so much open to discussion, *Nature et Formes de la Sympathie.*

206. "God is the greatest of all goods and more proper to each than anything else can be, *because He is closer to the soul than the soul is to itself.*" III *Sent.* d. 29, 1, 3, 3 (Cf. LAVELLE: "I always love something that is above me, because in myself I can only love that which is the very source of being and of life." *De l'acte,* 517.

207. Cf. SCHELER, *op. cit.,* p. 338: "In our conception . . . the person and the whole would exist independently of each other, but, at the same time, for each other; never simply for each

other, but both for God, as person; and it is only in God that they would live for each other."

208. PERE DE LUBAC said "centrifugal centre," and in this expression the paradox of the natural movement of love is perfectly seized.

209. "In the absence of this higher spirituality, which in the eyes of Christianity precisely invests it with all its significance, love falls into the rank of a *physical need* for the individual and a *social necessity* for the State. . . ." LACHIEZE-REY, *Les idées morales, sociales et politique de Platon*, 216–217.

210. Cf. the pronouncement of the Methodist Whitefield, at the moment of his marriage: "God be praised, if I know my own heart I am free of this silly passion which the world calls love," in D. V. HILDEBRAND, *Le mariage*, 23.

211. BERGSON, *Les deux sources . . .* , 326.

212. *Council of Trent*, Sess. 2, 4. Here we speak of marriage only in so far as it concerns this love "which penetrates all the duties of conjugal life, and holds a sort of primacy of nobility in Christian marriage." Enc. *Casti Connubii*.

213. An attitude admirably understood and lived by ALICE OLLE-LAPRUNE: *Notes sur le Mariage* in *Liens Immortels*, 137–149 . . . "For me, my husband is the Lord. And without restriction as without reserve, with an intention that is very direct, very vigorous and very supernatural, we shall fall in with his thoughts, with his mind, with his soul, not wearing ourselves out with argument. . . . We shall make a clean sweep of all the petty sophisms which chatter about an enfeebled personality and a ruined will. . . . Do we not know that it is precisely by this canalisation embraced for the noblest of all motives, that our wills acquire a ten-fold strength and that our personality will be more abundantly fruitful than ever before? Let us turn to St. Paul again and see whether he leaves any room for fear of exceeding in this respect. And the reason is compelling. We must always come back to it: for us our husbands are the Lord."

214. ST. FRANCIS DE SALES, *Treatise on the Love of God*, X, 1

215. ST. BASIL, *Reg. fusius tract.* 2 (P. G. XXXI, 908, 1).

216. ST. JOHN CLIMACUS, *Scala*, XXX (P. G. LXXXVIII, 1155a).

217. As regards the difference between *love* (which implies passion) and *dilection* (which implies a rational judgment), St.

Thomas writes: "But it is possible for man to tend to God by love, *being as it were passively drawn by Him,* more than he can possibly be drawn thereto by his reason, which pertains to the nature of dilection. And consequently, love is more godlike than dilection." *Sum. Theol.* I–II, 26, 3, ad 4.

218. Cf. St. Augustine, "Therefore we ought to love Him by whom the times were made that we may be delivered from time and be fixed in eternity where there is no more changeableness of times" (*Tract. in Jo.* 31, 5). And again: "The river of temporal things hurries one along, but like a tree springing up beside a river is Our Lord Jesus Christ. He assumed flesh, died, rose again, ascended into heaven. It was His will to plant Himself in a manner beside the river of the things of time. Art thou rushing down the stream to the headlong deeps? Hold fast the tree. Is the love of the world whirling thee on? Hold fast Christ. For thee He became *temporal* that thou mightest become *eternal.*" (*In I. Joan.,* 2, 10).

219. St. Francis of Assisi, cf. St. Thomas: Filial fear "implies in a way a certain separation (from God) inasmuch as he who fears presumes not to equal himself with God, but rather submits to Him; and this separation is to be observed even in charity, in so far as a man loves God more than himself and more than aught else. Hence increase in the love of charity implies no decrease, but an increase, in the reverence of fear." II–II, 19, 10, ad 3.

220. *"Formatio appetitus ab ipso appetibili,"* St. Thomas, *De Ver.,* 26, 4, c.

221. Cf. Rousselot, *Pour l'histoire du Problème de l'Amour au Moyen Age* (Paris, 1933), p. 28, 29, and 78, n. 3.

222. *De doctrina christiana,* I, 22.

223. *Sum. Theol.* II–II, 24, 12, c.

224. *Sum. Theol.* II–II, 19, 11, ad 2, and I–II, 87, 3, c.

225. *Car.* 5, ad 6.

226. Lagrange, on *St. John,* XIV, 15, *Commentary,* 381.

227. *The love of God is poured forth in our hearts by the Holy Ghost* (Rom. V, 5). Now this is the love that God shows us by giving His Son to death (v. 6, 8, 9) and which reconciles us to God by this death (v. 10).

228. *De peccat. meritis et remissione,* XXII, 36–37.

229. St. Maximus the Confessor, *Centuries on charity,*

3, 98 (P. G. XC, 1047) and St. John Climacus, *Scala,* 30 (P. G. LXXXVIII, 1155).

230. *De Caritate,* XI, 8.

231. This expression, applied to faith, comes from P. Menendez-Reigada, cited by P. Garrigou-Lagrange, *L'amour de Dieu et la croix de Jésus,* II, 574, n. 1.

232. *Living Flame,* Str. I, 4.

233. St. John of the Cross, *Vie,* R. P. Bruno.

234. St. John of the Cross, *Canticle.*

235. Dom Marmion wrote one day: "It is remarkable that since I gave myself more to God, I have gained a very lively feeling of my union with all the members of the Church, and with some of them in particular. It seems to me that I carry the whole Church in my heart, above all at Holy Mass and during the divine office, and in this way I no longer suffer from distractions as in the past" (*Vie,* by Dom. Thibaut, p. 172).

236. On this point, cf. the *Theologisches Wörterbuch zum N. T.* article *Agapé* (Stauffel), 51 sq.

237. That the problem is embroiled may be guessed from the Carmelites of Salamanca (in fact, John of the Annunciation), classical theologians if ever there were any, who write: *"Huic objectioni* (that charity is a love of concupiscence) *variae adhibentur solutiones,* quarum nulla placet. *Unde, illis omissis, ut legitimam tradamus, animadvertendum . . ."* (*De Car.* Disp., I, dub 2, n. 26).

238. *Sum. Theol.* II-II, 28, 4, c.

239. In classical terms: does it involve, with respect to God, a love of concupiscence or simply a love of benevolence? We shall avoid these expressions because, however exact they may be, they unduly restrict the terms of the problem. They cannot be applied to the love of God (or, for that matter, to the love of self) save after a strict theological criticism, and this is not the place for that. We think moreover that an expression such as "love of concupiscence" is an impossibility to-day in French: not to speak of the average Christian, the cultivated Christian is unable to think of this word without reference to certain scraps of Pascal and of Bossuet, to certain railleries of Voltaire's, and certain sumptuous rhymes of Baudelaire—and that makes the expression so much the less desirable.

240. *Sum. Theol.* I–II, 110, 1, c. "God directs righteous men

to Himself as to a special end, which they seek, and to which they wish to cling, according to Ps. LXXII, 28, *it is good for me to adhere to my God*" (*Ibid.* 109, 6, c.)

241. R. Lebreton, *Origines du Dogme de la Trinité*, I, 520.

242. *Sum. Theol.* I, 12, 7 ad 1.

243. St. Francis de Sales, *Treatise on the Love of God*, V, 3.

244. On all this cf. the theology of the divine missions, *Sum. Theol.* I, 43 (2, 3, 4).

245. St. John of the Cross, *Spiritual maxims and sentences*.

246. An habitual affirmation of St. Thomas, e.g. *Sum Theol.* II–II, 26, 13, c.; *De Malo*, I, 5, c.; *De Car.* 7, 10, etc.

247. *Sum. Theol.* I–II, 114, 4, c.

248. *Sum. Theol.* II–II, 24, 9, c.

249. III *Sent.* d. 29, q. 1, art. 1, 3, sol.

250. *Sum. Theol.* II–II, 26, 3, c. and ad 3.

251. III *Sent.* d. 29, q. 1, a. 3, sed c. 2.

252. *De Car.* I, 10; *de Spe*, I, 9; *Sum. Theol.* I–II, 62, 3, c.; II–II, 6, ad 3.

253. *De Car.* II, ad 15.

254. *De divin. Nomin.* IV, lect. 9–10.

255. *Sum. Theol.* II–II, 24, 12, c.

256. *Ibid.* I–II, 109, 3, c.

257. See, on this point, some excellent formulas of P. Rousselot, in *Le Témoignage de P. Rousselot* (Paris, 1940), p. 206–207.

258. *Sum. Theol.* II–II, 24, 9, c.

259. Rom. IX, 2–3. As for Moses see Exodus XXXII, 31–32: "Either forgive (this people) this trespass; or, if thou do not, strike me out of the book that thou hast written." As for St. Margaret Mary, contemplating God's chastisements: "O my Saviour, let rather thy wrath fall all on me, and let me be blotted from the book of life, rather than that all these souls that have cost thee so dear should be lost." As for St. Theresa: "One evening, not knowing how to tell Jesus that I loved Him and how much I desired that He should be everywhere glorified, I thought sadly that from the abyss of hell there never rose up to Him a single act of love. Then I cried that I would most willingly consent to be plunged into this place of torments and blasphemies so only that He might be loved eternally. . . ." (*Histoire d'une âme*, V, 104). It is a common cry, and that is why it constitutes a problem.

260. St. John Climacus, *Scala*, XXX (P. G. LXXXVIII, 1155).

261. Of R. Otto's book *The Holy* it will have to be said that it attained a great success without producing any echoes in philosophic thought. Cf. the curious and delusive chapter devoted to it by M. Pradines in *L'Esprit de la Religion*, p. 199 sq.

262. *Contra Gentes*, II, 68.

263. St. Gregory the Great, *Hom. in Evang.*, 37, 11 (P. L. LXXVI, 1272). And cf. 12, which we make use of in what follows.